Indian Gaming and the Law

EDITED BY

William R. Eadington

Professor of Economics and Director
Institute for the Study of Gambling and Commercial Gaming
College of Business Administration
University of Nevada, Reno

ISBN 0-942828-42-9

Published by
Institute for the Study of Gambling and Commercial Gaming
College of Business Administration MS 025
University of Nevada, Reno
Reno, Nevada 89557-0208 USA
www.unr.edu/gaming

Library of Congress Catalog Card Number
97-77846

Indian Gaming and the Law

Cover design by Creative Services, University of Nevada, Reno
Book layout by Diane Chester Berg,
Computer Support Services of Northern Nevada, Carson City

Printed in the United States of America

Contents

Indian Gaming and the Law

Contents

Contents

PREFACE

"The purpose of (the Indian Gaming Regulatory) Act is—

>   (1) to provide the statutory basis for the operation of gaming by Indian tribes as a means of promoting tribal economic development, self-sufficiency, and strong tribal governments;

>   (2) to provide a statutory basis for the regulation of gaming by an Indian tribe adequate to shield it from organized crime and other corrupting influences, to ensure that the Indian tribe is the primary beneficiary of the gaming operation, and to assure that gaming is conducted fairly and honestly both by operator and players; and

(3) to declare that the establishment of independent Federal regulatory authority for gaming on Indian lands, the establishment of Federal standards for gaming on Indian lands, and the establishment of a National Indian Gaming Commission are necessary to meet congressional concerns regarding gaming and to protect such gaming as a means of generating Tribal revenue."

Thus reads the "Declaration of Policy" in Public Law 100-497, the Indian Gaming Regulatory Act of 1988—IGRA. This Act came about as part of a political and economic process that began with challenges by the State of Florida to the legality of high stakes bingo games offered by the Seminole tribe in the late 1970s, and culminated in passage of an Act that triggered the most significant economic and social change to affect American Indian tribes since the founding of the Nation.

The emergence of Indian gaming in the fifteen years following the passage of IGRA has created an industry of surprising size and success. Indian gaming operations generated revenues of nearly $15 billion in 2002,[1] and have transformed the lot of many tribes in the United States presently involved in gaming. The largest casinos in the world—Foxwood's and Mohegan Sun in southeastern Connecticut—are classic cases of the directions that have emerged under IGRA since 1988. In 2003, each of these tribal casinos generated gross gaming revenues in the range of $1 billion, becoming the largest and among the most profitable casinos in the world. Tribal casinos in California generated about $6 billion in gaming revenues in 2003, closing in on Nevada's gaming revenues of just under $10 billion.

---

[1] Indian Gaming Regulatory Commission, www.nigc.gov.

Indian gaming has introduced a broad set of challenging, fascinating, and often contradictory issues related both to gambling and to Indian policy. The activity of gambling itself is viewed by many as a questionable, if not immoral, activity that attracts questionable, if not immoral, people. In spite of rapid expansion of permitted gambling throughout the United States and Canada from the 1980s to the present, gambling remains a highly controversial activity where consensus regarding appropriate public policy has become increasingly difficult to achieve. Because of concerns about the potential for social problems or scandals arising from gambling, jurisdictions have used a wide variety of legal and regulatory structures to protect the public's interests with regard to commercial gaming. But Indian gaming has posed special challenges.

The Supreme Court has consistently ruled that Indian tribes—because of tribal sovereignty—are not subject to state jurisdiction in areas of civil law. As states have removed prohibitions against gambling and allowed regulated and constrained forms of commercial gaming for various purposes, Indian tribes were then able to offer the same types of gambling allowed elsewhere in the state. Often, courts or compact negotiations under IGRA went beyond creating a level playing field with non-Indians, and gave tribes exclusive franchises to particular forms of gambling, especially casino-style gaming.

This interesting set of events has occurred at a time when various administrations in the U.S. were altering national policy toward Indian tribes by reducing direct subsidies and encouraging greater economic self-sufficiency and entrepreneurial activity to replace what has been considered the bankrupted paternalistic policies toward Indian tribes of the past hundred years. However, tribes have not had much of a comparative advantage in most economic activities. Gambling has now become a notable exception. For many tribes, commercial gaming has been a catalyst for economic development through revenue generation, job creation, and attraction of capital investment, in a manner that few other economic activities could match.

Passage of the Indian Gaming Regulatory Act in 1988 was met by affected parties with decidedly mixed reactions. Many tribal leaders thought that IGRA—because it forced negotiations between tribes and states for Class III gaming—was just another erosion of Indian sovereignty. Politicians thought that IGRA would contain Indian gaming and prevent it from spreading wildly and haphazardly throughout the United States. Some observers thought that passage of IGRA was going to serve as a major catalyst in the further proliferation of casino-style gaming in America.

In 2004—fifteen years after these papers and presentations were first made—some of the arguments and predictions contained herein are surprisingly prescient. Others have fared less well given the tests of time and the flow of events, but even these point out how difficult it can be to anticipate important future trends.

This book was initially distilled from papers and presentations made at the *North American Conference on the Status of Indian Gaming* in March, 1989, which occurred only months after passage of IGRA. This was a time when emotions were still strong and memories of the political process that shaped IGRA were still sharp among many participants. The contributors to this volume—all of whom were on the conference program—reflected a wide spectrum of political, legal, and academic expertise from both non-Indian and Indian backgrounds. The opinions put forth reflected the tremendous diversity of ideas and interests that lay behind the Indian gaming issues of the time, most of which are still relevant today. The interested reader will be able to find in these presentations the conflict and the controversy that the spread of Indian gaming and the passage of IGRA brought about.

ACKNOWLEDGEMENTS

The North American Conference on the Status of Indian Gaming occurred because of the inspiration and efforts of a number of individuals who felt that the emergence of Indian gaming and the passage of the Indian Gaming Regulatory Act needed a forum from which the many political, legal, social and economic issues that were related to the topic could be discussed and debated. The University of Nevada, Reno was willing to provide such a forum, based on the importance of the topic of gambling and commercial gaming to the long-term interests of the state of Nevada, and society at large.

It is appropriate and timely to once again re-issue *Indian Gaming and the Law* because of the continuing challenges confronting commercial gaming in general and Indian gaming in particular. This book still captures sentiments that are as vital and insightful today as when they were first expressed.

I would like to express my gratitude to all those individuals who worked to bring the North American Conference on Indian Gaming into existence in 1989, and to the various authors and contributors to this volume for their efforts and insights. I applaud the efforts of Judy Cornelius, Associate Director of the Institute for the Study of Gambling and Commercial Gaming at the University of Nevada, Reno, who was the coordinator for the *North American Conference on the Status of Indian Gaming* and who has been the major administrative presence within the Institute for the past 15 years. Thanks to Mikel Alvarez, a student at the University of Nevada, Reno and a member of the Cabazon Tribe for his suggestion of adding the new appendices to this collection and his encouragement to keep this publication in print.

William R. Eadington, Director
Institute for the Study of Gambling and Commercial Gaming
February, 2004

I

The Indian Gaming Act
and the Political Process

1

I. Nelson Rose*
Associate Professor of Law
Whittier College School of Law

For the past decade, a fight has been raging over what forms of gambling, if any, American Indians should be allowed to have on their own reservations. Ever since the Seminole Tribe in Florida won the right in 1979 to run high-stakes bingo games free from government control, the controversy has been fought in legislatures, the press, and cases going all the way to the United States Supreme Court.

In 1987 the high Court decided the landmark case of *California v. Cabazon Band of Mission Indians*, 480 U.S. 202 (1987) declaring that, once a state has legalized any form of gambling, the Indians in that state had the right to offer the same game, but without any governmental restrictions. This threw the ball into Congress's lap to do something, fast.

At times emotions overcame logic, with name-calling and hard feelings. The interested parties all felt they had a lot to win, or lose.

The stakes are not small by any means. Total gambling winnings by operations on Indian reservations has grown from zero to over one hundred million dollars per year, without slot machines, roulette wheels, crap tables, horse racing, Off-Track-Betting, state-wide lottery outlets or most of the other trappings considered to be essential to big money operations. In fact, although there are a few Indian card rooms offering poker and even some isolated blackjack tables, the game for Indian gaming operations is primarily bingo. For the small number of tribes operating high stakes games, bingo alone, not counting pull-tabs, in 1988 brought in over $110 million in gross win.

It is easy to see why the tribes thought they were literally fighting for survival. Before bingo was introduced, unemployment had run over 30% and as high as 70% on some reservations; many tribes felt their economic independence depended upon legal gambling. Perhaps more importantly, the question of who should control gambling on Indian land developed into a debate over who should control all Indian activities.

The Indian tribes legally are "dependent sovereigns" of the federal government, nations defeated at war with the United States, but still having much of the legal power of nations nonetheless. (Apparently the Seminoles are still technically at war with the United States, never having signed a peace treaty.) The Indians feel strongly about preserving their sovereignty, and they were willing to fight to the end to prevent federal or state governments from taking over completely.

But the Indians were not alone in their willingness to fight. Nevada and other states with legal gaming industries feared competition from unregulated Indian gambling. Worse was the specter of organized crime. A juicy scandal in an Indian casino could lead to a federal crackdown on all forms of gambling. Nevada casinos know the only way to prevent infiltration by organized crime is government regulation, but they certainly did not want to open the door to federal regulation of state licensed casinos.

Others joined in the battle. Management groups which run the games as well as suppliers of goods and services are often non-Indian; they did not want to find the federal government putting them out of business. Law enforcement joined the casino industry in warning about organized crime and the dangers of unregulated gambling. The federal and state bureaucracies that oversee Indian land, from the Bureau of Indian Affairs to the U.S. Attorneys to the state Attorneys General, added their voices to the debate. In fact, every industry and group that had something to lose or gain from gambling on Indian reservations was represented, except for the individual players, who have no organized voice in government.

Congress had the right to completely outlaw all gambling on Indian land, but that never was a real option, since it would have instantly created an economic depression on the reservations which would have required millions of dollars in federal aid. Although there had only been a few incidents of cheating and a scattered handful of unproved allegations of organized crime involvement in Indian games, virtually everyone understood that if the legal gambling was to continue, it would have to be regulated.

Although many Indian leaders took it as a personal affront, the need for some type of federal or state governmental regulation had nothing to do with whether Indian leaders were competent to manage tribal affairs. The problem was not that it was Indian gambling, but that it was gambling, period.

Gambling is the only business, legal or illegal, where the product being sold is cash, with no paper record. Organized crime is always attracted to cash businesses, but so is unorganized crime. The high-tech security systems found in every large casino are there to watch for cheating and stealing by employees more than by players.

Every government that has legalized gambling has soon realized that it has had to institute tough controls, and most have found that the criminals can be a lot smarter than the regulators. Even the largest organizations, such as the states of Nevada and New Jersey, have found that they cannot keep the games completely honest. A smaller government, such as a city or an Indian council, would simply not have the resources to do the background checks and continuing oversight necessary to keep a high-stakes casino game legitimate.

In drafting the Act, the most difficult issue to resolve was the basic issue of Indian sovereignty. How can the Indians be completely independent and at the same time subject to government regulation? Congress did not want to unilaterally impose federal or state controls; however, it was also not willing to allow the tribes to continue to run unregulated games. It looked like no solution was possible.

After many false starts and hot words, Congress passed the "Indian Gaming Regulatory Act." President Reagan signed the bill into law on October 17, 1988. The Act, now known as Public Law 100-497, is designed to end the heated debate. Actually, it only shifts the arenas to the states, federal courts and a new National Indian Gaming Commission. However, it does lay down some fairly detailed guidelines, which, hopefully, will answer the most important questions.

The solution to the question of Indian sovereignty was ingenious. Of course, whether it will work in practice is another matter.

What the Congressional negotiators did was break the problem into many different parts. Those forms of gambling that are considered the most harmless, social games and traditional Indian games, are left totally under Indian control; these are referred to as "Class I gaming". Next, bingo and card games such as poker are subject to some regulation by the newly created three-member National Indian Gaming

Commission, two of whom must be Indians; these types of gaming are referred to as "Class II gaming".

The most dangerous forms of gambling, casino games, parimutuel betting and lotteries, (Class III gaming) are governed by a complicated system that smacks of political brilliance. Congress acknowledged the Indian tribes as sovereigns; however, they also remembered the individual states are often considered sovereigns, and further, that one of the things a sovereign does is negotiate treaties with other governments. Therefore, Congress declared that a sovereign Indian tribe can operate a casino, race track, off-track betting parlor or lottery, if, but only if, it can reach an agreement, called a compact, with the state in which it sits.

Naturally, the Indians were concerned that no state would agree to allow a tribe to operate a competing game. So Congress wrote into the law a unique set of provisions, requiring the states to negotiate in good faith, and allowing the Indians to file a federal law suit if a state refused to sign a compact within six months.

Although some actors remain disgruntled, the political compromises of the Act gave virtually every interested party something to be happy about. The Indians can run high-stake bingo games, with only minimal federal oversight. Legitimate non-Indian management and suppliers can remain in business. States like Nevada that allow casino gaming can regulate these games on Indian land, if they are able to enter into a compact with their local tribes. And most importantly, everyone, especially the tribes, was able to save face.

As for the players, the most important result is that the games will go on.

The major architects of the great Indian gambling compromise, Senators Daniel K. Inouye (D. Hawaii) and Daniel J. Evans (R. Washington), should be given credit for having worked a political near-miracle by appeasing all, or at least most, of the political factions. But the miracle may turn into a Pandora's box of troubles for Congress.

The new Indian Gaming Regulatory Act will revolutionize gambling throughout the United States.

As mentioned above, the Act divides all gambling into three classes: Class I gaming is limited to social games played for minimal stakes and traditional forms of Indian gambling. Class I is completely within the control of the tribes and is not subject to control by either state or federal government, unless, I suppose, if someone is caught cheating. In practice, this will mean that the Indians will be free to play social games of poker as well as bet on kickball during tribal ceremonies.

It is likely that someone will suggest that Indians have always bet on races, including horse races, ever since horses were first introduced by the Spanish into America. However, it is clear that Congress did not intend to allow Indians to set up race tracks and call them traditional forms of Indian gambling. Indians can bet between themselves on races, but Class I does not include pari-mutuel betting.

Class II gaming includes bingo, in all of its variations from the regular five-by-five bingo card through pull-tabs to million-dollar satellite bingo, as well as commercially run card games such as poker, where it is legal under state law. Although the bingo games can be played for any stakes the Indians choose, the poker games must conform to restrictions set by state law on hours and pot size. In California, this means Indians can run cardrooms exactly the same as those in Gardena, except they cannot offer pai gow (a game of Chinese extraction, played with dominoes); they could however use a pai gow-style deck of cards.

Bingo, on the other hand, is wide-open. Controversy will continue for years over the meaning of what exactly is allowed under terms such as "lotto" and "instant bingo". Whatever these games are, they must be played on a card; electronic aids are allowed but not video substitutes.

A few existing Indian casinos were "grandfathered in". These will continue in Michigan, North Dakota, South Dakota, and Washington. These selected casinos cannot introduce new types of games, but I believe that the number of banking game tables they house will continue to grow.

Class II does not include slot machines, such as electronic bingo. However, Indians that were legally operating these devices have one year in which to try and convince the state in which they sit that the slots should be allowed to stay. An interesting question involves what Congress meant by this provision, since under the federal Johnson Act there were no legal slot machines on Indian land. One possible answer is that a "legal" slot machine or similar device need only to have been legal under state law, perhaps being called a "video lottery."

Congress expects Class II games to be the major form of gambling on Indian reservations. This will be regulated primarily by the Indians themselves with some limited supervision by the National Indian Gaming Commission.

But Congress may be in for a surprise. Class III gaming is the catch-all for every other form of gambling: lotteries; parimutuel betting on dogs, horses, and men; sports betting; slot machines; and casino games. It is, in fact, possible for the Indians to operate Class III gaming on their reservations.

Class III requires the Indians to enter into a compact with the state in which they sit, and Congress devised an elaborate scheme to force the states to negotiate in good faith. The negotiation is definitely stacked against the states and I predict that many Indians will be able to be operating dog tracks, off-track betting, blackjack, craps, and even slot machines within the next two years. In fact, within a few weeks of the bill being signed into law, all seven reservations in Montana had petitioned for the right to have Class III gaming.

The basic rule for both Class II and Class III gaming is that the Indians may operate these games, Class II if approved by the new Commission and Class III under a compact with the state, so long as any person in the state can conduct this type of game for any reason whatsoever. In practice, this means that high-stakes Indian bingo is now legal without debate in forty-five states, the only exceptions being Arkansas, Hawaii, Indiana, Mississippi and Utah. This will have an immediate impact on competing charity bingo games as well as those state lotteries and race tracks that are in close proximity to the great new bingo halls that will flourish.

Perhaps of more importance is the ability of Indians to force a state to negotiate regarding Class III gaming. Nevada, of course, has the most at stake in this issue, and has already entered into negotiations to allow Indians to open casinos subject to state regulation.

But casino gambling is not limited to Nevada or even to New Jersey. Arizona has a new statute allowing any person to set up a blackjack or crap table in a bar, so long as the bar does not take a cut of the action. The South Dakota constitution has been amended to allow low-limit casinos in Deadwood; Iowa just did the same for riverboat gambling; and for the past decade North Dakota has allowed charity blackjack in hotel/casinos. In fact, charities are allowed to run "Las Vegas nights" with virtually all casino games in fourteen states, including Washington, Michigan, and New York. Louisiana allows commercial casino gambling within its borders on federally navigable rivers. The Indians in all of these states will soon be demanding their right to set up their own casinos.

The argument has been made that the Act was only designed to create "a level playing field," meaning that the Indians can do no more than any other citizen of the state. This may have been the intent of some in Congress, but it is not the way the law now reads. There is nothing forcing the Indians to limit their games to the restrictions found in state laws. The *Cabazon* decision came about precisely because Indians in California refused to abide by that state's restrictions of a $250 cap for prizes on charity bingo games. The high Court held the Indians could operate under their own rules, and one of the main purposes of the new Act is to codify *Cabazon*, to write that standard into the federal statutes. It will be difficult for a state like Arizona to argue that it is worried about infiltration of organized crime and other wrong-doing in Indian casinos when it has literally no regulation of the casino gambling that is now taking place in bars throughout the state.

Along another line, in 1978, Congress passed the Interstate Horse Racing Act, giving the states sole control over off-track betting. In every state where off-track betting now exists, usually in the form of inter-track wagers, Indians can demand the right to set up their own off-track betting parlors. They are already negotiating for this right in California.

In fact, the only forms of gambling we probably will not see everywhere, for a while, are slot machines and lotteries. Indians should be able to negotiate for slot machines only in the eight states that allow slots: Nevada, New Jersey, Montana (video poker), South Dakota (in Deadwood and as video lotteries), Louisiana (video bingo), Iowa (on riverboats in 1991), Maryland (Eastern counties for charity), and now Oregon (video poker). However, the Shakopee Mdewakanton Sioux Community appears on the verge of entering into a compact with the state of Minnesota for "video games of chance." Lotteries, although available in many states, will probably not be successful for the Indians because the Act requires that the games be played on the reservation itself; although, Indians are investigating the possibilities of a national lottery and ticket sales by phone and mail. Of course, once the Indians open their slot machines on reservations throughout a state, like South Dakota, it will be politically impossible for legislators in that state, and in neighboring states, to resist the appeal of non-Indian charities to be allowed to operate slot machines too. State lotteries are going more and more toward electronic terminals, which will also open the door for Indian electronic lotteries.

A possible breakthrough of national significance involves sports betting. Indian reservations in Nevada, Montana, Oregon and North Dakota can negotiate to operate sports books, with very few restrictions. A little noticed provision of the new Act exempts all Indian gaming from the restrictions placed on sending bets through the U.S. mail or via telephone. Unless the state prohibits it in its compact with the tribe, Indians will soon legally be able to take bets on college and professional sports by phone from bettors located anywhere in the country. In negotiating the compact, a smart operator could agree to limit sales to out-of-state residents and to cut the state government in on a share of the profits. It would be hard for a state like Montana to resist, since it already allows betting operations, sports cards and calcuttas, on college and professional football, basketball and baseball run by non-Indians.

Regulation under this new Act will be haphazard at best. The Commission is expected to monitor all Class II gaming on all Indian land throughout the United States; yet, its budget is extremely limited. It can raise only $1,500,000 per year from fees from the Class II games themselves, with matching funds from the federal government. Even with the fines it can impose, the Commission's total budget will not be much more than $3,000,000. By way of contrast, the New Jersey Division of Gaming Enforcement and Casino Control Commission spent $51,577,100 in the fiscal year ending June 30, 1988, to regulate only twelve casinos in a geographic area smaller than most Indian reservations.

Even if it had the money, the new Commission does not legally have the power to do much to control Class II gaming. The Act makes it clear that the Commission Chairman has no choice but to approve Class II tribal resolutions that meet certain easily met standards, such as those providing the gambling profits go solely to the benefit of the tribe. Contracts for supplies and services over $25,000 annually are subject only to independent audits. Only management contracts will be given greater scrutiny and face greater limits, such as a 30% cap, in most cases, on profit sharing by non-Indians. The Commission Chairman does have the discretion to disapprove management contracts if he believes they are not fair to the Indians.

The new Act eliminates the anomalous situation where private individuals have been operating gambling games without control solely because they are on Indian land. These private individuals are now subject to the same licensing requirements as if they were not on Indian land. A few of these independent operators were grandfathered in, if they were legally in business on September 1, 1986.

The minimal Commission oversight is expected to eventually fade away. An Indian tribe that has operated Class II gaming for over three years may petition for a certificate of self regulation, which the Commission is required to grant so long as the game has remained honest. The certificate can be taken away for wrong-doing, but it is hard to see how the Commission would ever uncover any cheating or skimming, since once the certificate is issued the Commission does not have the right to review the operator's books, or even to inspect the premises. Thus, the Indians will soon be running their bingo games virtually free of government oversight.

The Act has a few miscellaneous provisions that will cause some confusion for years to come. As one example, Indians are exempted from the federal provisions limiting advertising of lotteries and similar games. It may have been accidental, but the Indians can now do just about anything they want in terms of advertising of any of their gambling games and are not subject to any control by state or federal government. It is not even clear if they can be sued for slander and libel.

All of the Indian games are subject to the reporting and withholding requirements of the federal income tax laws. Unfortunately, nobody knows exactly what those laws are when applied to some of the forms of gambling the Indians will be offering. Big winners will have to pay taxes, but it is far from clear whether the Indians themselves will be required to pay the federal excise tax on wagers.

An important issue left unresolved by the Act is the issue of state taxation. All Indian games run by tribes are exempt from state taxes. But a strong argument can be made that all parts of the

Indian gaming operation, from the concession stands to the management services, are also exempt. This means that non-Indians would not have to pay state excise, use, or sales taxes.

From a lawyer's point of view, the most radical change the Act brings about is three new federal criminal statutes. Two of these do nothing more than make it a federal crime to steal or embezzle money from Indian games. The third, however, revolutionizes Indian and criminal law by making it a federal crime to violate any state law involving gambling on Indian land. This goes well beyond the old Assimilative Crimes Act and will put the U.S. Attorneys in the business of having to enforce the most obscure anti-gambling statutes of every state in which there is an Indian reservation. The reality will probably be no enforcement at all, since even the federal government has limited resources and gambling crimes are the lowest priority offenses.

* Although the author is a licensed attorney at law, this report is not meant to be a legal opinion. The views expressed herein are the author's and do not represent any other individual or institution.

2

Harry Reid
U.S. Senator
State of Nevada

Enactment of the Act to Regulate Indian Gaming is certainly the most significant expansion of gaming activity since New Jersey voters chose to legalize casino gambling in Atlantic City in 1976. In the long run, though, it may prove even more significant than the actions in New Jersey. It's no secret that I was opposed to expanding gaming on Indian Lands. I think that it is still a poor tool for economic development in Indian Country and the social ills that it is likely to bring with it may completely overshadow any economic benefits.

In Nevada, we understand the social costs associated with large scale commercial gaming, and we've learned over the more than fifty years of its legal existence to deal with it and compensate for it. I also have first hand knowledge of the problems associated with commercial gaming as a result of having served a little over four years as Chairman of the Nevada Gaming Commission, from 1977 to 1981.

It was during those years that historians have already written to be the most turbulent times in the history of Nevada gaming. We closed a number of major resort hotels, including the Aladdin Hotel on two occasions for secret ownerships. We levied the largest fine in the history of administrative proceedings up to that time. It was quite clear that we were able to confirm the presence of organized crime in some of the gaming operations in the state of Nevada.

I think it goes without saying that when the commodity is cash, as it is with casino gaming, that it is difficult to control. But I don't think it is necessary to take my words, someone who was born and raised in the state of Nevada, on the negative effect of gaming on Indians. I think one only has to look at the final report of the President's Commission on Gambling which was commissioned by President Nixon, received and approved by President Ford in 1976. Even though this study was done in the 1970s, its findings are relevant today.

The Commission found that there were hidden costs associated with the proliferation of gambling. For example, it found that lower income groups spent a greater percentage of their income on gambling than did upper income groups. In fact, that report clearly showed that the poorer you were, the greater the tendency there was to gamble. Also, the more availability there was of gambling, the more people would gamble. Furthermore, the proliferation of legalized gambling led to increased illegal gambling and other general illegal activities. Thus the Commission concluded that legalization of casino gaming should be restricted principally to Nevada.

The Commission made this recommendation principally for reasons other than those I just mentioned. For example, they pointed out the geographical setting of the state of Nevada. Nevada is separated by the Mojave desert from the population centers of southern California and by the Sierra Nevada mountains to the population centers in northern California. The study found that to be extremely important, that it was difficult for people to get to Nevada. Clearly, the Commission did not believe that the expansion of high stakes gambling was in society's best interest.

I have to say that those studies undertaken about Atlantic City indicate that that is the case. There is some disagreement about the social and economic impacts of casinos in Atlantic City, but not a great deal. I think Atlantic City has proven what the Commission stated. At this stage the only people who have made money with the Atlantic City venture have been the casinos and their owners.

Following the Supreme Court's ruling in the *Cabazon* case though, there was little choice except for Congress to enact laws regulating gaming on Indian lands. The alternative would have been for the rapid and uncontrolled expansion of unregulated casino type gambling on Indian lands.

Therefore in the spring of 1987, there were two basic positions in regard to Indian gaming. On the one hand many tribes believed that the *Cabazon* decision and the concept of Indian sovereignty meant that gaming on Indian lands should be controlled exclusively by the tribes, with little or no oversight by the federal government. On the other hand, many law makers and state and local government officials believed that the states should have the right to directly regulate gaming on Indian lands. So it was clear to me at the time that neither one of these two positions was likely to garner enough support in Congress to pass, and therefore a stalemate was likely. We were going to have to find some realistic middle ground or face the consequences of continued inaction in this area.

I began discussions with Chairman Daniel Inoyue (D-Hawaii) and Chairman Morris Udall (D-Arizona), the Senate Indian Affairs Committee and the House Interior Committee chairs respectively. I also worked with Democratic Whip Tony Quayle to see if there could be legislation drafted that could pass both houses of Congress and be signed by the President.

There were two basic questions: how should different types of gaming operations be categorized or classified, and what is the appropriate level of regulation for each class of gaming? Some discussions were relatively simple. Traditional Indian games of chance were to be left to the sole control of the respective Indian governments. Also, bingo, with which Indian gaming operators have had years of experience, was to be left primarily in Indian hands as well with some federal oversight.

Other decisions were certainly more complicated. There was no intention of diminishing the significance of the *Cabazon* decision. It was understood that the *Cabazon* decision dealt directly with poker games on Indian lands, so percentage card games were included in Class II activities along with bingo. On the other hand it was generally agreed that casino style card games such as blackjack and baccarat, along with parimutuel betting and other casino style gambling including video and slot machines, should be subject to the tighter regulation required under Class III gaming operations.

The remaining difficulty, a major one, was to find an appropriate regulatory scheme for Class III gaming. It was clear that the Indian community would not accept direct state control. It was equally clear that the states demanded a role in regulating Class III gaming. The reason was very simple. If we had been dealing with gaming on Indian lands, operated by Indians for the participation of Indians, then such gaming would have been left solely to Indian control. However, there is no question that the majority of participants in Indian gaming and certainly a large percentage of the operators were and were going to be non-Indian.

State and local government officials and law officers felt that they had to have some role in saying that Indian gaming did not have detrimental effects on their citizens. To deal with this problem I suggested to Chairman Inouye that we use the concept of Tribal-State compacts to determine the regulatory structure of Class III gaming.

Under such compacts, states and tribes, as if they were foreign entities, would negotiate the regulatory structure for Class III gaming. We also built in safeguards for the tribes and states against bad faith bargaining on either side. This legislative process took a lot of time, but the compact approach to Class III gaming broke the logjam and allowed us to eventually pass the Indian Gaming Bill in both houses without even having a recorded vote, something that is very rare for an issue this controversial.

I believe it passed for two main reasons. First, the bill was as fair as we could make it, and it provided protection to states without violating either the *Cabazon* decision or the concept of Indian sovereignty. Second, although nobody agreed with every provision of the legislation, it was the only bill that could pass, and there were no alternatives that could become law.

The reason I've taken the time to discuss the way the law came into being is to emphasize the very careful compromise that was drafted. It was a fragile compromise, at that time, and it is still a fragile compromise. If such a compromise, though, is to work, everyone involved in Indian gaming, the Indian communities who wish to have gaming, the operators of the gaming, state and local governments, and federal regulators must understand the intent of the law, and agree to abide by it.

I've been overwhelmed by people talking to me about the Indian gaming law and I have to tell you honestly that most of them have not read it. In fact, the law is quite direct and forthright about the intent of Congress and indeed there were a number of colloquies that were entered into the record to make it even clearer.

So first, I would ask everyone who is concerned about the bill itself to read it. Unfortunately, we are already seeing efforts underway to stretch the limits of the Indian Gaming Act. For example, one provision of the law provides that certain Class III gaming operations that were in effect on May 1, 1988 and were also legal at that time could continue under the provision of Class III gaming for up to one year while the tribe and the state carry on negotiations aimed at arriving at a compact. Without naming names, I can assure you that we know of instances, for example, where efforts are under way to continue to operate video gambling devices under the provision of the law in states where such devices are clearly illegal.

I could list other problems of this type that have already arisen. However what is important to understand is that unless everyone works together to make this fragile compromise work, this compromise could collapse, and very quickly and we could find ourselves back where we started two years ago. Only this time the fight could become very negative, and the result could undermine the very future of Indian gaming itself. Hearings that have taken place in Washington regarding oversight of some of the Indian tribes in the United States certainly reflect on how much more difficult it would be next time.

I advise those interested in Indian gaming to do what is necessary to avoid reopening this fight. The Indian gaming laws are like any other law, they are living documents, and therefore undoubtedly have to be modified on occasion; thus, they are subject to change.

Over the years, for the Indian gaming laws to work properly, I am sure there will have to be modifications and changes. But we must stay within the confines of the intent of the basic compromise that underlies this very critical legislation, or risk destroying what is the fairest, and the only workable approach, in my opinion, to legalized Indian gambling.

3

Stewart L. Udall

Attorney
Santa Fe, New Mexico
Former Secretary of the Interior
Kennedy and Johnson Administrations

I went to Congress a long time ago, in 1955. I arrived in Congress just after a "drunken spree" when Congress decided the best thing to do was to terminate Indians. That was in 1954. I have watched Indian affairs and Indians, Indian leadership and Indian policy for nearly 35 years since then in a rather intimate way.

Our family came from Indian country, up near Zuni and Navajo country in northern Arizona, and my father always had strong feelings that Indians didn't get justice. Arizona was then the last state in the Union where Indians were not allowed to vote. We had had an Arizona Supreme Court decision which said Indians were wards of the State and therefore weren't eligible to vote. The first opinion my father wrote when he got on the Arizona Supreme Court overturned that opinion.

Watching history for this long a period of time gives you a sense of trends and directions and development. I think Indians, Indian government, and Indian policies have made some enormous strides in the last 35 years. Not enough has yet been done, but we have a totally different policy than prevailed in 1955. Now, instead of termination, we have self-determination.

In 1961, when I became Secretary of the Interior under Kennedy, I wanted two things to make a fresh start on Indian issues. I wanted an Indian Indian Commissioner, and I wanted an Indian solicitor, a lawyer who was an Indian to be the top person in the solicitor's office. However, I couldn't find any.

Today we have an cadre of highly qualified Indian lawyers. A lot of them are at this Conference, and many are coming out of law schools just as well trained and capable as any other lawyers. This has given Indians a strength that they didn't have before. More importantly, there is a competence in terms of Indian leadership today that is almost amazing compared to what existed when I became Secretary of Interior in 1961. This has been largely a process of education. There are more college trained Indians, although many of the Indian leaders never got much education, though they have demonstrated a lot of native ability. What has developed is just plain, pure competence of Indians to lead, to deal with their affairs, to deal with the state, and to deal with federal entities. I consider this one of the major beneficial historical developments of the last three decades.

There has also been an enormous change in Indian law. Charles Wilkinson, a scholar of Indian law who I respect immensely, says that modern Indian law began in 1959, with *Williams v. Lee*, an Arizona case where the state wanted to drag Indians off their reservation into a state court. There has been an enormous change since then, and most of the changes in Indian law have been favorable to Indian sovereignty.

Indians, as indicated by the Indian Gaming Act, may not be as strong in the Senate or the House as they would like to be. The place where they are really strong is the United States Supreme Court. What every lawyer interested in this issue should do is read Charles Wilkinson's *American Indians, Time, and the Law: Native Societies in a Modern Constitutional Democracy* (1987). Wilkinson develops the history of this change. The fact is that Indian sovereignty, which few people understood a few years ago, now has been defined through these law cases. One of the stupidest things that happens and has happened over the years is that people in state government in states where there are Indians – and particularly State tax commissions and sometimes even Attorneys General – either do not want to understand Indian sovereignty or just do not give a damn. They do some of the dumbest things possible, and the result has been, in the Supreme Court, that the Indians almost always win. Wilkinson documents these cases year by year.

The reason for this is that there has been hostility and there still is hostility, by some state government officials toward Indian tribes. Some of these people do not want to understand Indian sovereignty, and others do not like it. Their idea of a level playing field is that Indian sovereignty be abolished and Indians be placed under the jurisdiction of state law.

We all know that Congress has plenary, and ultimately if the Indians lose their sovereignty, it will happen, in my opinion, not through another termination. Instead, it will occur by a Congressional salami process of cutting off little pieces here and there, until some day it will all be gone.

This is why we have to look at carefully at the Indian Gaming Act. Senator Harry Reid and my brother, Morris Udall, were involved in this legislation, and I know it was a compromise. It is important to understand this, because four or five years ago when I first saw the first Indian gaming bills, I asked myself two questions. Where is the abuse with Indian bingo? And where is the evidence that there is an invasion of organized crime or criminal activity in Indian gaming? As was mentioned earlier in this Conference by a lawyer from Senator Inouye's staff, there was no evidence of criminal infiltration. So there was not a very strong case law to justify the legislation. Furthermore, the initial bills put the Secretary of Interior in charge of Indian bingo. That, to me, was a crazy idea.

The process has since moved forward. Now that we have these new legal trends which the Indians understand, and Indian lawyers and Indian leaders are better able to fight back, we find ourselves in a new situation. Something interesting has started to happen in the last two or three years.

From the time that Europeans first came to this continent over 450 years ago, the Indians held the land but did not have our concept of ownership. They had another view of ownership which is one of the things many of us admire about the Indians. From that time until a few years ago, there was a significant shrinking of the Indian land base. Much of that shrinking took place by just killing Indians in the beginning, by driving them off, by sending them west, by the Allotment Act, and many other actions. And yet to Indians, the most important resource they have for religious, cultural and other reasons has always been the land itself.

We have started to turn a corner. In 1988, with the help of Congress, there were forest lands that were acquired and transferred to Indian tribes to enlarge their land base. The Navajo Indians continue to buy ranches in Arizona. Arizona is a very interesting state. Twenty-eight percent of the land, more than any other state, is Indian owned and that percentage is increasing.

Different Indians tribes and groups are looking at this new trend with guarded optimism. I think we all ought to recognize this new development as beneficial. If other governments, states, counties and cities, can acquire land and have the power of eminent domain, why can't Indian governments? This is a promising turn of events.

There is also a major effort being made to define Indian water rights. The resolution of this issue is absolutely crucial. The federal government must play a stronger role and must put up some of the money to make Indian water rights settlements possible because we are either going to compromise Indian water rights or we are going to have bloody, long-lasting disputes in the courts. And if the states are smart and look at the long-term track record at the Supreme Court, they will recognize the Indians will probably win in most instances.

In another area, in the past year we have a new piece of pioneering legislation: Indian National Parks. There is going to be a Zuni Indian National Historical Park. This was an idea that I discussed with Robert Lewis, the governor of Zuni, twenty years ago. After much talk, the Indians finally decided they wanted to pursue it. This concept might be tried out in other areas too.

So there is progress and change that favors Indians rights and Indian initiatives. I think more and more people believe that America needs Indians to give us a diversity that we wouldn't otherwise have. One of the greatest things about Arizona is that the state has a number of different tribes and different cultures. This gives us a difference, it makes us a better state, and it gives our culture a versatility. I also see Indian gaming in this context.

I have ambivalence about Indian gaming, and from comments made by tribal leaders at this Conference, I am apparently not alone in my feelings. Actually, by having their budgets squeezed by the Federal government, Indian tribes in the 1980s deliberately have been forced to become more and more independent, to generate their own economic future, to do things themselves, to develop their own businesses. Some tribes have turned to Indian gaming because it was an available niche; opportunities were provided by bingo and gaming. This has become very important with some Indian tribes, although others have chosen not to experiment with gaming at all.

But the success of limited Indian gaming has encouraged some tribes to consider other gaming ventures. I believe the *Cabazon* case has brought this to a head, because there were Indian tribes that were talking about horse racing, casinos, jai alai or other gaming ventures, and the Supreme Court decision brought pressures from non-Indian gaming interests that produced the 1988 Act.

When I first explored the motivations behind the legislation, I thought that probably Nevada interests were behind this. Now I think I was wrong on that first assessment. I don't think that was the main thrust; rather, I think it was the states. States and state governments simply said, let's stop Indians, let's make them conform to our law and let's not let them have the freedom to introduce other forms of gaming. Let's stop Indian gaming in its tracks before it gains momentum and enlarges the status quo.

The idea that Indians might go beyond bingo to racing or to casinos or to sports betting or slots machines made a lot of people antagonistic. Some of them simply did not want the competition. Some of them wanted to stop the normal evolution economically and culturally that Indians would go through. And yet, Indians, because of where they are located and because of other factors, have enormous economic disadvantages. However, for those who are located near interstate highways, or near large cities, or in other places where they can enter into business and prosper, the prospect of additional revenue from gaming has been one of the few advantages some Indian groups had.

I have heard at this Conference that the country has changed its entire view about gaming in the last twenty-five years. Gaming used to be considered as something evil, horrible, undertaken by crazy Nevada people who were rooted in 19th century attitudes that developed in western mining towns. They were once considered bad anti-social people, but we all know what's happened since then.

We have a situation now where Indians are confronted with limited economic opportunities based on unusual circumstances. Gaming is one, and cigarette sales are another. States are taxing cigarettes to the point where the tax is greater than the value of the commodity; because they are exempt from state taxes, that is a niche where the Indians have established themselves. That is an area where they have been able to be competitive.

But my advice to Indian tribes as they develop these opportunities is not to make the differences between themselves and their competitors all that dramatic. They should have taxes of their own, to narrow the gap somewhat. By lessening their competitive advantage they can take some of the wind out of the sails of their critics.

I also suggest to those tribes who want to enter into Class III gaming compacts with states, don't rush in without careful thought. Rather, develop the best and strongest case you can. Choose the test cases carefully, because they will determine if the states are going to be fair. If it is going to be logical for Indians to have other kinds of gaming opportunities, both economically and geographically, this law is going to test the good will of the states. The record of most of the western states, I'm sorry to say, is a record of general hostility, usually directed towards anything Indians want to do that impinges upon what states have traditionally done or want to do in the future.

So this is my message to Indian tribes. I think that there are some favorable things in the Act as far as Indians are concerned. I think the fact that Senator Daniel Inouye from Hawaii has gotten interested in Indians is great news. Senator Bill Bradley's (D – New Jersey) interest is great news, too. We are going to need to groom some Representatives in the House to replace my brother. We ought to get about it. You need strong friends in high places. History shows a few of them can go a long way.

So the opportunities are there and I believe the Indians have the leadership now to seize these opportunities and deal with them in a sensitive way. If the states are going to smash Indian tribes in the face, the tribes are going to have to go to court. Let us see if the states will deal fairly with these compacts. This is where I agree with Morris Udall and Harry Reid. The Act is a law, so test it out, try it. If it doesn't work, go back to Congress and get it changed.

4

William N. Thompson
Professor
Public Administration and Management
University of Nevada, Las Vegas

I.   INTRODUCTION

The North American Conference on the Status of Indian Gambling generated several informative, interesting, and fascinating presentations on the subject of Indian gaming in North America. As a professor with formal training in the field of Political Science, I am always happy to have an opportunity to learn how our government really works. As I wish to cover some of the same ground covered by our political practitioners, albeit from the naivete of my Ivory Tower perspectives, I feel I would be somewhat remiss, if I did not make references to other presentations in the Conference.

First, with all due respect to the keynote speaker, former Interior Secretary Stewart Udall, I do not care to see the entire issue of Indian gaming given carte blanche to the United States Supreme Court. We are a democracy and I hope our elected officials can do their jobs. We should be able to have a coherent Indian gaming policy that is developed within the political branches of our government.

When this Conference was being planned, I felt that it would be appropriate to make a presentation on Indian reservation gaming in the state of Michigan. Michigan is in some ways typical of other Indian gaming jurisdictions, but in certain special ways it is also unique. Virginia Boylan, chief of staff for the Senate Select Committee on Indian Affairs, the committee that handled the Indian Gaming Regulatory Act, made a comment in her presentation to the effect that there were only three or four Class III Indian gaming operations in the United States today. I immediately suspected that Congress did not have an adequate pool of information when it passed the Act. In Michigan alone, there are seven Class III (casino games) operations on reservations controlled by five tribes. I suspect that there are more Class III Indian casinos in Michigan than any other state. However, such games are offered on reservations in several other states including Wisconsin, Minnesota, North and South Dakota, and Washington.

Michigan has a formal law on charity casino gaming – called the Millionaire's Party Law, which was passed in 1975. The law seemingly opened the door for the gaming. And the gaming, first initiated by a tribal member acting in an individual capacity and later imitated by actions on behalf of the tribes, was drawn into federal court litigation. Michigan also has one tribe that is attempting to acquire off-reservation lands for the purpose of having them become trust lands with Class III gaming. Michigan's situation is also confused because the state is one of four where Class III card games are given Class II status under the 1988 Act. Yet several of the Class III casinos offer more than just card games to players. The Michigan case is further complicated by the fact that there has been an active campaign to legalize casino gaming within the city of Detroit.

While I still feel that it would be appropriate to expound upon Indian gaming in Michigan, my examination of the Indian Gaming Regulatory Act of 1988 kept suggesting to me that an understanding of the Michigan situation and the situation elsewhere demands a closer analysis of the Act. There are too many problem areas in the Act that could cause major dislocations in the Indian Gaming enterprise. They must be addressed before we look at specific states and cases. The first thought I had in reading the Act was "Is this Law constitutional?" I think this question should be the starting point for my inquiry into the meaning of the Act. (The Michigan situation is included as a Case Study in Appendix II. below).

We have been told many interesting things at this Conference. For instance, Secretary Udall informed us that there was legislation that would have terminated all Indians in 1954; I never heard of this before. Virginia Boylan indicated that the Act that passed in 1988 was the only Act that could possibly have passed, and had it not passed, the alternative was that there would be no Indian gaming in America. Senator Reid said in his keynote speech that, had the Act not passed, it would have meant that Indian gaming would have rampantly spread all across the land. And Boylan and Reid, and Congresswoman Barbara Vucanovich all agreed that we had to "give the Act a chance.", that it was an "experiment," and that we should not look for loopholes, but accept it as it is "in the spirit" in which it was "intended".

I am afraid that I must dissent. Professor Nelson Rose informed us of many difficulties he found in the Act. I think I must continue his approach. You realize that we have had gambling since the beginning of humanity. And we have had Indian tribes for thousands of years. I think it is a little late in the game to be experimenting with Indian gaming. "Give the Act a chance?" I recommend we should do something that a majority of the members of Congress did not do – "give the Act a reading." To those congressmen and women and staffers who urged that we not play around and try to revise the Act, I can only wonder aloud if they have read the Act.

For example, section seven of the Act clearly requires that the new Indian Gaming Commission shall submit a report by the end of the year and the report shall recommend amendments to the Act. I think we should feel free also to offer suggestions for amendments.

(I am presenting as Appendix I. my suggestions for changes in the Act, changes which I believe can answer constitutional objections, and also changes which I feel will make the Act more coherent and workable.)

II.   PASSING THE ACT

A detailed reading of the Indian Gaming Regulatory Act of 1988 will be an uncomfortable undertaking, especially if you are not a lawyer. If you just read the text, you might be led to believe, as I do, that the Act is inconsistent, incomplete, vague, redundant, absurd, and unconstitutional.

In total, this suggests that what we have here is an ordinary piece of legislation produced by the "good old American legislative process". It is an old truism that there are two things that we should never watch being made – sausage and legislation. What we want is results, not processes. And it might suffice if we can just say that the sausage tastes good. However, the making of the Indian Gaming Regulatory Act of 1988 was typical of the worst kind of legislative action. Most of the members of Congress were not involved in the process, and they were quite happy not to be involved, either because the bill didn't affect their state (or so they thought) or they sensed that conflicting pressures coming from Indian interests, rival commercial gaming interests, state governments, and law enforcement officials made it a no-win situation. But most likely they just had better things to do with their time; there have been other important questions in front of Congress in recent years.

The Act involved political authorities and governmental actors at many levels – national, tribal, state, and local. There was a strong lobby effort from what was basically a unified group, the tribal interests. However, other interest groups (gaming regulators, state governments, the Department of Justice) produced a less intense and much more diffuse posture on the issue. Moreover, the congressional actors who were involved would have to consider a line of court cases that emphasized the need for some kind of national policy resolution that only they could give, yet at the same time gave them little guidance in drawing up that policy.

The *Cabazon* case of 1987 made Congress feel that the need for action was immediate. Adding to pressures for quick action was the fact that the bill moved through Congress while a national election campaign was developing into its final stages. The election also had the effect of taking public attention away from the process.

And so most members of Congress were happy to duck the issue. Even those most closely involved did not care to linger on the issue. When the bill came up for discussion and debate in the Senate Committee, the members actually proceeded to take a vote to recommend passage before the printed bill could be placed in front of them. Of course, they stipulated that their vote could be changed later if they had a chance to read the bill and they did not like it. They didn't, so they couldn't; and the vote stood.

On the floor of the Senate the major portion of the bill – the major controversial provision – was added by an amendment without debate. That provision authored by Senator Harry Reid (D – Nevada) authorized the establishment of Indian tribe-state compacts for regulating Class III gaming on reservations. The senators, not wishing to burden their colleagues with dilemmas of decision making, managed to maneuver the bill into a special status (by process of unanimous consent – therefore no expressed objection) whereby it could pass on a voice vote, a vote without individual senators having to go on record.

In the House of Representatives there were no committee hearings on the bill, and it too received a non-recorded vote of passage. Final congressional action on the bill took place in the Senate just two hours before the 100th Congress adjourned sine die.

It appears that the only person who had to officially go on record either supporting or opposing the bill was President Reagan. He signed the bill into law in October, 1988.

This kind of process inevitably produced a sloppy product. For example, in the course of passage the bill was amended so that a five person national gaming commission became a three person commission. One of the members is chairman, one is vice chairman. Section 4 (d) now reads: "Two members of the Commission, at least one of which is the Chairman or Vice Chairman, shall constitute a quorum." That is but one example of the care that went into refining this bill. So it is quite disconcerting that at this Conference we have to hear from Congressional spokesmen who quite obviously acquiesced in this process of speed and irresponsibility, not only defending their product as "the only possible bill that could have been passed," but actually boasting pride in the fact that it passed without a recorded vote. It appears to this observer that they got away with something. I might add that the next time they tried to pass an important measure without a vote – that being their own pay raise – they were not quite so lucky.

Congress has given us the Act and now they talk about following its intent. There was no intent except to duck responsibility and produce something that looks like a decision. The law delegates and defers real decision making; it is so vague and empty in parts that litigants, lawyers, and judges will have little to guide them toward final resolutions of just what our national policy on Indian gambling should be.

Again, all this is saying is that we have a typical piece of legislation to deal with. On the positive side, we must recognize that the Act may have the effect of forcing real decisions. Yet even here we might not reap benefits if the legislation is somehow ruled unconstitutional. Then the effort may all be for naught, that is unless Congress would move quickly to make corrections that could save the Act.

That constitutional problems were anticipated by Congress is clearly demonstrated in Section 22 of the Act: "In the event that any section or provision of this Act, or amendment made by this Act, is held invalid, it is the intent of Congress that the remaining sections or provisions of this Act, and amendments made this Act, shall continue in full force and effect." One little constitutional blemish therefore will not destroy the entire Act. But what will be the effect if a majority of the sections of the Act are flawed?

III.   CONSTITUTIONAL PROBLEMS.

(a)   Standing

Constitutional objections to the Act may be anticipated to come from one or more of several directions. Federal prosecutors were effectively estopped from appealing a District Court ruling in the *Bay Mills* case in 1988 (discussed in Appendix II.) because of the passage of the Act. The Court had refused to rule on the legality of Class III gaming on Michigan reservations, because the federal district attorney had sought a civil remedy rather than pursuing criminal charges against the Indian tribes involved. In order to get a specific ruling on the legality question, he would have to have the effect of the Act set aside. He conceivably could do so with claims that the Act was unconstitutional. He had originally claimed the Indian gaming was illegal because of the Assimilative Crimes Act.

Michigan also has an attorney general who is hostile to the expansion of gaming of any kind. As the governor's office moves to negotiate a regulatory compact with the tribes to allow casino type gaming, the attorney general could seek to invalidate the compact on the grounds that the Act is constitutionally defective. Similarly, there is a provision in the Act allowing off-reservation lands to be placed into trust for the Indian tribes. Such lands could then be used for gaming. One tribe in Michigan has purchased land in a nearby city, but twenty miles from the reservation, for the purposes of having a casino. The Act would permit such gaming if the Secretary of Interior and Governor of Michigan agreed. The attorney general could begin prosecutions against gaming at the location on the grounds that the governor can not give up state sovereignty by executive decree. In the process he could challenge the constitutionality of the entire Act. And of course, the Indian tribes could challenge the Act, claiming that it restricts their rights to commercial activity as guaranteed by treaties or other federal laws. Indeed, the challenge from the tribes has already begun.

(b)   *Indian Sovereignty and Equal Protection Questions*

The Red Lake Band of Chippewa Indians in Minnesota and the Mescalero Apache Tribe of New Mexico have initiated action requesting injunctive and declaratory relief in the United States District Court of the District of Columbia. In their suit against the Assistant Secretary of the Interior they ask that the Court declare the Act unconstitutional and prohibit the President from appointing the chairman of the National Indian Gaming Commission.

The essential claim of the Tribes is that the Act violates their sovereign prerogatives to conduct affairs on their lands as permitted by treaties and the Indian Self Determination Act. They especially object to the fact that the Act determined the legality of their gaming enterprise on the basis of state law, and that in order to conduct Class III gaming, they are forced to make agreements with state governments. Their claim is that their tribal standing is a matter of federal and not state law, and that any matters governing their commercial activities must be established through federal law, not state law. They hold that they can surrender tribal authority only to the federal government. Moreover, they feel that regulation of their affairs cannot be delegated by the federal government to state authorities. Indeed, they claim that "the primary purpose of the federal trust responsibility and guardianship is to protect tribes from interference from state governments."

The two plaintiff tribes object to the fact that the Act signalled out four states – South Dakota, Michigan, North Dakota, and Washington – for special treatment. Class III card games which were played on reservations in these four states on or before May 1, 1988 would be considered Class II games (along with Bingo) and could continue without the tribes having to enter into compacts with state governments. The Red Lake Band and the Mescaleros ask the question no one seems to be able to answer in any definitive manner: why these four states? Why not all states which had Class III Indian games on May 1, 1988? In my own quest to figure out the Michigan situation I asked the question to everyone I thought might be able to answer it. All I got was shrugs of shoulders and comments such as, "Well I guess that the tribes in those states (or the congressmen of those states) wanted the special treatment, and the Indians of the other states weren't able to speak up at the right time."

The Congressional Record does report commentary from Minnesota and Wisconsin senators asking why their states were excluded, but again no good answers are provided. I have to accept that it was just another case of "politics." But is this good politics? And, is this a case of constitutional politics? Given the very closed nature of decision making regarding the passage of the Act, can't we honestly ask: how could the tribes of the several states possibly lobby to have their Class III games treated as Class II games when there were only limited hearings in one house, and no hearings on the bill in the other house, when the committee staff of the Senate Committee was apparently ignorant of the extent of Class III gaming on reservations, when the Senate committee voted on the bill before a printed copy was available to them, and when floor debate proceeded so quickly that honest deliberations were not possible, let alone deliberations held in front of an informed public. The Indian plaintiffs ask: can there be a rational basis for treating reservations of four states differently than those in other states? Their rhetorical question is, of course, answered, "No." Classifications which treat people or groups differently under the law must have a rational basis to be constitutional. There is no rational reason for treating Michigan, South Dakota, North Dakota, and Washington differently. Indeed, it is very strange to see South Dakota in the list, because as of May 1, 1988, Class III card games in that state were categorically illegal whether played on the reservation or elsewhere. While the games had a legal basis in the other three states, they similarly had a legal basis in several other Indian gaming states as well.

The classification is not defensible, and in my opinion will not stand constitutional challenge.

(c)   Treaties, Compacts, or Something else?

Senator Harry Reid proudly claimed authorship of the most controversial part of the Indian Gaming Regulatory Act of 1988. In his remarks to the Conference, he indicated that the bill was at an impasse state when he talked to the leader of the fight for enactment, Senator Inouye (D – Hawaii). He suggested that Class III gaming be regulated in accordance with compacts the tribes would negotiate with state governments. His idea was not brought up until the bill had reached the Senate floor. It became an amendment that was accepted without extensive or even minimal debate. Like our electoral college, it was a "stroke of genius" that everyone recognized at once to be a solution to the problem of passing the bill. However, in their rush to incorporate this into law, the Senators did not consider just what they were doing, or what they were not doing. The rationale for the provision was that the Indians were sovereign entities, and the states were sovereign entities; therefore they should get together and mutually agree on the kind of regulation necessary for Class III gaming.

Senator Reid did not draw this idea out of thin air. The Fort Mojave Indian reservation at the southernmost point of the state of Nevada initiated serious plans to develop a major casino on their land, which is ten miles south of the successful gaming town of Laughlin, Nevada. The state of Nevada immediately became concerned that organized crime would dupe the Indians and take over their operations unless the casino would be fully regulated in the manner that other Nevada gaming halls were regulated – that is, so regulated that it would be impossible for the Mob to be involved. Of course, there was no concern that the Indians might compete with established gaming houses. The state hinted that they would challenge the Indian's right to have unregulated casinos. Rather than engaging in protracted litigation that they feel they would have won, the Indians sought a cooperative arrangement with the state of Nevada. They entered into a contract that was negotiated by the governor's office and approved by the Gaming Commission and the attorney general's office as well as tribal authorities. The contract provided that the Gaming Board of the state would enforce all provisions of the state gaming act on the reservation, and the Indians would pay for the cost of regulation.

Actually, the state would collect the same six per cent (gross gaming win) it collects from other casinos, determine costs of regulation, and return the balance to the Indian tribal treasury. The state was happy, the Indians were happy, and the project is proceeding full speed ahead without any legal impediments standing in its way, that is, unless the Indians, sometime down the road, would like to review their agreement in light of the Act.

The Fort Mojave agreement was clearly a contract written in accordance with state law. But is this what Congress intended under the Act? If so, why did congressional spokesmen talk about the sovereignty of the tribes and the state? Is it possible that Congress intended for the states and Indians to enter into treaties? Alternatively could they have intended that the agreements be Interstate Compacts as provided for in the United States Constitution?

Could the agreements be treaties? The answer is clearly "No". Article I, Section 10 of the Constitution clearly states that "No State Shall enter into any Treaty, Alliance, or Confederation..." Similarly as a matter of constitutional interpretation, Indian tribes are not foreign states with treaty making powers such as possessed by entities foreign to the United States. All negotiations with Indians that were previously covered by treaties between the United States and the Indians must now be negotiated through Acts of Congress with a recognition that the Indian interest is represented by the same 535 members who represent the interest of the United States Government.

But Congress did not use the word "treaty" when they adopted Senator Reid's provision. They used the word "Compacts." Certainly, our members of Congress know about Interstate Compacts. They are provided for in the Constitution (Article I, Section 10: "No state shall, without the consent of Congress...enter into any agreement or Compact with another state..."), and they have been a manifested ingredient of our federal system for nearly two centuries.

It appears that states have the authority to enter into compacts, and also it would appear that the sovereign standing of Indian tribes would place them on sufficient footing to also make compacts with states. The Constitution is silent upon the exact procedures states should follow in making compacts; however, the extensive history of the arrangements entered into over the past two hundred years leaves a mark of accepted methods. The National Resources Committee (*Regional Factors in National Planning and Development*, Washington: U.S.Government Printing Office, 1935; p.53) specified five precise steps in the process:

> "(1)   Congress authorizes the negotiation of the compact and outlines its purposes.

(2)   The State legislature authorizes commissioners
       representing them to meet and negotiate a
       compact.
(3)   The commissioners meet (under the chairmanship
       of a Federal representative) to negotiate and
       sign the compact.
(4)   The State legislatures ratify the compact.
(5)   Congress ratifies the compact."

The process requires state legislative action as well as congressional action at both the authorization-negotiation stages and the ratification stages. Representative political bodies are designated because of financial reasons. If a compact in any way involves the generation of public revenue or the expenditure of public revenues, legislatures should be involved as a matter of basic constitutional principles dating back to the Magna Carta. Certainly, the regulation of Class III gaming on reservations anticipated expenditure of funds and also the generation of revenues through taxes or fees.

Nevada maintains that the cost of regulation for the Fort Mojave casino is a contractual fee and a tribal tax which combine for an amount of six per cent of the gross gaming win at the proposed casino. The state portion of the fee-tax is to be at least one per cent. The tribal government agreed to this arrangement. Is taxation involved? What if regulatory expenses are less than one per cent of the gross win? They could be if the state chose to make them less. Then the state's one per cent would be in excess of actual costs; hence it would have to be considered a tax of sorts. As such, the legislature should have been involved in the process.

But the Nevada-Fort Mojave understanding was a state matter. The compacts of the Act are a federally authorized matter. Where a state on its own may make contracts, states will not be operating on their own with these compacts. State legislatures should negotiate the compacts, or at least ratify them. Yet many states are interpreting the Act otherwise. In some the governor is conducting the negotiations, and in others lottery commissions or gaming commissions. Can such actors draw up agreements committing state resources? Even if the legislative body is involved, there is a problem in that the Act specifies that the compacts must be negotiated within a time framework, 180 days, when many state legislative bodies are out of session. The ratification process may also be flawed in that the Act provides for the executive branch of the national government to approve of the compacts, rather than placing final approval in the hands of Congress.

Additionally there is a monumental problem in the fact that the two sovereign entities – tribes and states – are compelled to negotiate compacts in order for Class III gaming to exist on reservations. States must act in good faith and negotiate agreements within 180 days of notice being received by the Indian tribes. If the negotiation process does not proceed according to the desires of either party, outside elements will make the actual decisions on the contents of the compacts either through a mediation process or by action of the Secretary of the Interior. Clearly the two sides to the compacts are not acting as sovereign equals in the process. There is no equality, and there is only a minimal amount of sovereignty involved. If these are interstate compacts, the process is flawed.

The Act does not tell the states and the Indians what the position of the compact will be in the priority of laws. Will the compact be supreme to other state laws? Will it supercede the state constitution? On gaming matters? On other matters as well? Could the compact abrogate other Indian rights, rights they have gained in treaties? Could the compact address Class II gaming? Could the compact address other gaming within the state? For instance, could the Indians agree to state regulation of Class III gaming in exchange for a guarantee that there will be no other commercial Class III gaming in the state?

The Act does not specify how a compact may end. Can it end? Can a state change its law to remove the conditions allowing

Class III Indian gaming? Can they do so after the Indians have commenced the gaming? After the compact has been negotiated? What if the state supreme court rules that a Class III gaming provision in state law is unconstitutional? Would this negate a compact? This situation is very real in South Dakota. There a video slot law may be challenged in court. Will a state court decision take precedence over the compact process? This all raises another question: who is the final judge of the content and meaning of state law regarding gaming?

There are many unanswered questions regarding compacts. Some of the questions carry serious constitutional implications for the Act.

(d)   The Appointment process

United States Constitution states (Article II, Section 2): ". . . and (the President) shall nominate . . . by and with the Advice and Consent of the Senate . . . all other Officers of the United States, whose appointments are not herein otherwise provided for . . . but the Congress may by law vest the Appointment of such inferior Officers, as they think proper, in the President alone, in the Courts of Law, or in the Heads of Departments."

The Act establishes a National Indian Gaming Commission of three members. One of the members is designated chairman. The chairman is appointed by the President with the advice and consent of the Senate. Two other members are appointed by the Secretary of the Interior. A constitutional question arises in the examination of the Act. Are the associate commissioners inferior officers? If so, does the Act imply that the chairman is a superior officer?

The chairman is granted a salary one step ahead of the associate members on the executive salary scale. Yet all are full time officials. And all meet collegially, making decisions as a unit.

When the chairman is absent, one associate member who is designated as the vice chairman may act in his place. Yet there are duties the chairman exercises separately. Here too, the vice chairman may often act in his absence. Most of the independent decisions of the chairman may be overturned by the full commission. First, this introduces a faulty review process, as it implies that the chairman will sit in judgment over decisions he or she has already made. Second, it clearly implies that the associate members acting with the commission are superior, not inferior, to the chairman.

The problematic appointment process is confused further by the fact that the three commissioners must represent more than one political party (all three cannot be of the same party), and that two of the three must be Indians. There is no time table for appointments. There is no provision that the chairman or associate members must be appointed first. What happens when the President chooses to appoint a non-Indian as chairman? Must the Secretary appoint two Indian members? But what if the Secretary appoints one Indian and one non-Indian, must the President now make an Indian the chairman (with Senate approval, of course)?

Similar questions arise regarding political party representation. Is it proper that in a process where appointments are supposed to be made with a semblance of independence that a Secretary of the Interior can force the President to restrict his appointment choices? Of course Act supporters will suggest that the Secretary as a presidential appointee himself will coordinate the choice process, but why should this be? Should not all appointments be made in the similar manner? And shouldn't the roles of the three be better coordinated especially in the case of reviewing decisions made by one another?

(e)   Judicial Power and Executive Mediation.

In the event that a state government does not negotiate a compact with an Indian tribe for Class III gaming within 180 days after a request from the tribe, the tribe may initiate a cause of action in federal district court. If the court finds that the state had not acted in good faith in negotiations, the court may order that a compact be made by the parties within sixty days. If this is not done, both parties – state and tribe – must submit offered compacts to a mediator who is appointed by the Court. The mediator shall select one of the two proposed compacts. He then submits the selected compact to the Secretary of Interior for final approval or disapproval. If, however, the Secretary does not act within 45 days, the mediated compact takes effect. (Section 11, Act).

The provision on resolving impasses in the compact negotiation process raises several constitutional problems concerning judicial power and the separation of powers. It is an accepted constitutional principle that the judiciary should not be involved in exercising executive powers. Courts, for instance, cannot become involved in treaty writing (*The Amiable Isabella*, 19 U.S. 1, 1821). Courts may interfere with executive duties only if those duties are ministerial and involve no exercise of judgment or discretion. (*Litchfield v. Register and Receiver*, 76 U.S. 575, 1869). Moreover, an essential element of Judicial power is the element of finality. (*Hayburn's Case*, 2 Dall. 409, 1792).

While even consistently upheld cases may be modified in future court decisions, we can seriously ask if a change in constitutional law will be made for the compact provision of the Indian Gaming Regulatory Act of 1988. There should be doubt. Here the district court is clearly being asked to engage in an executive duty many steps before a final decision is rendered on the validity of a particular proposed compact. Here the district court is asked to appoint a mediator whose actions also are not final actions, and who is required to report his actions to the Secretary of the Interior who then exercises further discretionary power over the matter. The district court has been asked by Congress to exercise powers clearly outside its constitutional role.

The constitution does permit Congress to ask courts to appoint inferior officials. However, these appointments have usually been of officials who perform duties for the court, such as clerks and other judicial administrators. The mediator's duties are not performed for the court. Although there has been no direct holding on the point, the Supreme Court has tangentially indicated that officials appointed by the judiciary should report to the judiciary. In the case of *Ex Parte Hennen*, for instance, the Supreme Court ruled that the appointment of clerks of courts belonged to the courts, that a clerk of the courts was one of the positions contemplated by the constitutional authors when they allowed courts to make appointments of inferior officials, and that the appointment process was to be exercised by the department of government to which the officer to be appointed most appropriately belonged (13 Pet. 230, 1839). A strong case can be made that the mediator does not belong to the judicial branch.

(f)   State Sovereignty

Section 20 of the Act indicates that Indians may conduct gaming on newly acquired lands – not on reservations – if the Secretary of the Interior determines that the gaming is in the best interests of the tribe, will not be detrimental to the surrounding community, and if the governor of the state concurs. The Secretary must consult with the Indian tribe and "appropriate" local officials before making a decision. This section is indeed a wildcard provision.

There is no stipulation regarding which tribes may purchase lands, or where the lands may be located. Indeed, a California tribe could conceivably acquire lands in New York City for this purpose. The Secretary could consult with the mayor and win his agreement. After all, it was the New York mayor's insistence that Manhattan be included in a New York bill for casino gaming in 1980 that had contributed to the defeat of casinos in New York State. However, New York State is clearly a Class III gaming state as charities may conduct roulette, craps, and house-banked card games. To make it work would only require the governor's approval. It would not be too farfetched to expect a person in such a position to do something to help absolve our national guilt for centuries of mistreatment of Indians. What better symbol of reconciliation could there be than to grant the Indians a concession for gaming on Manhattan?

The Hannahville tribe of Michigan is in the process of seeking agreement for gaming facilities on newly acquired land in the city of Escanaba, approximately 20 miles off the reservation. The city council of Escanaba supports the plan, but the mayor opposes it. The matter may have to be finally resolved in the governor's office in Lansing. A Minnesota tribe has already made a land purchase in Duluth, and is conducting gaming there under conditions existent prior to the Act. When a state acquiesces in allowing an Indian tribe to conduct gaming on newly acquired lands, the state is giving up a major degree of sovereignty over the land. The compact provisions of the Act were written with at least a semblance of the notion that the tribes stood on equal footing with state governments. If this theory is valid, can we not also make an analogy between the newly acquired lands that will be used for Indian gaming and the creation of a new state out of land from an old state? If we can, we may apply the edict of Section 3 of Article IV of the Constitution which clearly requires the consent of the Legislature of a state before its lands are incorporated into another new state. Whether the analogy fits or not, the cession of state sovereignty over its own lands to any degree should be a matter for the representative branch of state government, and it should not be done by executive decree. Plano and Greenberg's *The American Political Dictionary* defines "Republican form of Government" as "a government that operates through elected representatives of the people."(4th ed., p.41).

As the Constitution requires the United States government to guarantee to every state of the Union a "Republican form of Government" (Article IV, Section 4) it would be appropriate that legislative bodies oversee matters of state sovereignty.

(g)   Freedom of Association and Employment

Despite the denials from Nevada spokesmen, the Indian Gaming Regulatory Act of 1988 has certainly received indelible markings from Nevada interests.   Senator Reid told us how he managed to insert a compact provision modelled (at least in his mind) after the Fort Mojave-Nevada contract for regulating casino gaming.

Section 11 of the Act was also influenced by Nevada experience. The section deals with tribal gaming ordinances. Tribes wishing to conduct Class II games must set down resolutions which will govern management and employment practices. As in Nevada, managers and key employees must undergo background investigations and be licensed. Nevada also sets down a broad standard for exclusion of persons from eligibility for licensure (Nevada Revised Statutes 463.170, 2a). The Act uses the exact same language with only changes in grammatical form and reference to tribes. But the Act goes further. Whereas in Nevada the standard applies to owners, managers, and other key employees, the Indian standard applies to all persons who would desire to be employees of gaming operations.

To comply with the Act, a tribal ordinance must contain "a standard whereby any person whose prior activities, criminal record, if any, or reputation, habits and associations pose a threat to the public interest or to the effective regulation of gaming, or create or enhance the dangers of unsuitable, unfair, or illegal practices and methods and activities in the conduct of gaming shall not be eligible for employment . . . " ((sect. 11, (b) (2) (F) (II).))

The quoted provision poses problems.   The right to employment is protected by due process clauses of the Fifth and Fourteenth Amendments as employment is considered within the rubric of "liberty" and "property". "The right to hold specific private employment and to follow a chosen profession free from unreasonable governmental interference comes within the 'liberty' and 'property' concepts provisions of . . . (the) Constitution that no person shall be denied liberty or property without due process of law." *(Greene v. McElroy*, 360 U.S. 474, 1959).

While the Nevada Gaming statute has been upheld by the Nevada Supreme Court in its application of standards for licensing key employees – in part on the basis that participation in the industry was a privilege and not a right – the case of a lower level employee in an Indian gaming hall might be seen quite differently. The Nevada case of *Rosenthal v. Nevada* (93 Nev. 36, 1977) was not a clear cut decision. In fact the trial court (district court) found the Nevada gaming statute to be absent of standards creating "a void in which malice, vindictiveness, intolerance and prejudice can fester." The State Supreme Court reversed the district court ruling. The United States Supreme Court denied certiorari denying all observers of benefit of having their final word.

Professor Nelson Rose would not have concurred with the high state court. In his *Gambling and the Law* (1986) he writes: "The First Amendment right to freedom of association is undermined both by refusal to license individuals on the basis of their past associations, and by putting restrictions on who they can associate with in the future. The U.S. Supreme Court has recognized the substantive due process right of a man to earn a living and engage in his chosen occupation, a right that cannot be taken away without a compelling state interest, except apparently in Nevada casino gaming." (P. 185)

Rose also points to procedural deficiencies in Nevada's licensing process. "The major federal constitutional right lost is the right to procedural due process. Without notice and the opportunity to be heard, none of the other rights mean a thing." (P. 185)   As with the Nevada Act, the Indian Gaming Regulatory Act is silent on procedural safeguards which may assure that a potential employee is not wrongfully labeled as unsuitable because he is not able to have proper representation or submit proper documentation to support his case for employment.

As alluded to in the Nevada district court hearing in the *Rosenthal* case, a major problem with the provision is vagueness. Courts have repeatedly set aside statutes which restrain liberties on the basis that the standards in the statutes are so vague that those subject to them cannot fully understand the conduct they must follow in order to enjoy their rights. (See: *Cramp v. Board*, 368 U.S. 278, 1961; *Keyishian v. Board*, 385 U.S. 589, 1967; and *Cox v. Louisiana*, 379 U.S. 536 and 559, 1965).

The standards set forth in Section 11 must be re-evaluated by Congress. Our national policy makers should not have rushed so fast to adopt and expand a state policy position that is so controversial and potentially flawed.

IV. SUMMARY AND CALL TO CONGRESS.

The Indian Gaming Regulatory Act of 1988 was the result of nearly six years of discussions regarding Indian gaming. However, while the issue was in front of Congress for a considerable length of time, the specifics of the actual bill passed were not. Indeed, the specifics seemed to be slipped through the legislative process in a manner suggesting that debate and open discussion were *per se* enemies of the policy making process. Sponsors of the bill indicate that quick passage was needed, because any other manner of deliberation would have resulted in no bill at all. The matter was so controversial that a blind committee approval was necessary in order to get a recommendation of favorable floor action. On the floor a maneuver to allow an unrecorded voice vote was necessary so that Congressmen could avoid having constituents know how they stood on the issue. Otherwise, no bill would have passed.

The result is that we have another piece of lousy legislation on the federal statute books. What is worse, there are several parts of the bill that could be rendered unconstitutional by court action. Indeed it is this author's position that any deliberative court must rule parts of the Act unconstitutional. Do we then return to the position where we have no bill at all? Perhaps that will be the case, unless Congress shows they can deliberate on the Act again and remove objectionable provisions, replacing them with appropriately constitutional provisions.

In this paper I have been admittedly quite negative. I do not, however, wish that negativism to represent my final position. Congress did pass a law. Congress did initiate a policy making process. That process can continue. A good Act can result. However, Congress must be willing now to review what they did and correct the deficiencies. For the most part this can be done in a non-controversial way, but not in all cases. Congress must in these cases be willing to make decisions that some people will not like. They must be willing to be public representatives.

APPENDIX I: A PROPOSAL FOR AMENDMENTS

(a)   Cleaning Up the Act

The Indian Gaming Regulatory Act of 1988 could be improved immeasurably with enhanced wording and with some non-controversial amendments. First, consider the National Indian Gaming Commission. Its three members should be appointed by the same authority. All three should be considered inferior officers so that Senate confirmation would not have to be involved in the appointment process. If Congress is reluctant to get into policy making on this issue, they should not be asked to be involved in the executive duty of appointments. As inferior executive officers, all three members of the Commission could be appointed either by the President alone or by the Secretary of the Interior. The appointing authority could designate the one member who would serve as chairman, and also the one who would serve as vice chairman. The single appointing authority would then be responsible for maintaining the proper party and Indian non-Indian balance on the Commission. A quorum would simply be two members. All decisions would be Commission decisions, although the three might delegate recommendation authority to the chairman. The chairman would then bring his preliminary analysis of an issue to the full board for final action. The full commission with the chairman participating would not be in the awkward position of handling appeals from the chairman's decisions. Appeals from Commission action could either be directed to the Secretary of the Interior, or such action could be considered final administrative action reviewable by the courts, as determined by the Act.

A second matter of minor concern should be the exemption given to four states so that Class III card games could be considered Class II games. All states and tribes should be treated the same under the Act. This could be accomplished by having all classes of Indian gaming (at least Class II and Class III games) regulated by the National Indian Gaming Commission, as will be discussed below. Barring such a decision by Congress, the exemption by the four should be dropped as soon as is practical. Perhaps the exemption could run for an additional year before the games would be subject to compact regulation.

(b)   Clearing up the Sovereignty Dilemma

The Sovereignty questions are difficult and they are clearly controversial. What is clear, though, is that the vast majority of tribes do not want any state regulation whatsoever. They should not be required to come under state regulation.

Court cases from *Butterworth* to *Cabazon* have held that Indian tribes can have gaming unregulated by states if the particular games involved are legal within the state. The Act goes further as it says the games may be permitted on reservations if they are permitted in the state "for any purpose, organization, or entity." A state government should determine what is legal and permissible within its borders. However, states have made rules for charity gaming and incidental games of chance (games which might take the form of casino games) before the issue of Indian gaming was joined. (For example, Michigan passed its Millionaire Parties Law in 1975.)

A state should be given an opportunity to review its gaming statutes and make revisions in light of their new effect. In two years (long enough for all legislatures to meet) the governor (with the approval of the attorney general) of each state should make a declaration to the National Gaming Commission regarding the games that are actually permitted in the state. The Commission would then presume the statement to be the definitive word on legality, but they would permit the statement to be challenged. The presumption could be overturned if it was shown to be clearly inaccurate, or if it were shown that other games were openly played in the state without any law enforcement effort to stop them. The National Commission would then declare to the Indians just what games were permitted on their reservations.

Such an amendment would serve the purpose of allowing states such as Michigan and New York to take another serious look at their charity games. Perhaps they would decide that charities could exist with just bingo. The Commission should allow a governor to amend his declaration at anytime; however, the Commission would allow Indian reservations a reasonable time, perhaps five years, in order to phase out their games. This time period would allow the Indians a chance to readjust their local economies. I would suggest that the Indian reservations be able to continue their present gaming practices for the two year period during which the states reviewed their gaming laws.

The essential source of Indian irritation with the Act is the provision for Indian tribe-State compacts for regulation of Class III games. These suggestions would allow for an alternative to the compacts.

In 1985 Professor John Dombrink, University of California-Irvine, and I served as gaming consultants to the President's Commission on Organized Crime. We were concerned with the proliferation of unregulated and under-regulated gaming across the country. While there was only minimal evidence that large scale organized crime was involved in the gaming, there were many recurring stories of local corruption and lapses in the integrity of the gaming operations. We suggested that there be a five year moratorium on all new gaming legalizations. In that time we envisioned that the federal government could sponsor and fund comprehensive and definitive studies on the social and economic consequences of various types of gaming. With a focused effort we could discern the extent of the problem of compulsive gambling, or the extent of organized crime involvement in each type of gaming. The five year time would also allow the federal government to set into place a National Gaming Commission. The Commission would then establish standards and rules for conducting gaming operations.

We proceeded to suggest that many states are already doing a good job in regulating gaming. They could probably do as good a job in the future as a new federal gaming regulatory body. Therefore we indicated that states should have the choice of accepting the federal regulatory mechanism or opting out for state regulation. State regulations would have to be as rigorous as federal standards.

The process of opting out is being utilized today by Nevada. State authorities negotiated to win the authority to implement federal Internal Revenue Service cash reporting requirements in casinos. New Jersey gaming regulators decided to let the I.R.S. enforce its own rules.

The approach we took in our report to the President's Commission on Organized Crime may well be utilized for Indian gaming regulation. I suggested above that we should give states two years before it is determined exactly what their gaming laws are. During that time we should build within the National Indian Gaming

Commission the capacity to directly regulate all Indian games (Class II and III).

The ideal of federal regulation is anathema to some state gaming regulators. Nevada interests have consistently opposed any federal intervention into gaming matters. The feeling is that gaming is strictly a state matter, a view expressed in the recommendations of the National Commission on Gaming Policy in 1976. However, there are other views. Thomas R. O'Brien, formerly the Director of the Division of Gaming Enforcement in the State of New Jersey, felt differently. In his opinion, New Jersey and Nevada had effective regulation. However, he reasoned that we would be encountering multifaceted dangers if another jurisdiction offered casino gaming. First, the new jurisdiction would lack expertise, especially at the critical start-up time for gaming. Second, as casinos became more available in more locations, the competitive formula would change. Casino enterprise and its beneficiaries – including state treasuries – would seek to maximize profits. Lax enforcement of regulations might result where a state would be seeking to attract new casino investors and to see the existing casino establishment reap more and more profits. With a major third gaming jurisdiction, O'Brien felt that federal regulation would be necessary . (Personal interview in Trenton, New Jersey, July 9, 1985). With Indians we are talking not about a third jurisdiction but rather thirty jurisdictions.

In recommending that the National Commission on Indian Gaming regulate Class II and Class III gaming, I am suggesting that the federal government has the capacity to develop gaming regulatory expertise. They should be able to do so just as well as any state faced for the first time with regulating Class III games. It is ironic that one of the reasons behind the creation of the Indian-State compacts for Class III gaming was that these games – table banked games – require a special expertise well beyond the skill level necessary for regulating bingo (Class II) games. The irony is found in the fact that the same decision makers that advanced that rationale also provided for exemptions so that Class III gaming on Indian reservations in

Michigan, South Dakota, North Dakota, and Washington would be regulated by the National Indian Gaming Commission on the same basis that Class II games are regulated.

I would suggest that the entire arrangement for Indian-State compacts be abolished. This would render moot all of the constitutional objections raised above regarding the compacts. However, if they are kept, some changes are in order to minimize constitutional challenges which are sure to move through the courts. First, the Act should specify that the compacts must be ratified by state legislative bodies as well as tribal councils, and that any mediators appointed to make decisions and report to the Secretary of the Interior should be selected by the executive branch of the government.

In place of compacts, the Act should permit states and tribes to make contractual agreements to allow Class II and Class III games on reservations to be regulated at the state level in accordance with their own desires. This regulation, if as rigorous as the national regulation, would permit the reservation to be opted out of federal regulation. There should be a federal tax on the gaming in order to pay the costs of the regulation (for instance, 3% of gross gaming win). A major portion of this tax (2 1/2%) could revert to any state which enters into a contract with the Indian reservations for gaming regulation purposes.

The Act should also be amended to provide that newly acquired Indian lands can be used for gaming purposes only if such use is allowed by the state legislature as well as the National Commission. Additionally, the Act should stipulate that any contractual agreement a state makes with an Indian tribe regarding gaming will affect gaming only on the reservation and will not speak to gaming elsewhere in the state.

In summary, I believe Indian gaming policy is a matter of national concern. Essential control over Indian gaming should be national.

APPENDIX II:SEVEN INDIAN CASINOS IN MICHIGAN

An enhanced understanding of the factors leading up to the passage of the Indian Gaming Regulatory Act and factors influencing the potential implications of the Act can be gained by examining specific jurisdictions. The Act did not come out of a vacuum nor will its effects be played out on a tabula rosa.

The Indian gaming experience of Michigan presents an interesting case study for several reasons. The state has several federally recognized Indian reservations. They introduced bingo games along with other charity groups in the early 1970s when the games of chance were legalized. In the mid-1970s charity casino nights were authorized in the state. However, it was not until the 1980s that casino games came to reservations. An individual entrepreneur attempted to start games on one reservation for his own personal benefit. He was stopped by an order of the federal district court. But when tribes instituted casino games as a collective venture, a federal district court refused to enjoin the activity.

Seven casinos now exist offering both Class II and Class III games. One of the five tribes operating the casinos is attempting to move gaming off its reservations into a nearby city. The effort is opposed by the state attorney general.

But Michigan Indian gaming should also be examined in the context of broader gaming policy. The case study starts by looking at general gaming law. The state of Michigan legalized pari-mutuel horse racing in 1933. In 1972 voters removed a constitutional ban on lotteries, and soon a lottery was established and bingo games for charity were authorized. In 1975 a law permitting charity casino nights was approved. The year of 1975 also saw a legislative study committee examine the feasibility of having commercial casinos in

Michigan. The report did not mention the topic of Indian gaming. Three times the voters of Detroit have been asked to vote on the desirability of having casinos in the Motor City. In 1976, 1981, and again in 1988, they rejected casinos. Proponents of casinos for Detroit, however, continue their efforts.

Indians offered bingo games on reservations soon after the charity games were authorized in 1972. High stakes bingo opportunities were not recognized until the late 1970s when tribes imitated the activities of the Seminoles in Florida and the Penobscots in Maine. In the 1980s, casino games were added to reservation gaming operations. Today there are seven Indian casinos in Michigan. All operate according to tribal ordinances which have been approved by the Bureau of Indian Affairs. One of the casinos received a grant from the Department of Housing and Urban Development to construct its gaming facilities. Tribes have also received loan guarantees from the Bureau of Indian Affairs for gaming operations. Each of the casinos is the largest employer on the reservation. Together they employ 800 workers, with over 95% of these being members of the tribes. Each has from 60 to 195 employees, and payrolls ranging from $500,000 to $1.5 million per year. As a result of gaming operations, reservation unemployment rates overall fell from 63% to 22%. On the Bay Mills reservation the rate fell from 70% to 10%, while with the Leelanau facility, Indian unemployment fell from 77% to 10%. All management employees at all the reservations are members of the tribes. Furthermore, there are no outside management contracts.

The capital investment for each of the seven facilities exceeded $1 million. Gross gaming wins realized have been as high as $1.6 million on one reservation for the year. As a result of this economic activity, tribes have made economic investments in other enterprises including motels and printing shops. Funds have also gone for building houses, health care, education, substance abuse programs, and meals for senior citizens.

In addition to bingo, the casinos offer blackjack, baccarat, poker, craps, and wheel games. They also sell pull tabs, but there are no slot machines. Maximum betting limits are as low as $5 per play in one casino, and as high as $100 in another.

The Saginaw Chippewa reservation near Mount Pleasant (in the center of the Lower Peninsula, about 65 miles north of Lansing) has 900 members living on 500 acres of land. They began high stakes bingo games in 1981. In 1987 they started blackjack games. They soon moved the card games into a separate building that is 60 feet by 100 feet. As of 1989, they have 31 blackjack tables, six poker tables, a craps table, and a big wheel. Maximums range from $5 to $25. All dealers are Indian, all customers are non-Indian. Crowds of 600 persons wait to enter the card room when it opens. Often they have to give numbers to players as they wait. The facility is open from 5 p.m. to 12 midnight on Wednesdays, Fridays, and Saturdays, and from noon to 7 p.m. on Sundays. The tribe is basically Methodist in outlook, and therefore alcoholic beverages are not available at the facilities. The tribe plans to use profits from gaming to purchase additional land for the reservation. (*Lansing State Journal*, January 14, 1988)

The Keeweenaw Bay Indian Community has two casinos. One, the Ojibwa, is near Baraga, the other is at Watersmeet. Together they offer bingo and 20 tables of blackjack. In 1987 their payroll was $740,000. The Keeweenaw Bay Indian Community is probably responsible for Class III Indian gaming in Michigan, because they approved Fred Dakota's private casino operations in January 1984. (*Detroit News*, January 17, 1988; *Lansing State Journal*, December 27, 1987)

There are two casinos near Sault Sainte Marie. The Vegas Kewadin (meaning "Vegas of the North") is located in the city, while the Bay Mills casino is at the town of Brimley. The Vegas Kewadin began operations in November 1985. It is open on Wednesdays from 6 p.m. to 2 a.m., and on Fridays, Saturdays, and Sundays from

6 p.m. to 4 a.m. A bingo hall stands across the road from the Class III gaming hall. The gaming hall has two big six wheels, 36 blackjack tables, as well as poker and craps games. The hall also offers two airball games (simulations of roulette) and pull tabs. Bet limits are $100. The casino has a bar lounge and a restaurant. It draws three hundred gamers an evening. Eighty per cent of these are from Canada. The facility employees 180. (*Lansing State Journal*, July 13, 1986)

The Bay Mills casino opened in 1984. It has suffered from the competition of the Vegas Kewadin. Its employment force is now only 20, and it has dropped its number of tables from 17 to 12. It also found it necessary to drop maximum bet limits from $100 to $15.

The tribe of Chippewas that operates the casinos has had plans for expansion. Their gaming literature indicates they will open casinos at St. Ignace, Manistique, and Munising – three cities in the Upper Peninsula of Michigan.

The Grand Traverse Band of Ottawa and Chippewa Indians operates the Leelanau Sands Casino in Peshawbestown, twenty-five miles north of Traverse City. The Sands is on a reservation of 135 acres which is home for 1800 tribal members. The goal of the casino is to allow the reservation to be economically self sufficient. Gaming proceeds have supplemented government funded programs for the elderly and the young. Health care and job training have been emphasized along with senior citizen housing. The tribe is also building a 26 room motel with casino revenues. The casino opened in 1984. By 1987 gaming revenues were $1.6 million for the year. The facility has twelve blackjack tables, and accepts bets up to $100 per play. (*Detroit News*, January 17 and April 17, 1988; *Detroit Free Press*, April 1, 1988)

The Hannahville Indian Community opened its "Chip-In Casino" in December 1985. It now employees 71 tribal members in a facility offering craps, blackjack, poker and pull tabs. Most of its gamers are from Wisconsin. In 1988 the community decided that it needed larger facilities. The tribe signed an agreement to purchase property in the downtown district of the city of Escanaba. The new expanded casino will employ an extra 99 persons. The tribe then began procedures to have the property made part of their reservation. At the time the procedures required that the Bureau of Indian Affairs accept the land in trust for the Indians. The state attorney general's office immediately voiced objections to the plan. In a letter to Secretary of Interior Donald Hodel, Attorney General Frank Kelley called the tribal proposal "an effort to shelter the casino from state gambling laws." He continued, "the state of Michigan recognizes the very pressing need of tribes for significant economic development. However, we cannot and will not condone the use of commercial casino gambling as a means to accomplish this end." (*Mining Journal*, September 20, 1988) The attorney general also feared that approval of relocation of an Indian casino into a city would create a precedent to establish other gambling centers near other cities. Facing such state opposition, the tribe reached out to win approval of the local citizens. They asked the Escanaba city council for a resolution of support. They won support of the council members who voted for the resolution with only one dissenting vote; that vote was from Mayor Jean Jokipi. The mayor worried about the community's image. "We have been very concerned with economic development. The real carrot on the stick for luring business is the quality of life." Comments from citizens at an open hearing before the council were mixed. (*Mining Journal*, September 17 and 21, 1988). The matter remains unresolved. With the passage of the Indian Gaming Regulatory Act it appears the plan will now have to win approval of the governor of Michigan.

Two federal court cases have influenced the development of Indian casino gaming in Michigan. The tribal code of the Keeweenaw Bay Indian Community was amended in 1981 to provide for licenses to provide for licenses to conduct both non-profit gaming and gaming for profit. In December 1983 Fred Dakota and his wife Sybil, both members of the tribal community, opened a casino in their garage on the reservation. On January 17, 1984, the facility was licensed by the tribe. They opened a new casino building in July. The Dakotas operated blackjack, craps, poker, and pull tab games for profit. The casino employed 35 persons, most of whom were tribal members. Patrons included members of the tribe as well as residents of Michigan, Wisconsin, Illinois, Ohio, Oklahoma, and Oregon.

In September 1984 both the United States District Attorney for Western Michigan and the state attorney general brought a civil action in federal district court seeking a declaratory injunction to stop the gaming. The plaintiffs utilized the Organized Crime Control Act of 1970 to assert that the gaming was illegal. The state of Michigan dropped out of the case in November 1984 as the question involved became a matter solely of federal law, i.e. was the gaming a violation of the 1970 Act.

On June 28, 1985, Judge Wendell Miles agreed that it was, and he issued the requested injunction. The Dakotas appealed, but to no avail. On July 18, 1986, the sixth circuit of the United States Court of Appeals upheld the lower court ruling. The government had claimed that the conditions of the Organized Crime Control Act were met because the Dakotas' enterprise involved more than five persons, it had been in continuous operation for over thirty days, and that it had realized gross revenues in excess of $2,000 in a single day.

The defendants did not contest these facts. However, they did object to the most critical point – that the gaming was in violation of state law. The courts, however, felt that it was. They emphasized that Michigan law prohibited commercial gambling. The courts refused to read that a Millionaire's Party Law passed in 1975 made casino gaming a civil-regulatory action as opposed to being a criminal prohibited action – a distinction used in the *Butterworth* cases and in other federal cases. Millionaire parties were strictly for non-profit charities and not for commercial profit seeking enterprises. (*United States v. Dakota*, 796 F. 2d 186, 6th Cir., 1986).

Following the lower court ruling in 1985, Michigan tribes took the ruling judge's position to mean that only profitable commercial gaming was prohibited by the Organized Crime Control Act. Accordingly, several tribes established casinos that were to be operated by the tribes with all benefits going to tribal council treasuries. The tribes also structured their gaming to exclude any non-Indian participants from holding management positions with gambling functions. In doing so, they also met one other objectionable item in the Dakota's enterprise. The Dakotas had hired as a consultant, manager, and trainer of dealers, a person who had been convicted of a felony for misappropriating funds at a North Dakota charity gaming facility. He had served ten months in a North Dakota penitentiary and was on parole when he was hired. The Dakotas were allegedly knowledgeable about the person's background. (Walter Funkenbusch, "Gambling on the Reservation," in *Gambling Research*, William Eadington, ed., University of Nevada, Reno, 1988).

The new tribal casinos that opened after the initial *Dakota* ruling may have been structured to satisfy what the Indians believed a federal judge desired. However, the new casinos did not satisfy the federal district attorney, John Smietanka. On November 15, 1985, he filed another civil suit in the federal district court sitting in Marquette, Michigan. Again he sought an injunction against the gaming operations. Smietanka commented, "The U.S. Attorney's office cannot and will not ignore the burgeoning of casino gaming upon federal Indian reservations...The tribes have interpreted the (*Dakota*) decision differently than the government." There were five defendant tribes: Bay Mills Community, Sault Sainte Marie Tribe, Keeweenaw Bay Indian Community, Grand Traverse Band, and the Hannahville Indian Community. Their spokesman indicated that they would defend their activity, because they were engaged in a "proper and lawful course of conduct." He claimed that the facts of the case were "so different" that the *Dakota* ruling should not apply. (*Lansing State Journal*, November 16, 1985)

The court's reaction to the case suggested that justice was not about to move swiftly. The *Bay Mills Case* was assigned to a different judge, Douglas Hilman, and transferred to the Grand Rapids chambers of the district court. Government motions were not heard until November 21, 1986, with initial briefs filed during early 1987. A full hearing was not held until December 1987, and final briefs not received until April 1988. The federal government made the same claim in *Bay Mills* as it made in the *Dakota* case. The tribes were engaged in activities which were in violation of the Organized Crime Control Act of 1970, and they should be enjoined from conducting casino games. By the time Hilman ruled on the case on August 13, 1988, the tribal casinos were economically viable on-going enterprises upon which the reservations had become very dependent. The United States Supreme Court had given its *Cabazon* decision, and Congress was moving toward passage of the Indian Gaming Regulatory Act.

Judge Hilman took notice of the positive contributions gaming was making to life on the reservations. Casinos were providing one-third of the reservation employment. He cited an anthropologist who concluded that the "tribal governments are heavily dependent on gaming for their economic welfare." The judge also indicated that the economic benefits had spread into surrounding non-Indian communities. He recited that the federal government had supported the gaming through Housing and Urban Development grants and Bureau of Indian Affairs guaranteed loans for the construction of the casino facilities.

However, Hilman could not bring himself to a discussion of the merits of the case. Rather than siding with or against the government's case, Hilman raised an issue presented by neither plaintiff nor defendant. He examined the issue of the process the district attorney should use to stop the gaming activity. Hilman asserted that "as a general rule, a court may not enjoin the commission of a crime." He reasoned that criminal defendants should be given procedural opportunities for their defense that are not available in civil tribunals, i.e. tighter evidence rules. Therefore, this not being a special case, he dismissed the complaint, admonishing the district attorney that he must seek a criminal indictment if he wished to have the gaming declared illegal. The case was dismissed, and within two months new federal legislation had been passed. (*United States v. Bay Mills*, 692 F. Supp. 777, West. Dist., Michigan, 1988; also, *Lansing State Journal*, August 14, 1988; *Mining Journal*, August 14, 1988).

The Indian Gaming Regulatory Act seemingly estopped any attempts at appeal. However, as noted in the body of the paper, such an appeal could be accompanied by claims that the new legislation is unconstitutional.

After the Act was passed in October, 1988, four of the five tribes conducting casino gaming moved quickly to notify the state of their intention to negotiate compacts so that they could continue Class III games. In the meantime they continued their operations. Class III games offered on the reservations included dice games. Michigan reservations were exempted from Class III regulation of casino card games. However, because of dice games and wheel games, the four tribes are seeking to have Class III treatment of their casinos. There is an assumption that a Class III agreement can encompass all the casino games even though the exemption could allow separate treatment of Class III card games. However, a bifurcation of games conducted in the same house by the same employment force could be very difficult.

The four tribes contacted the governor's office. The governor's staff worked with the attorney general's office to prepare for negotiations. With the time clock running out – they had six months from October, 1988 – the Indians had as of late March, 1989 not yet sat down with the state authorities.

The fifth tribe, the Mount Pleasant Saginaw Chippewa tribe, wanted no part of state regulation. Their attorney indicated that they wished to have Class II treatment of their casino games. Such being the case, they may have to give up craps and wheel games.

They are also quite concerned that the Act will not permit them to expand their gaming hall facilities to permit additional card tables. At the time the Act was passed, they had plans to build a new hall for the casino games. They are concerned that the Act may not permit this. Nonetheless, they do not wish to join the other tribes which are collectively approaching the state for a compact agreement.

The state presents an interesting case in that it appears there will be a compact for six casinos, and Class II rules for a seventh casino. Perhaps, the Saginaw Chippewa tribe can later seek a compact if they are satisfied with the nature of the compact given the other tribes. If they do so, the state will be faced with the question of equitable treatment of different tribes. All these issues await the passage of time in the near future. Given the structure of the Act, it will be somewhat of a miracle if their resolution is not directed into the hands of the federal judiciary once more. In the meantime, the solidification of casino gaming on Michigan reservations will direct extra pressure on legislative policy makers to consider again the question of non-Indian commercial casino gaming in Michigan.

II

Views from Supporters of the Act

James E. Ritchie, Esquire
O'Connor & Hannan
Washington, D.C.

The issue of importance before the North American Conference on the Status of Indian Gaming is not whether Indian gaming operations should have regulatory, accounting, and security controls, but rather what type of controls. Any activity which involves large (and sometimes even not-so-large) sums of money, whether it is bingo on an Indian reservation or stock trading on Wall Street, is going to attract greedy and unethical elements of our society who will employ whatever means are necessary to get a part of that money the "new fashioned" way - by stealing it.

We have all been made aware in the media of Ivan Boesky, who pled guilty to illegal insider stock trading in New York several years ago. However, you may not have heard of Stewart Siegel. He pled guilty to rigging bingo games at the Barona Reservation in California in 1986. No doubt there are other Ivan Boeskys and other Stewart Siegels who are at this very moment involved in fraudulent schemes designed to siphon profits from unsuspecting victims. Just as honest stock brokers are working with the Securities and Exchange Commission to revise the rules which govern stock trading, so must Indian tribes work with the National Indian Gaming Commission and state gaming regulators to implement a system of controls which will identify the Stewart Siegels of the world.

No control system, however sophisticated, will ever stop all thieves from attempting to ply their trade. The best of systems may deter a few of the amateurs, and should hopefully catch even the highly skilled professionals. The worst will only give honest participants a false sense of security in the integrity of the game. The situation created by enactment of Public Law 100-497, the Indian Gaming Regulatory Act, is unique.

Nevada implemented its system of regulatory controls long after gaming had become established in the state. New Jersey, on the other hand, was able to put controls in place prior to the opening of its casinos. Indian gaming operations will fall into both these categories. It will be necessary for existing Class II games to conform to as yet unwritten regulations imposed by the National Indian Gaming Commission. Relatively few tribes are currently involved in Class III games, so those which plan to open such games will have prior knowledge of the regulatory controls which will apply as a result of the compact negotiation process.

I think most people would agree that the New Jersey example, having a set of established regulations from the start, is the preferred method. As of March, 1989, President Bush had not yet named his candidate for the chairmanship of the National Indian Gaming Commission. Given the speed at which most things in Washington happen, it may be some time before the Commission and its supporting cast are in place and ready to function.

Various sections of the Indian Gaming Regulatory Act were written in response to problems which had been experienced by a number of tribes. The most common problem involved the actions of bingo management contractors and the terms of the contracts themselves. As a result, the Chairman of the Commission will be responsible for:

1. approving all such contracts;
2. conducting background investigations on individuals connected with management companies; and
3. reviewing independent audits of the gaming operations.

Having read the testimony by Indian leaders who appeared before Congressional committees, as well as media accounts of alleged improprieties of a few contractors and tribal members, I believe that these three particular functions are the most vital to the tribes concerned. Performing these functions in an effective and efficient manner will not be easily accomplished. About a hundred bingo halls are already in operation, and a significant number of these involve management contractors. The volume of data that must be reviewed in a relatively short period of time is staggering, and the geographic dispersion of Indian bingo halls complicates the problem even more. These factors alone make the Commission's initial organizational decisions a critical element in determining its ultimate degree of success.

The Chairman and the Commission would do well to look at the regulatory organizations and procedures of Nevada and New Jersey, but I also believe that some new and innovative methods will be necessary. Areas that might lend themselves to such methods include a centralized system for checking background information on persons involved in Indian gaming. Likewise, a nationwide system to license suppliers and their products would also greatly simplify matters for the Commission and gaming tribes. Such a system might also be utilized by state governments which either sponsor or license similar gaming activities. There are probably a number of issues which will have to be resolved before the systems I described could become fully operational, issues such as information sharing among separate jurisdictions and standardized specifications for gaming devices.

Those who attended this Conference who will be working with the National Indian Gaming Commission have a rare opportunity to help define the regulatory systems which will be employed by the Commission. I am sure that many tribes represented at the Conference have implemented their own control systems which have proven successful. The Commission ought to be made aware of those that could serve as models for the systems the Commission will ultimately select.

Finally, I believe that the Commission, with the cooperation of gaming tribes, the Bureau of Indian Affairs, and other Federal agencies, will succeed in meeting the objectives Congress had in mind when it passed the Act. The ultimate objective is, of course, to ensure that tribal members will receive the maximum benefits available from the gaming operations.

2

B. W. "Butch" Tongate

Legislative Consultant
O'Connor & Hannan
Washington, D.C.

I would like to begin my remarks with a reference to Napoleon. It is my understanding that during his military campaigns, Napoleon always kept on his personal staff the dimmest corporal he could pick from the ranks. Whenever he needed to send an order to one of his field commanders, Napoleon would write it down on a piece of paper. Napoleon would read the order to the corporal, who would then tell Napoleon what the order meant. If the corporal was right, then Napoleon had a reasonable level of confidence that his field commander would also correctly interpret the order. If the corporal was wrong, then Napoleon would rewrite the order until the dim-witted corporal could understand it.

Perhaps if Congress tried this approach, the laws it passed might better produce the results it intended. In the case of the Indian Gaming Act, they did not, so at this Conference we have a most distinguished group with each delegate trying to determine what the law means, both personally, and to the affected clients or constituents. It is my understanding there are close to 500 people in attendance at the North American Conference on the Status of Indian Gaming, and if each one has read the Indian Gaming Regulatory Act, there are probably close to 500 different interpretations as to what it means.

It is not appropriate for me just to continue the debate on the constitutionality of the provisions of the Act. The courts, with the help of skilled attorneys, will eventually settle that. In the meantime, the law is here now, and it is going to have to be implemented. Perhaps I am too pragmatic, or perhaps I should have been a corporal in Napoleon's army, but it seems to me that it would be in everyone's best interest to implement the law the way Congress intended it.

If flaws are found during that process, they should become known. They can be corrected. If Congress sees that, in general, the Act is working, they will be willing to make adjustments to it.

One way to help understand what Congress really intended in formulating the Act is to read the Committee Report and the Congressional Record of debate that occurred on the bill. It is my understanding that sometimes federal judges will do exactly this when they do not "get Congress' drift" from the statute itself. In fact, that's what a judge did recently when deciding whether to grant the Omaha tribe's request for an injunction against the U.S. Attorney.

If one examines Sections 2 and 3 of the law, the "findings" and the "declaration of policy", and try to put those words into simple terms, basically what the Act is saying is that, after careful examination,

Congress found that gaming really is the lifeblood of many tribal economies, and they did not intend to adversely affect that relationship. They also found that, while the Secretary of Interior has to approve management contracts, it is not very clear what he is looking for when he reviews them. Furthermore, there is no existing federal law that tells anyone how to regulate anything having to do with gaming.

One thing that was not included in the findings, but which Congress undoubtedly knew because it had been discussed at length in the hearings, was that some tribes, but by no means all, were suffering because there were not any regulations to prevent those kinds of situations where tribal governments lose control of their operations, and as a result, lose revenues.

Much has been said about problems associated with bingo management companies. I have no doubt most bingo management companies are legitimate businesses, run by honest individuals just trying to make a living. However, because there were a few that were less than honest, Congress felt compelled to impose a regulatory scheme to address the problems that it recognized. There has also been a lot of discussion about organized crime in Indian bingo. In my opinion, gaming operators and law enforcement officers ought to worry just as much about dis-organized crime as they do about organized crime. It is also my opinion that Congress, in passing this legislation, also hoped to put an end to the rash of lawsuits that resulted from the absence of a statutory basis for Indian gaming. I fear what we may see now, as a result of the new Act, is an epidemic instead of a rash.

In creating a statutory basis, Congress basically established a framework of regulatory controls, and empowered the Chairman of the Indian Gaming Commission to come up with specific rules to address the problems it perceived for Class II gaming, and it provided a mechanism for states and tribes to mutually agree on the regulations necessary to ensure that Class III activities are conducted legally and in accordance with acceptable standards. It effectively gave the Chairman powers in the three areas that any regulatory system must address to be effective: licensing, auditing, and enforcement.

By requiring background investigations on primary management officials and key employees, undesirables will hopefully never get into a position where they can skim profits or rig games. Would an effective licensing program have prevented Stewart Siegel from getting into a position where he was able to rig bingo games at the Barona reservation with prizes amounting to almost $100,000? In my opinion, it probably would have worked.

An audit system helps keep the honest people with licenses honest. In the case of management contracts, by requiring that tribal leaders have access in all financial transactions, Congress hoped to eliminate situations where tribal leaders were kept in the dark as to how much money was generated in gaming operations and how much was spent on supplies and services. This was considered to be a real problem on a few reservations.

Neither of these measures, background checks or audits, would have been effective if Congress had not given the Chairman and the Commission powers to enforce the rules and regulations. Fines, closures, suspensions, and denials are really the only tools – short of prosecution – that a regulator has to ensure the integrity of gaming operations. These powers taken together are absolutely critical to the long-term success of gaming, and they ought to be addressed in Class III compacts as well. Whatever it costs to implement a comprehensive regulatory system, it is minimal compared to what a tribe could lose if a corrupt official or even a disorganized criminal finds and exploits a gap in the regulatory controls.

What should tribes do during this interim period before the Commission is in place? They ought to make sure that their current regulatory systems include measures similar to those described in the

Act, and that those measures are being followed. Even if the law is eventually determined to be unconstitutional, it is going to be in the tribes' best interest to do that. If they find any gaps or shortfalls, they ought to make the necessary corrections. If they lack expertise in a certain area, they ought to consult with other tribes or other qualified professionals who can help them.

It is likely that most tribes with Class II gaming will want to apply for self-regulation as soon as possible. Strict compliance with the regulatory procedures defined by the Act and by the Commission will undoubtedly be a requirement for certification for self-regulation.

What can state governments do in light of the Act? That is more difficult to specify, because the situations will vary from state to state and possibly from tribe to tribe within a given state. It is my recommendation that states look at the same three areas – licensing, auditing, and enforcement – for each potential Class III game in their state, and consider how each area might be addressed in a state-tribal compact. States should also identify key individuals in the government or their gaming or racing commissions who can provide the required expertise in each of these areas.

As another concern, should states that allow "Las Vegas nights" for charities once or twice a year have to worry about regulatory controls for full-blown, high stakes commercial casinos? I do not think so because, in my interpretation, that is not what Congress intended when it drafted the gaming bill.

What can the Commission do? If and when the Commission ever gets in place, it can avoid reinventing the wheel. First of all, it does not have enough money to do that. Secondly, there are any number of existing systems that could be used as the basis for Class II regulation. It ought to tap those existing resources, and hire acknowledged experts in the various disciplines, perhaps on a contractual basis, to produce maximum results as quickly as possible.

Perhaps I am looking at the world through rose-colored glasses, but if we accept the fact that there is going to be a National Indian Gaming Commission and there are going to be state-tribal compacts, I do not believe the kind of development I have just discussed has to be a particularly painful process. I believe it is in everyone's best interest – the tribes, the states, and the gaming public – to see that all gaming, including both non-Indian gaming and Indian gaming, is thoroughly and effectively regulated.

3

Anthony Chamblin
Executive Vice President
Association of Racing Commissioners International
Lexington, Kentucky

The Association of Racing Commissioners International was formed in 1934. It represents fifty-five racing commissions throughout the United States, Canada, Mexico, and the Caribbean and about eighty associate member groups in North America and abroad. Each state in which legalized financial wagering is conducted has at least one regulatory commission. Delaware, Kentucky and Pennsylvania each have two; one for jockey type racing, another for harness racing, in which a horse pulls a cart and driver. Alabama has four county racing commissions, three for dog racing, and one for horse racing.

Racing commissions are responsible for establishing and enforcing rules and procedures promulgated to maintain the integrity of parimutuel wagering. Commissioners allocate dates to operators of parimutuel facilities after issuing operating permits to those operators. Commissioners provide the standards for inclusion or exclusion of participants, and set the parameters of approval for contracts, policies and procedures utilized at parimutuel facilities. We regulate all forms of course and harness racing, dog racing, and jai alai.

In a sense, the Association of Racing Commissioners International office is the parimutuel sports equivalent of the commissioners' offices in major league baseball, professional football, basketball, or hockey. The difference is that whereas the commissioners of those sports have broad authority, we deal in racing with the sovereignty of the forty-two states in which parimutuel wagering is legal. We can only recommend policy, not mandate it. The primary role of commissioners is that of unbiased regulators. They are appointed as representatives and protectors of the public trust. The parimutuel industry survives on a base of strictly guarded integrity. Every facet of a commissioner's action is geared toward maintaining the fairness of the contest to assure a level playing field for the participants. Through internal industry screening and the work of investigatory organizations, the industry which provides nearly $1 billion a year to state governments in the U.S. in direct parimutuel taxes is built on public confidence, which transcends state lines or geographic locations. Without confidence, the public will not wager. Without wagering, the parimutuel industry would die.

There is an interwoven network of checks and balances established throughout the industry to insure the continuance of that confidence to the best of our abilities. It is our position that parimutuel wagering on Indian land, whether in the form of racing, jai alai, off-track betting, or simulcasting, should be governed by an equally restricted set of standards and an equally communicated exchange of information.

As an observer of the Indian gaming issue, I have learned that many Indians are weary of hearing that gaming activities on their lands present a threat to the public welfare and the welfare of Indian tribes, and individuals who may represent criminal elements are preying upon such activities. I recognize that Indians have heard these horrified claims many times before. The stereotyped claims are made by white men that if Indians are allowed unlimited hunting and fishing privileges, they will destroy the resources. If Indians are not subject to zoning, they will build slums. If Indians are allowed to run gambling, organized crime will control their operations.

I do not personally subscribe to these generalities. I understand why Indians consider them to be insulting. It does in fact seem peculiar to hear white people say or imply that because we have some people in this country who are crooked, then Indians should not be allowed to gamble on their sovereign lands. However, it would be naive to believe that the potential for corruption in Indian gaming does not exist, just as it would be naive and certainly inaccurate to believe that the same potential does not exist in state regulated parimutuel activities. Perhaps Indian gaming has been fortunate in avoiding corruption up to this time. But as the stakes increase, as all states in which gambling is legal have realized, the need for strict regulation and law enforcement oversight is necessary for the preservation of integrity.

Nearly $20 billion was wagered on parimutuel sports in this country in 1988. Millions of dollars are churned daily by hundreds of thousands of patrons. Those who would belittle the need for heavy regulation and enforcement are only kidding themselves. There also are other concerns with racing that do not exist with other forms of gaming, such as bingo. Racing also requires extensive background checks of operators and licensees by law enforcement agencies.

Finally, there is the problem of market saturation that exists in most areas. Faced with competition from other forms of gaming, legal and illegal, as well as competition from other sports, entertainment, and cable television, most racetracks have been struggling economically in recent years. That is why most are eagerly embracing off-track betting and/or simulcasting as methods of increasing revenues. The long term effect of this marriage may not be happy because both off-track betting and simulcasting seriously dilute live on-track attendance.

I would like to offer a brief review of the current status regarding the possibility of parimutuel wagering on Indian lands in states around the country. In Arizona, the Javapai Apache tribe has expressed willingness to build a track. The Javapai County Fair in Prescott is interested in moving its race meeting to that location. Several years ago, the Bureau of Indian Affairs in Arizona approved jai alai there, but the State of Arizona has been successful in preventing implementation of that gaming activity to this day.

In California, Governor Deukmejian has delegated the horse racing board in conjunction with his office to negotiate with the tribes. The Cabazon and Morongo tribes in California reported that track or satellite wagering is being considered. In Colorado, the Ute tribe made application for parimutuel wagering in 1985 but currently no formal applications are pending. In New Mexico, no applications are pending at this time, but in recent years the Santa Ana Pueblos showed interest in having either a horse or a dog track, and the Sandia Pueblo attempted unsuccessfully last year to negotiate interstate simulcasting agreements with Pennsylvania tracks. In Oklahoma, which was all Indian land at one time in history, at least four tribes, the Apaches, the Cheyenne, Arapahos and Comanches, have expressed interest. The Comanches have proposed building a horse track near Lawton. Governor Bellman has designated former Undersecretary of the Interior Ross Swimmer to negotiate the compact on behalf of the state. With reference to the problem of over-saturation, the Oklahoma Horse Racing Commission has a rule prohibiting any new parimutuel racetracks until such time as the state's aggregate combined wagering revenues total $230 million for each of two consecutive years. This rule of course preceded the Indian Gaming Act and thus its legal significance may be nil.

In Oregon the Warm Springs tribe attempted to get an Off-Track-Betting facility at one time, but no formal activity is pending currently. In Minnesota, legislation is pending to expedite the process of complying with the federal Act. I understand that informally in South Dakota a number of tribes have indicated an interest in gaming activity including parimutuels. In Montana the parimutuel commission has had an initial meeting with seven or eight tribes. The state recently passed a simulcast bill, and the Crow tribal council has conducted its own horse race meeting for many years. In Wyoming, which now has a network of seven off-track betting teletheaters, there have been many rumors indicating interest in parimutuels by Indian tribes, but no formal activity has yet surfaced. And in Wisconsin, at least one tribe has shown preliminary interest in simulcasting horse races from a race course in Chicago. The Racing Board has also received a request from an individual who wants to manage simulcasting activities on Indian lands.

In summary, the Association of Racing Commissioners International supported the compromise reached in Public Law 100-497, the Indian Gaming Act, because we believe the legislation represents the government's best effort to arrive at a regulatory scheme that will balance the interests of the federal, state and tribal governments, that will respect law enforcement concerns, tribal sovereignty and economic development, and that will insure the integrity of the gaming activities legalized by the Act.

III

The Fort Mojave Project

1

Nora Garcia

Chairperson
Fort Mojave Indian Tribe
Needles, California

The Fort Mojave tribe is located in the three states of Arizona, California and Nevada. The Tribe controls about forty-eight thousand acres that are spread over the three states around the southern tip of Nevada. The majority of that property is located in the state of Arizona and is laid out in a checker-board pattern.

There are approximately 625 tribal members on reservation in two villages in California and Arizona. We are governed by a seven member tribal council. When I came on the tribal council in 1981, the tribe had already been talking about the "Fort Mojave project" for 25 years, but because of other priorities, such as establishing perfected water rights on the tribal reservation in the three states, the tribe felt there were other issues that needed to be taken care of first. Development of a resort area had always been on the back burner, but because of the limited resources and the limited time to spend on a major issue such as this, the tribe held off moving in that direction. Furthermore, the market itself was not there until the 1980s. Since we are located just ten miles south of Laughlin, Nevada, and since Laughlin has become a boomtown which has just grown in leaps and bounds throughout the 1980s, we felt the time was right to pursue this. Four years ago we started working with Tim Carlson, who now is CEO of the MoVada Group.

Since we began working with Mr. Carlson and MoVada, we have seen four new casino properties develop in the Laughlin area, which continue to expand the market that is currently there. We expect that this trend will continue and that we will be part of it with our development. Indeed, we hope that future Conferences on the status of Indian gaming will be held on the reservation in our facilities one day.

In arriving at its decision to enter to an intergovernmental agreement with the state of Nevada, the tribe did not act arbitrarily. We did a careful analysis of everything relevant to the project and our tribal interests. When I first came on the tribal council in 1981, there were a number of issues that needed to be addressed, such as social problems, inadequate funding, limited resources, and the lack of people capable of handling the all-encompassing problems confronting the tribe. The council talked about the smallness of the tribe and we realized our capabilities and resources were very limited and the magnitude of the undertaking was substantial. The effort to bring our four thousand acres of land to a level where we would have valid gaming rights was an undertaking very monumental for the tribe. We talked many times about how we could handle this effort – whether we were capable of undertaking it as a tribe. The more that we looked at it and weighed the alternatives, it became evident that this was something too big for us to handle.

Thus, based on a number of long deliberations and discussions, we entered into a contract with the state of Nevada through the Nevada Gaming Control Board in October of 1987. Prior to this contract, we had testified in Washington in 1985 that we were out of step with most other tribes throughout the United States in the pursuit of our endeavor.

Our tribal lands are located at the southern tip of Nevada adjacent to the Colorado River. We feel we have tremendous potential with this acreage. The resources have not yet been developed to their full capability. There are twelve miles of shoreline on the Arizona side and approximately four miles of shoreline on the Nevada side.

The other issue we evaluated was the credibility of casino style gaming as a viable business and its marketability to visitors to the region. Would people come to the reservation? There had been a number of stories that had circulated concerning organized crime in Indian gaming operations. A majority of these cases were apparently isolated cases; however, when people from outside Indian country view a tribe and its business operations, they tend to generalize the worst image to all of us, across the board.

Another thing that our tribe looked at was the fact that Indian tribes are not all the same. Every tribe has its own agenda. Each tribe is diverse in its resources, its level of government, and its expertise. We considered our own strengths and weaknesses when we decided to enter into this agreement with the state of Nevada. The state would regulate gaming on the reservation. With regard to the lease of our land, the first thousand acres that we leased out has been through the Bureau of Indian Affairs process for about a year to this date (March, 1989); I am not surprised when other tribes state it is taking a year or more to get an investigation or even a review of a project. We have had a number of similar cases in dealing with the Bureau of Indian Affairs. However, much of that is due to the process and the code of Federal regulations that must be gone through and the number of hoops that we have had to jump through just to get this project conditionally approved pending an Environmental Impact Statement. This has been very frustrating, because one just does not know what the next stumbling block will be, and sometimes it seems like nothing is ever going to happen.

I have always tended to blame myself that we did not push hard enough on our project, but that is just the process that must be dealt with. Hopefully, after this lease has gone through the process, others that are pending will go much more smoothly, and the transition of Indian land to other uses will take place more quickly. Historically, we have had all kinds of people who have approached the tribe with the promise to save the tribe from itself and the bureaucracy. We have seen fly-by-nighters come to our "rescue", and we have seen people who had good intentions, but because of the problems of awaiting decisions or approvals from the Bureau of Indian Affairs, they could only hang around for a short period of time. Often, investors did not have the patience; they had to move on. The process in itself was a hindrance that all tribes have to deal with, so although gaming was potentially very lucrative, and it carried potential for our tribe, the issues were not yet resolved. We did have the compact with the state of Nevada, but we needed gaming legislation at the Federal level to ratify the compact.

At the present time, we believe we finally have the conditional approval to go forward, pending Environmental Impact Statements. I think that in itself, Bureau of Indians Affairs approval and the timeliness of necessary processes is something that should be evaluated in terms of time frame for getting similar projects under way and getting some dirt turned. I think these are things that we, as tribal leaders, need to work on so that we can recommend changes when dealing with economic development on the reservations.

I believe each individual tribe and each reservation has different potentials and different needs to address when dealing with states in negotiating compacts. Each tribe has a different way of approaching the negotiation issue, and it should be done strictly on a government relationship between the tribes and the states. Hopefully, the Bureau of Indian Affairs will gear up for this process as long as it is going to be run through the Secretary of Interior until the Federal Indian Gaming Commission has been set up during the transition time.

2

Tim Carlson
President
MoVada Group
Las Vegas, Nevada

The Movada Group, with which I am associated, has worked with
the Fort Mojave tribe since 1985. There are only three principles
in the Group. First, there is Bob Cashell, the former Lieutenant
Governor of the state of Nevada and a license holder in the privileged
gaming industry in the state. He holds licenses at present for three
separate gaming properties. He is quite an individual in his own right,
who started as a truck driver. Driving through Reno years ago, he
stopped at Bill and Effie's Truck Stop west of Reno, and he decided
that he wanted to buy it. He did, and turned it into Boomtown, which
was sold in 1988 for fifty million dollars. He is the chairman of the
MoVada Group.

Jerry Dondero, who is the president of the MoVada Group, spent twenty years with Senator Paul Laxalt (R., Nevada) working in government. He was initially trained as a teacher. Now, he has an excellent background in lobbying in the Washington, D.C. arena.

I spent eight years as the Economic Development Director for the Las Vegas based Nevada Development Authority. I was fortunate enough to work with the community in an area where I dealt extensively with business leaders. I learned quite a bit about economic development, which is the dominant issue relating to Indian gaming in this country.

Gaming has been construed to be an economic development issue adopted by those of our nation who have been on the continent longer than the Europeans. From my experience, economic development is not an easy issue with which to deal. Gaming also is not an issue with which it is easy to deal. Furthermore, developing on Indian land is not an easy issue with which to deal.

Raising the capital that is going to be needed to develop the Fort Mojave project has itself been a tenuous process. This is because of poor regulations in the Federal system, along with a lack of trust and a lack of belief that the American Indians can accomplish what they are capable of. It is also based on the issue of how one brings the entrepreneurial spirit onto a piece of land that has been tied up for so many years with Federal problems.

In working for two years with Indians on the Fort Mojave reservation, learning as much as I possibly could and using my experience and background in economic development, I believe this project can be accomplished. The spirit is there, as is the desire and the need. All the ingredients are there. We truly are in a new era, one of growth and development. It is up to the Indian tribal leaders at this Conference to take the message back to the Indian people. I believe the key to the development process is in bringing non-

Indian developers onto the reservation. They should become a part of the process; they should become partners in development projects.

However, if Indian and non-Indian partnerships are going to be forged, there is going to have to be give and take. In the past, dealings have been one-sided, but now I believe we are moving into an era of change, an era of opportunity, one which, to my knowledge, has not existed within the Indian nations before. The opportunities are great, if the proper steps are taken.

These words have been said many times to Indians before: if the proper steps are taken. But it is important to understand the perceptions and thought processes of an entrepreneur looking at the development process on the reservation. The key to this process in any investment is the market and location. The following discussion should provide some understanding of what is available at the Fort Mojave Reservation and why investor groups, such as myself and my partners, have seriously considered pursuing a project of this magnitude and vision.

The Fort Mojave project is one that will mean something to everyone in the Indian nations if it succeeds. In my opinion, it will become a cornerstone of other such partnerships, and this is why it is so important for it to succeed. This is not just for the monetary return to the Mojave tribe, but also to demonstrate that such undertakings can be accomplished. This will help to dispel doubts about the ability to achieve successes on Indian lands. It will point out that things can actually occur in a positive manner on a reservation. With our experience, we hope to be able to spread this knowledge and help other tribes go through the process with their own projects, by speeding up the process, and by dealing with the Bureau of Indian Affairs in an effective and meaningful manner. We also hope to weed out some of the bad regulations that people working with the Bureau of Indian Affairs constantly have to deal with.

The Fort Mojave reservation sits on the Colorado River, close to Lake Mojave, which was created by damming up the river in the early 1950s. Just south of the dam is the city of Laughlin, Nevada, which interestingly enough is not an incorporated city. Rather, it is in the unincorporated portion of Clark County. At present, there are approximately four to five thousand residents in the city of Laughlin. Across the Colorado River is the Arizona town of Bullhead City, which has about twenty thousand residents. South of Bullhead City and Laughlin is the reservation and the 48,000 acres of Indian land. The tribal land straddles the California border, the Arizona border across the river, and the Nevada border; these lands essentially form the very southern tip of the state of Nevada.

In that tip lie the one thousand acres which will be developed by the Movada Group in our first phase. I mentioned before that a businessman's key considerations are market and location. Investment potential in this particular location is phenomenal. Just ten miles up the Colorado River are nine operating casinos. The monthly payroll is in excess of one million dollars. In 1987 and 1988, four new casinos were opened. Ten years ago, if we could have moved a little faster, we might have been able to capture even more of the market that we intend to capture now. We feel that in the state of Nevada, which always is a casino gamblers' haven, major growth is going to continue in the southern portion of the state, much of it at the southern tip, feeding into the Laughlin market.

The aspect of major importance about Laughlin is the fact that it is exactly the same distance from Los Angeles to Las Vegas as it is from Los Angeles to Laughlin. Laughlin is a very interesting market. It is a down-to-earth market, much like old Las Vegas, where people enjoy wearing jeans and t-shirts, and just having a good time on the river. In my opinion, Laughlin is adding to the Nevada market another location for which the visitor, the individual who can and wants to enjoy gambling, can also pursue other activities. The river is providing a tremendous family attraction as it always has.

The water sports at Lake Mojave attract millions of people. In 1987, 2.3 million people visited this area. The Fort Mojave Indians deserve the opportunity to expand and capture a portion of that market, and that is what our project is all about. They can expand this market because they are at the right place at the right time.

This is an exciting time for the Fort Mojave tribe, as well as for the MoVada Group. We are projecting our first phase to cover one thousand acres. Hopefully, things will be going so well that we will go through our first, second and third phases in the first two years following ground-breaking. That is what we believe the market will bear. In going through our development strategy, we plan on developing a casino site which would be adjacent to a forty acre lake and some residential living units. For our second phase, we are planning to add a golf course and two other hotel-casino sites, as well as expand the lake. Water is not a real issue with this development because the tribe was smart enough to deal with that in the years past. Water rights for the tribe itself are in the neighborhood of 129,000 acre-feet of water per year for the entire tribal lands. Fortunately, 12,000 acre-feet of that allocation is used on the Nevada side, so the tribe has 12,000 acre-feet of water rights that can be applied immediately to this project. Out third and hopefully final phase or project will follow with additional casino-hotel and residential unit development.

We are hoping to offer a dramatic destination resort. We want a facility which will bring travelers into it off the Needles Highway; these visitors make up sixty-five percent of the Laughlin market. We hope to bring them in with striking architecture contrasted against the sand dunes and the river bank. The golf course will be like an oasis, and we have all the water needed to make everything green and beautiful.

All these are just basic ideas we are hoping to bring to reality. But it has a chance of becoming reality because of the attitude and the direction that the leaders of the Fort Mojave tribe have taken themselves. They have adopted the entrepreneurial spirit that they have been hearing about and reading about for so many years. It is because of this spirit that they have entered into an intergovernmental relationship with the state of Nevada.

Today we are in a position to move forward. We are going through the steps that are necessary to go through in order to solve all the problems in front of us.

We are aware this is not a sure thing. It is not a 100% done deal because we are still dealing with all the agencies that Indian tribes have worked with for so many years. Frustration is a major part of the process, but people are honestly working hard to overcome the obstacles. The Bureau of Indian Affairs is working hard to help get this project accomplished. However, they have antiquated rules and regulations which they must follow.

Hopefully, I will be able to report in the future what we have been able to accomplish. The MoVada Group and the Fort Mojave tribe are, in a sense, vanguards. I pledge that as an officer of the MoVada corporation, we will share the failures along with the successes. We will show what we have been able to accomplish by developing such a project in the right location and in the right market.

IV

Observations from Tribal Leaders

Eddie Tullis
Chairman
Poarch Band of Creek Indians
Alabama

This Conference has generated a real discussion on whether or not it was appropriate for all us Indian people to come to Reno to talk about gaming. I believe it is appropriate, in the respect that we need to realize that when we talk about gaming, it is one of the major problems in Indian country today. It is a problem because it is setting what I perceive to be a precedent that Indian tribes will have to deal with well into the future, and this is only the beginning.

It is also my opinion that we as tribal people lost something when Congress passed the Indian Gaming Act. I don't want anyone to leave this Conference thinking that a bunch of dumb Indians don't realize that something was lost. Some of us see it as a slicing away, as Secretary Udall said in his presentation, of tribal sovereignty. To Indian tribes, that is an issue of paramount importance.

Some tribal leaders see the opportunities opened by Indian gaming as a way to try to balance the slicing away of tribal sovereignty. Certainly, at this Conference, we have had an opportunity to hear from some people who are at the forefront of doing that, of trying to balance the fact that we are losing some tribal sovereignty, but at the same time developing some economic opportunities for some of the tribes. For example, the Fort Mojave project is going to create significant opportunities for their tribal people, and that is something about which we can be proud.

However, I believe a major reason the Indian Gaming Act became law was in reaction to Indians' economic opportunities that emerged with the successful Indian gaming operations with the Seminoles and the Pequots. For many of us tribal leaders, we consider this issue strictly an economic problem that we have in Indian country. Many of us are concerned about the fact that the state of Nevada and particularly representatives of Las Vegas and Reno were in the forefront in the fight against Indian gaming. We understand their position, not from a tribal sovereignty perspective, but strictly from an economic perspective.

Nevada's interests can use the smoke screen of organized labor or organized crime or anything else they would like to use to constrain Indian gaming. Indian people on the reservations have created situations that are significant economic entities, and as such, have threatened Nevada. Thus, economics is what has motivated the interests from Nevada. It is also what motivated people from many other states to get involved against the Indian position. The end result has been that not only did the tribes lose by acquiescing to the Act, thus helping Nevada; they've also created some real problems for other places.

I will use my own tribe as an example. In the State of Alabama until just recently, anytime someone wanted to invest some money in a game of chance, they would catch a plane and fly to Las Vegas or Reno. When the Poarch Creeks started playing bingo, many Alabamians said, "If we want to gamble, we can go down to Atmore and spend our money with the Poarch Creek. We don't have to fly all the way to Nevada."

The people in Nevada are conscious of that. We heard Nevada's senior Senator at this Conference state that he believes just because Nevada has an isolated location away from the major population centers of this country, it should be the only state that has the right to provide organized gambling. What in the world do they think some of the Indian reservations in America have? We possess some of the most isolated real estate in the world on some of the reservations. So why don't Nevadans note that they are not unique in their isolation, that we should also have the right to have organized gambling on the reservations? In my opinion, it is strictly economics.

Thus, it is important we realize the tribes lost a slice of their tribal sovereignty with the Act. However, this is not going to shut out many of the existing Indian gaming operations. Some operations will close down for economic reasons because there are so many bingo halls out there, and we are beginning to see market saturation in some areas. But many Indian tribes in the last few years have taken the financial resources that have been raised from bingo and are beginning to do other things. And just as with Nevada and its gaming, we are beginning to see people in other states concerned about Indians becoming a competitive economic threat in other areas. Such people are motivated strictly by economics.

I particularly think the most significant thing about the Indian Gaming Act is that it removes opportunities from the Indian tribes. It has done this by eliminating our capacity to raise the financing that is necessary to do some of the things that need to be done on the reservations. We have been operating under major handicaps. We cannot raise capital by mortgaging our property. The Bureau of Indian Affairs is so slow that any person with a little bit of financing who wants to invest in a hurry on Indian land certainly would not want to get involved with the Indian tribe because the Bureau of Indian Affairs would drag the process out so long that the opportunity might pass. And now the Indian Gaming Act has removed much of the financial resources that we have recently had available. So we've lost that opportunity to do some things that the tribes needed to do.

With this opportunity disappearing, every taxpayer in this country, along with government entities such as the counties, the cities, and the states have lost something too. Many have lost opportunities for Indian tribes to invest in the economies of the local area. If you go around Indian country now, one of the major changes taking place is that Indians are involved in a lot of activities, not just gaming. If the Bureau of Indian Affairs ever generated a good comprehensive report on the economic development in Indian country, there would probably be an uprising from many entities, claiming the Indians are impacting their livelihoods, and they might run to Congress to get Congress to take away that opportunity from the Indians.

Thus, Indian people have lost a lot more than just the chance to be involved in a gaming activity. We have lost a lot of opportunities to provide service to our people that would be beneficial for us in the long run. However, as always, we will find a way to survive. But it is going to be much harder for us to take advantage of the fact that we now, as a matter of government policy, have self-determination for American Indians. Self-determination in itself is great if the resources exist to take advantage of it.

We Indian people also are conscious of the fact that those interests who have been involved in the past with the Indian Gaming Act are not stopping now. We know of activities that are going on right now from the side of those who are asking to give this bill an opportunity to work, which is itself a great argument. Of course, the same interests did not want to use that argument when Indian tribes were saying, let's see if the Indians can regulate their own gaming operations, or prove first that there are organized crime problems in the Indian operations before they went to Congress with the bill.

But now these interests are saying, "Let's give this law a chance to work." But we know for a fact that many of these interests are actively conniving to go back and further restrict the abilities of the Indian tribes. This would be another slice taken away from tribal sovereignty.

Indian tribes are going to survive and we will find other avenues to do it. Gaming has been a great one for us. I think if anyone went out in Indian country, they would have to admit that there has been great progress made. This setback is not going to stop us from taking advantage of those opportunities that are out there. We are going to continue to be involved in fighting for our opportunities, especially as long as we are aware of opposing interests who are dedicated to slicing away those tribal sovereignties in any way they can. We are going to be involved in trying to make sure that does not happen.

I want to make one other point about the interests who have been involved in this activity who now see a major opportunity for them to again have a real impact on Indian country. This is with regard to the decision of who will be appointed as the Indian Gaming Commissioners. If these interests are so supportive of the new Indian Gaming Act, and they think it has so much benefit by creating such a level playing field, why is there activity going on now to try to influence who the appointed commissioners will be? Indian people are going to lose another opportunity to have some impact if we don't stick together and if we don't recognize the fact that there are interests who will take every opportunity to try to slice away at our tribal sovereignty.

2

Wendell George
Chairman
Planning Committee
Colville Confederated Tribes
Washington

I would like to begin by giving you some background on my tribe because that will provide a perspective of why we have pursued Indian gaming the way we have. The Colville Reservation is in the state of Washington, in the north central part of the state. The Colville Confederated Tribes number about 7,000, and there is a fourteen member council. The tribe possesses 1.3 million acres, of which 800,000 acres is forest land, which is our primary source of income. However, our forest land has been cut over two or three times, and the tribe realizes that it is not going to support us as it has in the past.

Thus, for the last couple of years, the tribe has been looking for diversification. Tourism is an excellent choice because it is a non-polluting industry, and the gaming industry is an excellent option for us because it also does not harm the environment. There are other types of industries that we have considered but rejected because they did not fit what we have as one of our primary criteria for any business: that the environmental impact should be zero. We have done this because we believe we have a pristine reservation. We are very proud of that, and we intend to keep it that way. We are also in a remote location. So we are not going to bring in industries that pollute us in any way.

The Colville Tribe has been involved in national politics for quite a while. One of our members was a charter member of the National Congress of American Indians when it was started. The National Congress of American Indians has had its good times and its bad times, but in the past it always had a focusing point that brought Indian people together. One of the few good things about the Indian Gaming Act is that it has brought the Indian community back together. It is a single issue, but it is really much broader in the sense that we have to discuss jurisdiction. Jurisdiction is a very general term, but it manifests itself in many areas, and bingo and Indian gaming are just two of them.

In his presentation to this Conference, Stewart Udall spoke of self-development. That movement started in 1969, when President Nixon was influenced by a bunch of Indians. We managed to get a statement adopted that resulted in a self-determination policy. It was not implemented very much in the 1970s, but the idea was there; this was the first time it really was acknowledged by the federal government. It was not until the Self-Determination Act was passed that we actually had something to put our hands on. It still was not all that we needed, but it was a start.

The Act recently went through some 638 contracting modifications (regulations). My tribe decided that the Self-Determination Act was one of the key elements to self-determination. As a result of this, we put together a task group of sixty-five people from our tribal council and our chief administrators to undertake a two day workshop on how to get our input into improving the regulations. We found that the door was totally open to us; however, we had to step through that door and make sure that those regulations were in our favor. Otherwise, our opinions, in terms of what we felt was best for the Indians, would be overlooked, because the regulations had been put together by the Bureau of Indian Affairs and by others from tribes without much in common with our needs and interests.

The same situation applies here. We have a set of regulations that is going to be imposed on Indian tribes that is going to be the key to how the entire Indian Gaming Act is implemented. What our tribe learned in our workshop is that we have to keep our minds on what the legislative intent was. If we deviate from that norm, then we could lose a lot.

The legislative intent of the Indian Gaming Act is good for Class I and Class II gaming. It maintains tribal sovereignty. It does not allow the states to control in areas where they were trying to control us. So my advice is that all interested tribes should put our heads together and make certain that the regulations that come out are favorable and consistent with legislative intent. We should also make sure that we influence what has to be put into the regulations relating to Class III gaming.

There are a couple of topics dealing with interpretations of the Indian Gaming Act that concern me. One interpretation was offered that anytime an Indian gaming operation had any gaming that fell into the Class III category, all its Class I and Class II gaming would also have to be treated as if it were Class III gaming, and this clearly would include bingo. This bothers me greatly because I had thought bingo was safe under the definition of Class II gaming.

Another topic that has been raised deals with the historic role of the federal government with respect to gambling and gaming. It was pointed out that gambling in the United States has historically been treated as a privilege, and that early regulation was undertaken by the federal government, but regulatory responsibility was then delegated to the states. From the Indian perspective, this is the whole problem. Within the Indian culture and the Indian community, gambling is more than a privilege. It is our culture, and it is our tradition. It is inherent in everything we do. When we try to make these arguments with anyone outside the Indian community, they do not understand this. It is for this reason that we cannot delegate control of our gambling to the state.

The only reason we are willing to delegate to the federal government is because of the fact that we've had federal relationships from the start. They have not always been good relationships but, generally speaking, they have been better over the years than working with the states. For example, in my state of Washington, we have had particular problems. We had to fight the state on cigarette tax issues. We had to fight the state on our liquor tax. We have had to battle with them on fish and game, on zoning, and on other jurisdictional issues.

The Colville Tribes have asked for a Class III gaming compact negotiation. We sent a letter to the state of Washington the day after we heard about it, and we have yet (as of March, 1989) to hear an answer back from the state. I don't anticipate an easy time with the state because they have a history of being very tough to deal with. The only thing that is favorable in the state of Washington is the fact that they have finally decided that it has cost the state too many millions of dollars to take every issue all the way to the Supreme Court. Thus, because of the economics of it, they are now willing to negotiate on some issues, though not everything. So we will try negotiation first, and if that does not work, we will probably have to fall back to litigation.

Another area of concern about the Indian Gaming Act has to do with the definitions of the Classes of gaming. When the definitions were made, they did not take into consideration either Indian culture or the Indian definition of various types of gambling. We have had horse racing from the start, and we have had card games from the start. We have also had bingo and dice games from the start. These were all in primitive forms, but Indians were playing them before there were any white men on this continent.

So far, we have identified two methods that opponents to Indian sovereignty have used in their strategy to try to defeat our goals and objectives. One of these is misinformation or disinformation. Many statements are made that are just slightly off center from the truth. Perhaps it is because the person making the statement just does not understand the issue, or perhaps the misstatements are intentional. It actually does not make much difference if it results in the same kind of harm. The other strategy is the divide and conquer technique. This is being used again, as it has been used with Indians before. If opponents to Indian sovereignty can get the tribes fighting amongst themselves, then they have lessened the opposition. They are attempting that strategy right now, and that is why I am happy to see so many Indian tribes represented at this Conference, so that we can compare notes and compare strategies. As long as we stay together, we are going to have strength.

One objective of our efforts is that we are going to try to keep everybody informed through a networking organization. The purpose of the organization is to give information to the Indian community. Information becomes the basis on which tribes can decide what to do. Tribal decision-making is similar among most tribes; I can't make a decision for my tribe and I'm sure that other councilmen can't make a decision without going to their tribal councils. But the information should be disseminated so everybody sees it and then makes their decision. I anticipate there will be several amicus briefs filed for the two cases challenging the Indian

Gaming Act in the works in early 1989. It is my hope that with the dissemination of information, there will be some key legal points that will be discovered through litigation; that we can make some inroads administratively through the regulations or through the legal amicus briefs. I think our main objective at this point is to win what we have to win, and the critical issues all hinge around the treatment of Class III gaming.

If Class III gaming is ultimately interpreted the way we want it, all the jurisdiction will be deferred to the tribes, which is a very good possibility in some states. If it is interpreted the way the states want it, jurisdiction will lie with the states. If and when it gets to that situation, I would be willing to bet that the intent of the *Cabazon* decision will be violated.

3

Harold A. Monteau

Tribal Attorney
Chippewa-Cree Tribe
Montana

One of the key issues confronting the Indian Gaming Act is the question of judicial challenges. This topic makes a lot of state government representatives nervous. In Montana, after the passage of the Act, all seven Indian tribes issued a notice of intent to negotiate for Class III gaming with the state. It will make the state of Montana nervous that there is ongoing litigation on the constitutionality of the Act and that the seven Indian tribes in Montana may to some degree be supporting that litigation.

However, before the Indian Gaming Act was passed, the Indian tribes in the United States and the individual states had the sovereign authority to enter into cooperative agreements at any time they wanted to, under state law and under tribal law. There are some states that would have to pass particular provisions in order to enable them to make such compacts, but the opportunity has always been there. This point is especially brought out by the compact that was recently negotiated in Nevada between the Fort Mojave tribe and the state. That compact was not negotiated pursuant to the Indian Gaming Act; rather, it was negotiated pursuant to state law and tribai law. Thus, as the litigation takes place, if there are some holes blasted in the Act, or if the Act itself is declared unconstitutional, Indian tribes still have the opportunity to enter into cooperative agreements in the area of gaming.

I would also note that I was a little disturbed by the presentation of Senator Reid which more or less issued a thinly veiled threat to Indian tribes, stating that if they do proceed to litigation on the Act, there might be repercussions from Congress. Indians have never been a people to back away from that sort of thing, and it is not going to stop us now. Furthermore, I can speak for more than just tribal attorneys. This is an issue that reaches all attorneys, including attorneys general of the various states and U.S. attorneys. Each one of us has taken an oath to uphold the United States Constitution. If there is something in this Act that does not set right with the Constitution, we have the responsibility to see that it is corrected. It does not matter whether we personally support the issue or not.

There are some parts of this Act that we find particularly offensive as Indian people. They are of course the parts dealing with the tribal-state compacts. I was told one time by a non-Indian person, "My goodness, you Indians are just buggy about that sovereignty stuff." I appreciated that, because we are buggy about that sovereignty stuff. The reason we are is that, without sovereignty, we do not survive as Indian nations.

I want you to think about the philosophy of some of the organizations that are advocating the abrogation of treaties, the disappearance of tribal governments, and for that matter the dispersion of Indian people into the so-called American mainstream. There is a term for that, and it is a harsh term, but I think it is particularly applicable. If you support that concept, then you support racial genocide. The disappearance of a race is nothing other than that. The disappearance of a nation is nothing other than that. I think Hitler was a little more harsh in the way he tried to carry it out, but I also think that we have to review American policy as it pertains to the American Indian in light of this perspective.

The United States in 1988 finally endorsed the anti-genocide treaty that has been in existence since shortly after World War II. It took the United States this long to recognize that certain people on this planet are in danger of disappearing. I do not think Congress particularly had Indians in mind when they finally ratified that agreement. However, the Indians of America are going to let them know we are here and that we are going to hold them to the propositions set out in the anti-genocide treaty.

I think all of the Indian policy should be reviewed with the idea of whether that particular policy is designed to someday facilitate the disappearance of Indian people. In my opinion, there is a lot of policy around that does facilitate that end. That is why we Indians are so buggy about that sovereignty stuff.

I would like to also say a few words on negotiations. The Fort Mojave Compact, though a good compact, is not a prototype for tribes and other states. That compact arose outside the parameters of the Indian Gaming Act. One thing that both the state and the tribes should keep in mind as they negotiate is that a lot of the responsibility can be put back right where it belongs, in the hands of the federal government. We do not have to have an intrusion of state law enforcement on the Indian reservations under the compacts that are envisioned by this Act. Instead, we could have contractual relationships with the state governments for the provision of the expertise that they may have. There actually are not many states that have developed expertise in gaming regulation to any great degree, but there are a few. It is my observation that many states that do have some gaming regulation are presently a bit overwhelmed by what they already have to regulate, in terms of the gaming that is already going on outside Indian reservations. These states are going to be hard put to dedicate further resources to regulate what goes on inside the reservations. Therefore, tribes should think about what type of contractual relationship they can negotiate, and they should think about the federal government maintaining the law enforcement responsibility under those contracts. It does not necessarily have to be the state law enforcement intruding. It does not necessarily have to result in a burden to the tribe in terms of law enforcement. I think law enforcement responsibilities can be placed squarely back on the federal government.

One of the reasons that I advocate this position is that, eventually, I feel there is no reason for Class III gambling not to be placed under the auspices of the Federal Indian Gaming Commission. The taxpayers are already paying for it, and the Indian tribes are going to be assessed to pay for it. There is absolutely no reason why the Commission cannot assume its full duties and regulate Class III gaming also.

There has been an aspect of tribal government that has been ignored at this Conference. Many tribes are developing the regulatory capabilities that seem to have been ignored in prior discussions. We also tend to ignore the sea of regulatory bureaucracy that the Bureau of Indian Affairs has generated over the years. As Indians are well aware, bureaucracies can be terribly complacent in their responses. However, it is up to the tribes to improve on that because the Bureau of Indian Affairs is the agency that we deal with. I believe we have seen improvements in this area in recent years, and are seeing them continue on a daily basis.

I would like to issue a warning to the states. The abrogationists that I mentioned before, people who want to abrogate Indian treaties and do away with reservations, will come out of the woodwork. They will attempt to obviate in any way that they can. They will try to prevent the tribal-state compacts for their own reasons. They are going to be very verbal. They are going to be loud. They are going to spend some money trying to get the states to come over to their point of view. But the states should really take a close look at these organizations, and who they represent. Recently, in the state of Montana, a particular issue arose over a state fish and game agreement. These abrogationists were deluging their legislative representatives with phone calls and letters on a daily basis. The Indian tribes had meetings with the local chamber of commerce and the county commissioners, with Ducks Unlimited and Trout Unlimited. What we learned from these groups was that the abrogationists, those calling the state legislature, do not represent the majority. They are just particularly vocal about their positions. Therefore, we asked the chamber and the commissioners, and the wildlife groups to let their legislators know that. They did, and as a result Montana will probably soon be signing a fish and game agreement with the Flathead Reservation. I believe this situation was indicative of the type of misinformation that can be circulated in a political environment.

Finally, some comments of support for the lawsuits challenging the Indian Gaming Act are in order. It is my belief that any time there is a new law passed, there are going to be court cases arising from that law. No one should become particularly alarmed about it; this is the American way. Otherwise we would just have an administrative legislative branch. The judiciary is there for a purpose. Just as many people have said to give this Act a chance, I am saying the judiciary is going to have to clean up some of the great ambiguities that have arisen within this Act. We had no opportunity at the time this Act was passed through the halls of Congress to comment on what we perceived were the constitutional weaknesses in the Act. We have heard statements from supporters of the Act that this was one of "the greatest bills that showed the greatest compromise in the Congress last year"; or that "a lot of good deals had to be scrubbed in order to grease the wheel so the Act would get through on unanimous consent". It was claimed that a lot had to happen in terms of agreements in the House of Representatives so it could pass there.

That is not the way the Indian tribes perceived it. We perceived the use of unanimous consent as a means of cutting off any debate on the state-tribal compact aspects of the Act, which it effectively did. It also cut off those states that did not particularly agree with those provisions in the Act.

I do believe that this Act needs to be revisited. Do we need an Act? Perhaps. I think there may be some grounds for saying that the stability created by some form of federal regulation is needed. But I do not believe that we need to have the type of conflict that the tribal-state compacts portion of this Act is creating. As I mentioned before, there already exists the sovereign authority under tribal and state law to enter into cooperative agreements on any issue, including Indian gambling, on reservations.

V

Alternative Perspectives and Implications

1

John R. Mills

Professor of Accounting
University of Nevada, Reno

I.   INTRODUCTION

The 1988 passage and signing into law of the Act for the Regulation of Gaming on Indian Lands[1] will significantly change the way Indian Gaming is regulated and operated in the United States. This Act effectively allows, on a state-by-state basis, Indian tribes to engage in any gaming activity already permitted by the individual states. It is also likely that this Act will serve as a watershed for commercial Indian gaming ventures, and lead to a rapid evolution in the scale, nature, mix, and sophistication of commercial gaming on Indian lands.

The Act also establishes within the Department of the Interior a Commission to be known as the National Indian Gaming Commission. The Commission's function is to promulgate such regulations and guidelines as it deems appropriate to implement the provisions of the Act and to monitor gaming on Indian lands. Funding for this agency will come from fees assessed for gaming activity but is limited to not more than $1.5 million for any fiscal year. An additional $2 million is also appropriated to fund the operation of the Commission for each of the fiscal years beginning October 1, 1988, and October 1, 1989.

The Commission's funding contrasts dramatically with that of Nevada and New Jersey, the two states that currently regulate gaming. The Nevada Gaming Control Board has a total budget for fiscal year ending June 30, 1989 of approximately $16 million. This amount funded approximately 380 employees for monitoring over 1,200 gaming licenses. The New Jersey Division of Gaming Enforcement and Casino Control Commission spent $47 million in 1988 to regulate only twelve casinos in a geographic area smaller than most Indian reservations.

The contrasting differences in funding has raised concerns over the ability of the National Indian Gaming Commission to effectively monitor and enforce any regulations that the Commission implements. There is more concern that lack of proper monitoring will allow entry by organized crime, or other criminal elements. Large amounts of cash moving through Indian Gambling centers can represent "vast opportunities for skimming and laundering"[2]. There are indications that this possibility already exists. A protected federal witness who said he has direct ties to organized crime told a Senate investigating committee that he personally knew of organized crime infiltration into gambling operations of twelve Indian tribes.[3] He indicated that organized crime now sees Indian reservations as ripe territory for future inroads into illegal gambling and drug operations.

The financial constraints facing the new Commission may limit its capacity to fully monitor all Indian gaming licenses. However, the Commission may be able to maximize its coverage with a minimum of expenditures if it follows the path taken by the Nevada Gaming Board. The Nevada Gaming Board has been able to hold down staff and expenditures by implementation of minimum internal and external audit standards. Such an approach places a large amount of the enforcement requirements on internal audit staffs and their external audit CPAs.

II.   ANALYSIS OF INDIAN GAMING LAW

Three purposes were expressed for passing the Indian Gaming Law. These were:

    a.   to promote tribal economic development, self-sufficiency, and strong tribal governments;

    b.   to provide a statutory basis for the regulation of gaming by an Indian tribe adequate to shield it from organized crime and other corrupting influences, and to ensure that the Indian tribe is the primary beneficiary of the gaming operation; and

    c.   the establishment of a National Indian Gaming Commission along with the establishment of Federal standards for (Class II) gaming on Indian lands.

In keeping with the above objectives, net revenues generated from tribal gaming can only be used to fund tribal governmental operations or programs, provide for the general welfare of the Indian tribe and its members, promote tribal economic development, donate to charitable organizations, or help fund operations of local government agencies.

The Act requires that the Commission be supplied with annual outside audits of the gaming operations, which may be encompassed within the existing independent tribal audit systems. The Act also requires independent audits for all contracts for supplies, services, or concessions for a contract amount in excess of $25,000 annually.

The Act separates gaming into three classes with corresponding levels of regulation. Class I gaming is considered to be social games for prizes of minimum value or traditional forms of Indian gaming engaged in by individuals as a part of tribal ceremonies or celebrations. This form of gaming is left 100% under Indian control and is not subject to control by either state or federal government.

Class II gaming includes bingo and card games such as poker. This type of gaming will be allowed only if the individual state allows such gaming. For example, if the state allows social bingo at church functions, then it must allow Indians to partake in bingo on their reservations. Although the bingo games can be played for any stakes the Indians choose, the poker games must conform to the restrictions set by state law. Class II gaming must be approved by the new Commission and will be monitored by the same. Congress expects that Class II games will constitute the major form of gambling on Indian reservations.

Class III gaming includes all other forms of gaming not covered by the other classes. This catch-all class would include lotteries, sports betting, dog and horse betting, slot machines and casino games. This type of gaming will also be allowed only if the individual state does not have a blanket prohibition against such gaming under any circumstances. Any gaming falling under this category requires an Indian tribe interested in offering such gaming to enter into a compact with the state in which they reside. The Act requires the state to negotiate in good faith and is subject to settlement by an independent mediator, which may leave the state little choice in the type of gaming allowed on the reservation. The individual state compacts will set specific standards and regulations for the implementation of Class III gaming and thus should fall under state statutes.

The Act provides the Commission with the authority to create regulations or standards for all Class II types of gaming. The commission can therefore develop common practices for this type of gaming across all states. However, that consistency is not applied to Class III types of gaming. The result could be fifty different standards for each type of Class III gaming.

Class III gaming has the potential to generate large sums of revenues for the Indian community. But, without proper development of controls, this form of gaming also has the potential to destroy any trust in the creditability of Indian gaming. The result would be an erosion of the Indians' economic base which is based on commercial gaming.

III. NEED FOR MINIMUM ACCOUNTING CONTROLS

The Nevada Gaming Control Board has spent years developing controls for all aspects of gaming and specifically gaming in a casino environment. The Board was also instrumental in the development of the AICPA's audit and accounting guide, *Audits of Casinos*[4]. Yet, years of experience has shown the Nevada Gaming Board that simply requiring proper internal controls without sufficient testing of these controls can result in the perpetration of various frauds and skimming schemes. For example, between October 1974 and May 1976, at least $7 million in slot department revenues were taken from four Las Vegas Casinos[5]. This represented at least 20% of these casinos' slot machine revenues.

In this case, the skimming was undertaken through schemes where slot machines were rigged to falsely indicate that they were paying out to customers one-third more than they actually were. Then, when the coins were collected and taken to the counting room, the electronic scales used to weigh the coins were rewired to underweigh the coins by one-third.

In this instance, the accounting control procedure was to have an auditor compare the indicated coin count by weight with the total after the weighed coins had been wrapped in containers, each holding a designated number of coins. Such a procedure would have shown that the number of wrapped coins was one-third more than the weighed coins.

The casinos could have circumvented the procedure two ways. The easiest approach would be to keep the auditor out of the count room. Such a technique would eventually make the auditor suspicious, so the second approach appeared to be more commonly used. In many instances, the auditors provide advance knowledge of the days they will arrive to audit the casino. Therefore, the second alternative was to adjust the weights before the auditors arrived and then when they left, adjust them back to the incorrect weight.

Examples of slot fraud are not limited to Nevada. Slot fraud also resulted in the removal of all slot machines in 1972 from Army bases[6]. Congressional inquiries and subsequent audits of slot machine operations disclosed that grossly inadequate internal controls engendered an environment of mismanagement and potential fraudulent practices which were of particular embarrassment to the Army.

Credit frauds have also been high on the list of schemes associated with gambling. The simplest fraud is to extend credit to customers with payment made to them in chips. The customers then turn around and redeem the chips at another cashiers' cage and fail to repay the debt. The casino makes no attempt to collect on the credit extension. To top it off, the casino then turns around and writes the credit off as a bad debt, thereby expending the transaction.

Another approach that has been used is to extend credit to parties affiliated with junkets but leave the responsibility of collection to the junket operators. All payments are made to the junkets but in some cases the junket operators never pay the casino directly, thereby allowing the casino to write off the account as a bad debt while at the same time skimming the money off through the junket.

It is also quite easy for credit fraud to be exercised against the casino. Examples abound of cases where casinos have been duped out of hundreds of thousands of dollars through phony credit schemes. For example, a group of 54 conspirators defrauded the Paradise Hotel-Casino in Las Vegas in 1977 of at least $325,000 in cash by using fictitious names, fictitious addresses, and in some instances legitimate credit references. Posing as formidable businessmen, they lulled the Paradise management, causing them to deviate from their normal procedures utilized to protect themselves from such frauds.

In each of the above examples, control procedures were in place that, if properly followed, should have caught the fraudulent acts. The results clearly point to the need for minimum compliance testing of these procedures. Any type of controls are only effective if they are properly implemented. As a result, the Nevada Gaming Control Board has recently developed and implemented requirements for Minimum Internal Control Standards ("MICS")[7] as well as minimum agreed upon procedures for independent accountants' evaluation of "MICS"[8].

IV.   A LOOK AT CONTROL PROCEDURES

Gaming operations are subject to a greater than normal risk of loss as a result of employee or customer dishonesty because:

a.   it is not practical to record all individual table game transactions,

b.   cash receipts or equivalents are not recorded until they are removed from the drop boxes and counted, and

c.   the revenues produced are not from the sale of products or services that are readily measurable[9].

The minimization of these risks require the development of procedures that can control the authorization, accountability, and safekeeping of gaming operations' major asset, cash.

Nevada and New Jersey require casinos to file with regulatory agencies reports describing, in narrative and diagrammatic form, a set of detailed operating procedures for all gaming and gaming-related activities. The report essentially describes the accounting system and system of internal control that must be established before a casino can open its doors. These procedures include paper controls, physical safeguards, and human controls.

The application of paper controls leaves a trail of documentary evidence which is easily tested for compliance by the inspection of transaction documents and records along with appropriate signatures and stamps. Physical safeguards such as safes and cashiers' cages provide self-evident controls. People controls represent activities such as supervision or accountability for transactions.

People controls, i.e. people-to-people checks, frequently leave no audit trail of documentary evidence and are more difficult to continually observe. Misunderstanding of these types of controls can often lead to attempts to circumvent the controls with the resulting possibility of fraudulent actions. The high frequency of non-documented cash transactions in casinos means that people controls play a larger role than what may be found in other industries. Assurance that these controls are working can only be achieved by corroborative inquiries and actual observation of routine operations.

The breakdown of people controls are common across all industries, but are extremely costly in industries dealing with large amounts of cash transactions. This fact, along with the vast disparity in compliance testing of these controls by external auditors, resulted in the Nevada Gaming Control Board's issuance of guidelines entitled "Independent Accountant Minimum Internal Control Standards Compliance Questionnaire for Group I and Group II Licensees"[10].

V. GUIDELINES FOR CONTROL STANDARDS

The Board believes that the use of the Questionnaire should remedy the disparity in the amount and scope of compliance testing of minimum internal accounting controls. It will also ensure that each licensee's compliance with the MICS is consistently evaluated by the independent accountant to the degree intended by the Regulation.

The guidelines provide a set of minimum requirements that must be met for evaluation of any casino's internal controls. In issuing the guidelines, the Board elaborated on several of the following points.

The accountant must read the licensee's system of internal control to determine compliance with the MICS as required by the Regulation. Once this initial desk review has been completed, only a review of system amendments would be necessary in subsequent years.

The Board also specified that the independent accountant should place minimal reliance on the work of the licensee's internal audit staff for purposes of this internal control work. The Board took this approach due to their experiences and the feeling, "internal audit departments have only a limited degree of independence."

In addition, to ensure the integrity of the results of drop and count observations, the Board stipulated that observations of count and drop should be unannounced. For purposes of these procedures, "unannounced" means that no officers, directors, or employees are to be given advance information regarding the dates or times of such observations.

The guidelines also define the minimum applicable revenue centers to be tested. A questionnaire must be completed for each gaming revenue center contributing more than 5% of annual gross gaming revenue. If the revenue centers with revenue greater than 5% do not aggregate to more than 90% of total gross gaming revenue, additional revenue centers should be selected until the 90% threshold has been exceeded.

Finally, the Board provided the following procedures as the minimum agreed upon procedures that must be performed. However, these guidelines are not intended to limit the independent accountant to the performance of only these specified procedures.

     a. At least one unannounced observation of each of the following: slot drop, table games drop, slot count, and table games count;

     b. observations of the licensee's employees as they perform their duties;

c. interviews with the licensee's employees who perform the procedures addressed by the MICS; and

d. compliance testing of various documents referred to in the MICS. The scope of such testing is indicated on the questionnaire where applicable.

VI. THE QUESTIONNAIRE

Regulation 6.090(9) requires the independent accountant to use "criteria established by the chair" in determining whether a Group I or Group II (Nevada) licensee is in compliance with the Minimum Internal Control Standards. (Note: in Nevada, a Group I licensee is one that generates gross gaming revenues (GGRs) in excess of $1 million per year; a Group II licensee generates less than $1 million per year in GGRs.) The Questionnaire represents a series of checklists put together by the Gaming Control Board's Audit Division to be used by the independent accountant in determining whether the licensee's operations are in compliance with MICS. The checklists cover the operating areas of table games, slots, manual keno, computerized keno, bingo, manual race and sports book, computerized race and sports book, card games, and cage and credit.

While the Questionnaire provides guidelines for all operating areas, as a result of the "90% rule" discussed in the guidelines, a majority of the locations throughout the state require only the completion of the questionnaire for slots, table games and perhaps cage and credit. The intent of the 90% rule is to limit the independent accountant's review to areas with material monetary activity only.

The Questionnaire is very specific regarding the procedures to be performed by the independent accountant, including the designation of the scope to be used for compliance testing. The Questionnaire has been developed using the MICS as a basis for the questions included in the checklists.

The scope and content of the questionnaire can be seen by using table games as an example. Table credit play compliance testing has a designated scope that selects two master credit reports per day for two days per year. Each day should be in a separate month. Table games compliance also requires that fill and credit testing include the selection of five fill and credit slips per day for two days per year. The sample should include both fill and credit slips. Again, each day must be in a separate month.

Compliance testing for minimum internal controls requires that any deviations or non-compliance from procedures designated as minimum standards be disclosed. The results of these compliance tests are disclosed in the Independent Accountant's special report.

VII. INDEPENDENT ACCOUNTANT'S AGREED UPON PRO-CEDURES REPORT

The special report required by Regulation 6.090(9) identifies the procedures performed (e.g., compliance tests of both the written system and the procedures in effect), specifies the revenue centers tested (as well as Cage and Credit, if applicable), and describes all instances of procedural noncompliance with the MICS or approved variations. Additionally, the report describes all instances where the written system does comply with the MICS. Finally, it identifies procedures in effect that deviate from the submitted system, and any material internal control deficiencies in the gaming, internal audit and accounting areas that are not addressed by the MICS but are noted by the independent accountant.

The function of this report is to provide the Gaming Control Board with information that enables the Board to maintain strict observance of internal accounting controls and thereby minimize the exposure of potential fraudulent acts.

VIII. CONCLUSION

The Indian Gaming Law has the potential to increase gambling in every state without approval by the citizens of that state. Furthermore, most states do not have the expertise, ability, or funding to implement procedures or oversee proper monitoring of the various types of gaming that could result from this law. Yet, the Act only provides authority for the Commission to create standards for Class II gaming.

Any regulations dealing with Class III gaming must be worked out in compacts between the Indian tribes and the individual states. The result could be a diverse group of rules or standards that could possibly pit one state against another or Indian tribes in competition against each other. Years of experience in Nevada have clearly shown that a diversity of standards can ultimately provide opportunities for major skimming or other fraudulent acts. The result would be detrimental for all concerned parties. The creation of standardized set of minimal internal and external controls such as that now existing in the State of Nevada can go a long way toward providing the solid economic foundation that commercial gaming could bring to the Indian community.

[1] AICPA, *Audits of Casinos*, American Institute of Certified Public Accountants, Inc., 1984.

[2] -----, *Business Week*, August 19, 1985

[3] Chuck Raasch,"Senate panel told of mob role on reservations", *Gannett News Service,Reno Gazette-Journal*, February 9, 1989, p. 1 ff.

[4] AICPA, *Audits of Casinos*, American Institute of Certified Public Accountants, Inc., 1984.

[5] Miller, Ken, "Skimming Can Be Done Simply or Intricately", *Reno Gazette-Journal*, July 17, 1985.

[6] Farinella, Robert, "Re-Introducing Slot Machines on U.S. Overseas Army Bases: Objectives, Restrictions and Accomplishments", in *Gambling Research: Proceedings of the Seventh International Conference on Gambling and Risk Taking*, 1988, University of Nevada, Reno, volume 1, pp. 280-293.

[7] State of Nevada, *Minimum Internal Control Standards for Group I and Group II Licensees*, Gaming Control Board, October 1987.

[8] State of Nevada, *Guidelines for the Preparation of the Special Report and Supporting Checklists Required by Regulation 6.090(9) for Group I and II licensees*, Gaming Control Board, March 31, 1989.

[9] AICPA, *Audits of Casinos*, AICPA, New York, New York, 1984.

[10] State of Nevada, *Independent Accountant M.I.C.S. Compliance Questionnaire For Group I and Group II Licensees*, Gaming Control Board, March 31, 1989.

2

Jerome H. Skolnick
Professor of Law and Criminology
University of California, Berkeley

After listening to the various papers and presentations that have been made at this Conference, I recognize that most of the sharp, analytical observations on the Indian Gaming Act have already been said. Earlier presentations have done a very detailed analysis of the new gaming law, and have detailed all of the problems and possibilities of that law.

In my presentation, I will try to put some of the issues that have been brought forward into a broader perspective. When I began to think about how to accomplish that, I realized that I wrote an article as part of a conference that took place recently that might be pertinent.

I received a call a couple of years ago from a professor at Duke University Law School. He said they were going to have a conference on the topic of vice, and they wanted me to do the lead article on this topic and explain what it is. I saw it as a challenge, so I decided to see what I could do. The first question that came to mind was, what is the difference between a vice and a crime? I thought there is a difference but it's very hard to define. So I looked up vice in the dictionary, and it said vice is evil or immoral conduct, but that is true of crime also. So what's the difference between a vice and a crime?

A crime is something that we all recognize as evil and immoral. It has no dualistic quality. Everyone agrees that murder, rape, and robbery are evil acts. However, vice is something that is sometimes called evil and also can be very enjoyable. As a result, there is a good deal of ambivalence about vices. This Conference on the Status of Indan Gaming has addressed itself to a phenomenon about which American society is most ambivalent about how it feels: gambling.

If you think about the concept of ambivalence, what does it mean? It suggests two poles, a positive one, and a negative one. Freudian psychologists talk about love-hate relationships of parents toward children, of children toward parents, and even of spouses toward each other. The whole idea behind the concept of ambivalence is that people are able to maintain quite inconsistent attitudes towards the object of the ambivalence. I suggest it is this kind of inconsistent attitudinal structure that can exist at the social level as well as the individual psychological level.

Let me cite another example. Perhaps it is the best example of social, and indeed, moral ambivalence: the attitude towards alcohol. Will Rogers may have captured this best when he was asked during the 1920s what was the sentiment of the American people, were they wet or were they dry? And he said, "Well, are

Americans dry? Watch them vote. Are Americans wet? Watch them drink."

In my opinion, American society is similarly conflicted regarding its attitudes towards gambling. Gambling is very popular, but in many segments of American society gambling is looked down upon, and is regarded as immoral and wicked. During the 1970s, I undertook a study of casino gambling and its regulation that resulted in the book, *House of Cards* (Little, Brown & Co., Boston, 1978). In the book, I said that gambling, especially casino gambling, was a "pariah" industry. It was an industry that was stigmatized. At that time, at least part of the public perception of gambling was attributable to the fact that Nevada's casinos were viewed as being dominated or infiltrated by mobsters, by organized crime.

It was also true that many visitors to Nevada were titillated by that association. Many players would go to a casino like the Flamingo in Las Vegas because of its historical association with Bugsy Siegel. Being associated with organized crime did not reduce business. At the same time, casinos were looked down upon as places that were connected with crime, with prostitution, and with other sorts of undesirable activities. Gambling itself was looked down upon that way.

If you consider the association of gambling with charity nights, charity bingo, and Las Vegas nights, they also almost perfectly represent the moral ambivalence that gambling generates. The players in these charity events are told it is all right to sin, provided that the profits are directed towards good works. So we find this kind of curious and self-contradictory phenomenon linking charitable fund raising to gambling. In a similar vein, the legalization of lotteries as they have developed in the United States are also morally justified on the worth of generating income for education from sinful activities.

Lotteries have always had this kind of morally contradictory character. If one looks back historically in America, the budget of the first city in what was to become the United States, Jamestown, Virginia, in 1640, was maintained through a lottery. However, the lottery was closed down some years later because there were no controls over the way the lottery was run, and it was found that there was a lot of cheating taking place.

This has been an aspect of the history of gambling throughout both United States and British history. The lotteries provided a good deal of income for the cities in England in the 18th century. But in the early nineteenth century, lotteries were shut down in England because they were thought to be an immoral way to raise money. Many U.S. states had lotteries in the 19th century but by the end of the century, all legal lotteries in the United States had been abolished. The first renewal of the lottery took place in 1964 in New Hampshire, again as part of a sin tax notion. One selling point was that people from other states could be persuaded to bet the lottery in New Hampshire; thus, some of the state revenue generation would be shifted to residents of other states.

It is interesting to note that there was no lottery by the federal government during the Second World War to raise money. Obviously lotteries do raise a great deal of money. Why didn't this take place? Because there was a good deal of ambivalence about whether it was morally correct to raise money from this supposedly sinful activity.

Why should gambling be regarded as a sinful activity by anybody? One reason is the modern casino gambling business in America was indeed started by organized crime. The atmosphere around the casino industry is now much different that it was only fifteen years ago when I began to study Las Vegas. During the 1960s the state of Nevada had a terrific problem keeping mobsters out of the casinos.

However, there are other reasons that people give for regarding gambling as a sin or something evil or immoral. Gambling violates the Protestant ethic. According to the Protestant ethic, one is supposed to earn one's rewards. Many people feel people are not supposed to be chosen by fortune, though many others think that's perfectly all right. My point is that we are ambivalent about this as a society. Thus, there is a lot of conflict over the legitimacy of gambling.

There are others who point to other kinds of problems associated with gambling. It induces people to spend beyond their means, and it may bring crime, prostitution, and other disreputable activities in its wake. I must say I was somewhat astonished earlier in this Conference at hearing Nevada Senator Harry Reid spelling out, one by one, the potentially socially destructive results of having gaming in a community. He was obviously offering a mixed message. He was saying to the Indian tribes that they would have these potentially destructive results if they pursued casino-style gambling. However, the citizens of Nevada, who have lived with the casino industry for more than fifty years, have learned to deal with them. Therefore, casino-style gambling ought to be limited to Nevada.

There may be something to this argument. There is a case to be made, one that has been made in Europe in the past, that casino gambling should be restricted to spas and watering places. Casinos should be restricted to places where people have to make an independent decision to visit those places and gamble. They should not be located in major metropolitan areas easily accessible to the general public who then wouldn't have to think about making a decision to go and gamble.

It is my opinion that at this point in time, we are at an extraordinary turning point in the development of public attitudes towards gambling. If I was astonished by what I heard Senator Reid say, I must say I was even more astonished when I read the *Cabazon* decision. This Conference has generated a lot of analyses of that decision from a legal perspective. I want to suggest that there is another way to look at that decision. One thing the court does is to take a rather positive view of gambling as a recreational activity, which itself it quite striking.

Quoting from the decision: "The tribes," writes Justice White, "are not merely importing a product on to the reservation for immediate resale to non-Indians. They have built modern facilities which provide recreational opportunities and ancillary services to their patrons who do not simply drive onto the reservations, make purchases and depart, but spend extended periods of time there enjoying the services the tribes provide."

Justice White goes on to compare the tribal bingo enterprises to the Mescalero Apache Tribe resort complex, which features "hunting and fishing". What is emerging in this decision is the notion of the legitimacy of gambling as a recreational activity, moving it from the pall of immorality to the light of positive recreational activity. When the Supreme Court of the United States in its authoritative voice makes this kind of pronouncement, even though it is dicta and not law, it is providing a vision of the acceptability of gambling in American life as well as on the tribal lands.

It can also be noted that the *Cabazon* decision turns on what a skeptic might describe as a splitting of a legal hair. The question raised in the decision is: Is the California prohibition against gambling and bingo a regulatory or criminal prohibition? The Court answers this by saying it is regulatory, not criminal. Therefore Public Law 280, which had given California and some other western states criminal jurisdiction over Indian lands, does not apply.

I found that quite interesting because the Court could have come down on either side if it had wanted to. The Court itself is troubled by the implications of that pronouncement. In a footnote, one which could become famous, which is a humorous footnote in some ways, the Court writes: "Nothing in this opinion suggests that cockfighting, tatoo parlors, nude dancing and prostitution are permissible on Indian reservations within California." In other words, those activities are quite distinguishable from gambling. Those activities are morally reprehensible and anyone who practices those activities is engaging in a crime. Those are criminal activities.

But gambling is not morally reprehensible. Gambling is therefore a regulatory kind of activity and it does not fall under the police powers of the state.

Of course, the control over these other activities might well be considered regulatory, but it is not. Gambling is different. Gambling has come to take a place in American society which is recognized as far more legitimate.

There is another feature of the *Cabazon* decision which indicates how much I think the position of gambling in the American social landscape has changed, and also how difficult it is to define it. If you look at most recent cases involving criminal law or criminal procedure, you will find a fairly consistent lineup of the Justices. You will usually find Justices White and Rehnquist always on the conservative side, usually along with Justices O'Connor and Scalia. Almost always on the other side are Justices Brennan and Marshall, often joined by Justice Blackmun and sometimes Justice Stevens.

The line-up for *Cabazon* is very interesting. In this case Justices White, Rehnquist, Brennan and Marshall joined on the prevailing side, the Court's conservatives and liberals forming the majority. A middle of the road Justice Stevens writes the dissent joined by two conservatives, O'Connor and Scalia. It is scarcely possible to imagine such a Supreme Court lineup in another criminal law or procedure case. Indeed, I cannot think of any decision involving the Fourth amendment where Justices Scalia and O'Connor fall on one side, and Justices White and Rehnquist on the other.

The question is, why should that be? I suggest it is because there is no consistent set of values associated with the idea of gambling in the minds of the Justices. I think that Justices Brennan and Marshall voted pro because they generally vote on the side of ethnic and racial minorities, and oppressed peoples, and that is the way they envisioned the decision. However, that still leaves unexplained Justice Rehnquist's positive vote, as well as Justice White's writing of the decision. This is very hard to explain because usually they are very deferential to law enforcement, and especially to state law enforcement. The only thing I can think of is that they reasoned as follows: If the states are going to benefit from this activity that we are not very happy about, then the Indians ought to be allowed to do that as well.

However the Justices arrived at their individual decisions, it is important to understand the jurisprudence of the *Cabazon* decision. It rests on what could be called the jurisprudence of balancing. The Supreme Court does not hold that the tribes are sovereign and therefore the tribes may have gambling.

What the court does is to balance. On the one side, it balances legitimate state interests in preventing the infiltration of organized crime. On the other side, it balances federal interests in Indian self-support and similar Indian interests in tribal self-government. In other words, the court is not saying Indian tribes are sovereign and are nations who therefore can do as they please. Rather, the Court is saying that there are federal interests in Indian self-support, tribal interests in Indian self-support, and also sovereign interests in self-government; at the same time there are state interests in preventing the infiltration of organized crime. But those former interests outweigh these latter interests.

When you get into a jurisprudence of balancing, it is usually weighing values. How does the Court know how much weight to give to state interests in preventing the infiltration of organized crime, or how much weight to give Indian interests or federal interests in self-government? This kind of balancing jurisprudence is very different from the jurisprudence of rights.

In a jurisprudence of rights, one wins not by balancing the interests in question against other interests, but because it is one's right to do something. For example, a person has a right to counsel. The Court could say a person has a right to counsel because the interest of the state in not giving a right to counsel, and its costs, are outweighed by a person's right to counsel. However, that is not what the court says with respect to right to counsel, or the right to vote. It says a person has a fundamental right to counsel. A person cannot have a fair trial without a right to counsel. One cannot have a free society without a rule of one man, one vote. That is a jurisprudence of rights.

A balancing jurisprudence by contrast almost invites legislation because it is legislative in the way it is framed. What is the state's interest in law enforcement? What is the federal interest in Indian self-support? What is the Indian tribe interest in self-government? In a sense, the Indian Gaming Act was almost inevitable given the kind of balancing decision that came from the United States Supreme Court.

I believe that the Justices were very influenced by this self-support notion, as well as by the values of economic development and the values of self-determination, all of which are conservative values. They write in their decision: "The tribal games at present provide the sole source of revenues for the operation of tribal governments and the provision of tribal services. They are also the major sources of employment on the reservations. Self-determination and economic development are not within the reach of the tribes if they cannot raise revenues and provide employment for their members. The tribes' interests obviously parallel the federal interests."

Thus, the Court is saying that here is a legitimate economic activity. The Court is not saying that this activity should be uncontrolled, or that there is no state interest in controlling this activity. Rather, it is on balance recognizing that there is an economic interest here that should go forward. In effect it throws the entire issue to the legislature to determine how to balance out the trade-offs. Indeed, a legislature is in a better position than a Court to find facts, to balance interests, and to play politics, because a balancing rationale is a kind of political rationale in itself. A legislature, with its hearings and its political processes, is in a better position to weigh all of those interests.

That is what happened. The Congress wrote the Indian Gaming Act after lots of politicking. What emerged is a bill that is a compromise, as many people have pointed out. But so is *Cabazon,* and that also should be recognized.

With this as background, the Indian Gaming Act can be examined in a different perspective than has been done elsewhere. After all the analyses that have been presented, this Act, in gambling terms, is best described as a wild card. It is replete with ambiguities. Because of these ambiguities, everybody seems to be unhappy with it.

I want to suggest that the states and the casino industry may regard certain aspects of this bill as a defeat, but of course as compared to the *Cabazon* decision, which is also a wild card, it is no defeat. It probably should be regarded by the states and the casino industry as a victory.

I have also heard tribal speakers at this Conference who are asking for a conception of sovereignty that, in my opinion, really reflects a concern for dignity. Unfortunately, it is very difficult for the Congress or the courts at this stage in U.S. history to offer the kind of dignity which goes along with independence, particularly involving an activity about which in the broad perspective of American society there is so much ambivalence.

Based on *Cabazon* and the Indian Gaming Act, I want to suggest that, in fact, the last three years have been very positive for gambling in the whole landscape of American society. *Cabazon* can be read as it normally is, allowing Indian tribes to have gambling if there is the same kind of gambling in the state. More importantly for the future, it also can be read as a decision in which the United States Supreme Court authoritatively says gambling is a legitimate recreational activity like hunting and fishing.

As a result of the Act, the tribes are scarcely limited, if limited at all, with respect to Class II gaming. The Cabazon Indian tribe clearly can run bingo and so can any other tribe. Furthermore, except in what seem to be the most egregious circumstances, there will be internal tribal control of bingo on the reservations as the Act provides.

Because of the affront to dignity, tribes have understandably bridled at having to negotitate with states over Class III gaming. But if this is examined more practically, I wonder how much of a difference this really will make.

In a state like Nevada, the tribes clearly will be able to open casinos. But as a former student of casino gambling, I want to suggest that just because Indian tribes are permitted to have Class III gaming does not mean that Class III gaming will be profitable. Any one qualified person can open a casino in Reno or Las Vegas. But then the problem is competing against the rest of the casino industry. Such competition might make it quite difficult to turn a profit.

The fact that tribes are permitted to have Class III gaming does not mean that Class III gaming is necessarily going to be profitable. This is clearly the case in Nevada, where it is uncertain as to whether any casino is going to be profitable. If tribal casinos develop in other jurisdictions where they would have a regional monopoly, that could be profitable. However, it is unclear that a *Cabazon* sort of balancing will occur in another jurisdiction. For example, how a court will look at this issue in a state like New York, which has Las Vegas Nights, is hard to predict. They might reason that bingo in California is one thing, but casinos in New York quite another. It is another wild card. It's not clear which way the court would rule.

Everyone tends to interpret victory into defeat in terms of its most recent manifestation. But I want to suggest to the tribes that it would be worth considering interpreting victory in defeat in much longer range terms. The tribes won in the Supreme Court, whereas the gaming industry prevailed in the Congress. From a longer range historical perspective I suggest that everybody associated in the gaming industry, those who already have an interest in this industry, along with the tribes who have a future interest in this industry, have won a great deal in the last three years.

If we go back twenty years in the state of Nevada, when I first began my studies of this business, the state of Nevada was struggling to improve its image by introducing better controls. At that time, casino companies were not publicly traded. They were not allowed to be. Nevada's major industry was in many ways in quite serious trouble in the 1960s. In the 1960s, the state operated under the remote but quite possible threat that the Congress would outlaw casino gambling in the United States. After the Kefauver Hearings in the early 1950s, it became perfectly clear that the casino gambling business was started by mobsters, was infiltrated by mobsters, and that mobsters ran the state of Nevada; there is little question about that.

Gaming Control in the late 1960s and 1970s in Nevada really emerged in response to the threat of Federal intervention and the widely held perception that Nevada's casinos fueled organized crime in places like Chicago, Detroit and Kansas City. This perception was not unjustified.

When I wrote *House of Cards*, I wrote about the gaming industry and called it a pariah industry. Why did I call it a pariah industry at that time, in 1975? It is because at that time the gaming industry was still experiencing considerable difficulty in obtaining any kind of capital for its expansion from respectable institutional lenders like banks or insurance companies.

When I first started my research in Nevada, the first priority of the Gaming Control Board and the Gaming Commission was trying to figure out how to get the Teamsters Central States Pension Fund, headed by Jimmy Hoffa at that time, out of the state of Nevada. In the early 1970s, that fund held a quarter of a billion dollars of loans against Nevada casinos and in fact surreptitiously controlled many of those casinos.

Since that time, there has been a remarkable transformation. Casino companies now trade on major stock exchanges as publicly held corporations. It may turn out that, in the future, *Cabazon*'s most important legacy will not be its rather weak balancing holding, which could easily shift. Future courts could say that the state's interest in law enforcement is now more important than it was when the original decision was rendered. Rather, the importance of *Cabazon* might be in its dicta; the statements indicating gambling is a legitimate business serving a socially useful, recreational purpose.

I will conclude this presentation by offering, with some temerity, a suggestion to everyone in the gambling business and everyone considering entering the gambling business. The suggestion is: be prudent. Gambling is now poised on the positive pole of the moral ambivalence. But history shows that society could move to toward the negative pole, if it appears that gambling is associated with economic failure and bankruptcy. If this economic failure leads to infiltration by organized crime, or leads to a perception of sleaziness and tawdryness, then public opinion, which I think if reflected in the Court's opinion in *Cabazon*, might change.

The Court says in *Cabazon* that the tribes have a strong incentive to provide comfortable, clean, attractive and well-run games in order to increase attendance at the games. Who am I to suggest that sometimes the U.S. Supreme Court writes platitudes? But this is a platitude. The observation is true of all businesses, be they gaming facilities, hotels, motels, or restaurants. They all have incentives to run very fine facilities. But we all know that not all hotels, motels, restaurants and gaming facilities are clean, well-run and attractive. Incentives help, but they don't necessarily work. They can be undermined by overexpansion, by moving too quickly toward an apparent economic paradise which results in economic failure. This could result in a lack of vigilance in a time of need, resulting in decline.

I suggest to you that as result of *Cabazon*, the Indian Gaming Act, and general economic expansion, the gambling industry is on a roll. Furthermore, the tribes are going to roll with it. However, I also want to point out that as every professional gambler knows, lucky streaks can change. You have to know when to hold them, and you have to know when to fold them. And you should never push your luck too far.

3

William R. Eadington
Professor of Economics
University of Nevada, Reno

Much of the attention of the analysis on Indian gaming at this Conference has concentrated on passage of the Indian Gaming Act, the political infighting that took place in the halls of Congress prior to its passage, and the reasons why people are happy or unhappy about the results. However, of far greater importance to all affected parties are the long term implications of the Act: what does the Act, in conjunction with the economic and social trends taking place in America with respect to the popularity of gambling and the spread of commercial gaming, imply for the future of Indian gaming?

This analysis poses a speculative glance into the future. Our horizons should not just cover the next two or three years. Rather, we should look ten years, twenty years, thirty years and more into the future. There is much that can be learned by looking at past and present trends and projecting them into the future to see what they portend.

These observations also reflect the analytical processes of economics, rather than politics or the law. As it stands, I am the only economist participating in this Conference, whereas many of the other contributors have been trained in, and are actively involved in the practice of law. It is my opinion that economists can offer some interesting insights to this situation which are not immediately obvious, but which portend interesting possibilities that need to be evaluated.

In my opinion, these possibilities are of critical importance to the self-interest of the Indian nations who have considered venturing into Indian gaming operations, as well as to the states that will have to deal with the issue of regulation of Class III gaming. These possibilities also involve the other affected parties, the non-Indian commercial gaming industries that already exist or that will be created in the future throughout the U.S. and Canada, and ultimately the gaming customers themselves.

Economists are sometimes criticized for making predictions about the future. John Kenneth Galbraith was once asked, "Why do economists forecast?" His response was "Because we are asked to do so." Economists have no crystal ball, but they are trained to analyze economic processes and empirical data in a systematic matter that allows them to gain some insights into the implications of past and present trends as to how they might turn out in the future.

The distinction between the way an economist looks at an issue like Indian gaming, and the way an attorney, a legislator, or a regulator sees the same issue, can be illustrated by analogy. Consider a person in the process of constructing a new house for the purpose of taking up residence in it for an extended period. As a rational self-interested individual, he would consider the various costs and benefits of different grades of building materials and alternative house plans, and he would ultimately have to decide how much in the way of resources could be allocated to building the structure. He might also evaluate alternative techniques that could be applied to construction, and how much insulation should be used to protect the residents from the elements outside. He would have to weigh the trade-offs, the benefits and costs, in terms of what kind of heating systems and other amenities should be built into the house.

These construction decisions are analogous to the debates that transpired concerning the formulation of the Indian Gaming Act by Congress. The Congressmen and Senators played the role of architects in shaping the blueprint of the law. The regulators in the various states are mandated to play the role of construction crews, going from the broad blueprint of the Act to the specifics of putting together workable facades. The attorneys are playing the role of building inspectors, checking to see that building codes and standards have been adhered to, and challenging earlier decisions when they believe that not to be the case.

The important question is, what kind of a structure does this process generate? The economist looks at the entire process from a slightly different perspective than the others. The economist would ask what the house is going to be like once it is inhabited. The question of how comfortable the house is for day-to-day living is not just an issue of how it was built, but also a question of how compatible the house is with the external elements that will affect life inside the house. What is the nature of the weather patterns that will push against the exterior of the house? What are the forces that will test the strengths or weaknesses of that particular structure? If the weather outside is mild, a shoddily constructed, poorly insulated house could fare well. If the external economic environment is mild, a weak set of laws and regulations could fare well for Indian gaming.

However, one of my personal forecasts for the intermediate and long term future is that the competitive economic environment confronting gaming industries, including the Indian gaming industries, are not going to be mild. Therefore we need substantial construction standards and practices, along with a good structural foundation, for the laws and regulations dealing with Indian gaming. It is critical that decision makers consider these needs in anticipation of what is likely to occur in the future.

Because economists have very different ways of looking at public policy issues from those trained in the law, they often come up with different sets of recommendations. Attorneys and the legal system often involve themselves with questions of deciding who owns what. Litigation often centers on the question of claims of ownership on existing property. To a large extent, the debate on Indian gaming has been a question of who has the right to offer gaming services to the general public, and who has the right to control those individuals who are offering gaming services. On the other hand, economists usually deal with resource questions in terms of how the productive base of resources can be expanded to increase the amount of production, or the incomes, or the well-being of society at large. These are very different perspectives.

Children as they are growing up learn to fulfill their needs and react to their environments much as attorneys do through the legal process. Children learn that they can get what they want through negotiation. They can get what they want through fighting or crying or whining. They can get what they want through being stubborn, or bullying, or persuasive, or whatever they have discovered will work, but they can get what they want by somehow transforming the property rights of someone else, often their parents or their friends, to themselves.

However, as children go through adolescence to adulthood, they establish a better realization of what the world is really like. As they get jobs and start earning a livelihood from their own labor resources, they start seeing things slightly differently, more in an economic fashion as compared to a political fashion. This perspective is based on the premise that each individual is the owner of certain resources, that these resources can be transformed into income through market transactions, such as selling one's labor to an employer, and then the income earned can be used to buy what the individual wants. For society at large, this leads to an expansion in the base of available commodities, rather than just dividing a fixed amount of commodities through property rights determination.

This is a process that enhances the realization of what living and dealing in the economic world is like. However, because of the emphasis on litigation and property rights determination, many attorneys miss this nuance of a market driven economy and tend to see things as a politically determined zero-sum game. In a similar vein, the long-term relationship between Indian tribes in the United States and the federal government has created a situation where the way Indian tribes receive their allocations, their share of the pie, is determined far more by political forces than by economic forces. If Indian tribes are going to be successful in competing with other gaming industries in the delivery of gaming services to potential customers, they will have to change this perspective.

What general trends are likely to take place with commercial gaming industries over the next twenty or thirty years? As a first approximation, one could examine what has happened to commercial gaming industries in this country and throughout the world over the past three decades. Given this long view, it is amazing how much change has taken place. Legal commercial gaming industries thirty years ago were virtually all perceived by society as illegitimate, with few exceptions. Much of the gambling that did take place was illegal, though society was often ambivalent about enforcing anti-gambling statutes. Gambling as an activity and as a commercial enterprise was considered inappropriate, immoral, corrupt and destructive. Gaming industries were considered "pariah" industries, a term coined by Jerome Skolnick in his seminal book on casino regulation, *House of Cards* (Little, Brown & Co., 1978).

However, by the 1970s, the transition toward legitimacy was well underway, with the spread of lotteries, with corporate entry into casino operations, with government operated off-track-betting in New York and other states, and with the emergence of casino gaming in Atlantic City. Yet in terms of sophistication, of product development and marketing strategies, and sheer financial size and strength, the gaming industries of today have evolved substantially from those of just ten years ago. In short, over the past thirty years, commercial gaming has been on the fast track toward legitimization.

Assuming continuation of past trends, the gaming industries of thirty years from now will be far more sophisticated and legitimate than those that exist today. They are also likely to be more consolidated organizations, perhaps dominated by the larger, diverse private sector companies in the leisure and entertainment industries. Furthermore, government operated gaming, such as today's state lotteries, could also be far more extensive and pervasive.

What does this imply for the competitive environment for commercial gaming? If we just look at recent trends toward legalization in the United States alone, we find now that some form of gambling is present in virtually every state; Utah and Hawaii are the last two hold-out states. As of 1989, major casino gambling is constrained to the states of Nevada and New Jersey, but by 1991, Iowa will have riverboat casinos, and small-stake casinos will be operating in Deadwood, South Dakota. These trends undoubtedly will continue. In twenty or thirty years, it is not inconceivable that casino style gaming will be available to virtually every community and every citizen in the United States.

Unless there is a significant shift in the direction of the trends that we have seen for the last thirty years, this kind of progress is almost inevitable. This has very significant and important implications for Indian gaming. If in fact commercial gaming continues to expand, then the ultimate issue of economic viability and of profitability for gaming operations will heavily depend on which competitors can attract the consumer base. Successful competitors will be those organizations which can best provide the entertainment product, the resort services, the gaming action, and the atmosphere that will be appealing to broad market niches of customers in a highly competitive environment.

In my opinion, those gaming operations that have the greatest consumer appeal and loyalty are going to be successful; they will be the survivors. Such operations will also be the ones that can attract financial capital for the investment necessary to develop facilities that will provide the high quality experience that individual consumers will demand. Those facilities that can attract the financial capital will be the profitable entities. On the other hand, there will be many gaming operations in various arenas of commercial gaming industries that will not be survivors.

Performing well in an uncompetitive environment versus performing well in a highly competitive one is like night and day. For example, one need only examine the airline industry and its experience in the last ten years under deregulation to get a sense of the differences. One could also examine the bankruptcies and closures of casinos in the Reno-Sparks market between 1978 and 1989 to gain a sense of the victims competition can create in the gaming industry.

A very important factor to attract financial capital, which is a necessary ingredient to remain profitable in the long run in a competitive environment, is to be able to exist in a stable economic environment. The environment must be stable in terms of its regulatory structure, its legal structure, and its competitive structure. Referring to the analogy of the house, if the house is well constructed from the beginning, it may weather the storms. But if the house is built poorly, as if constructed on sand, and then the storms come, the house may crumble and disappear. Indian gaming does have the potential of becoming, or for many tribes remaining, an important revenue generator and source of employment. But if these benefits are going to be long lasting, Indian gaming will have to have a stable and survivable structure to work within.

The issue here is not legal survival. Nor does it deal with claims on the prominence of Indian sovereignty or alternative interpretations of the Indian Gaming Act. Far more important are the fundamentals of economic survival in a competitive environment. If Indian tribes win their arguments against the Indian Gaming Act and in favor of self-rule and self-regulation, as many Indian tribes at this podium have advocated, the victories will be hollow. If the law is successfully challenged, and even if Congress gives the Indian tribes all that they ever asked for in a new Indian Gaming Act, I would guarantee that in twenty five years Indian gaming will not be a viable economic entity for Indian tribes. They would be in no position to survive the competition from legitimate, highly regulated, highly capitalized gaming operations.

Self-regulation does not have credibility. Regulation by the states under compacts may not initially have credibility, but they have much greater potential to develop it than self-regulation ever will. It is instructive to look at the history of gaming regulation in Nevada and to note that thirty years ago Nevada had virtually no credibility. Nevada had problems in the gaming industry that the state itself continued to deny existed, but nonetheless the problems were fundamental realities. Teamster financing, hidden ownership, individuals of questionable character and background who had been with the industry from its inception, clear links to so-called organized crime; these were the realities of the Nevada landscape. At that time, the gaming industry could not attract financial capital from legitimate sources; thus, it could not expand to fulfill its profit potential until those fundamental realities changed.

The realities did change and are continuing to change over time. As a result, Nevada is very prosperous. Nevada has benefitted substantially by these changes. But not everyone in Nevada has benefitted uniformly. The casino operations that have survived, those that have prospered, are the ones that are highly capitalized, that have substantial facilities, that have utilized scientific management techniques, that have applied the expertise of well trained individuals in marketing, accounting, finance, the law, and other general management skills. They are not the "mom and pop" operators. They are not the casinos managed by the rough and tumble guys who learned how to run a gambling joint illegally in the back room in some bar in some city elsewhere in the United States. The gaming industry has evolved to become as sophisticated as virtually any industry in the United States. Furthermore, the gaming industries are going to continue to evolve, and that is the reality that Indian gaming operations have to keep in mind in evaluating their viability in the long term.

The question of Indian sovereignty is a significant issue among tribes; for them, it is a source of tremendous pride. It is felt by many Indian leaders that the loss of Indian sovereignty could carry with it a threat to the very Indian way of life and to their fundamental values. However, with respect to Indian gaming, I would recommend that tribes not confuse pride with common sense. If Indians challenge the Indian Gaming Act successfully, if they are able to remove the constraints that Class III gaming have put forth, if the price of this victory is going to be an economically non-viable Indian gaming industry, would it have been worth it?

When the rest of the United States has legalized gaming, what will Indian gaming operations have that will make their customers loyal to them? Many Indian leaders have stated that the Indian Gaming Act that became law was really the Nevada Bill, and it certainly did have strong support from Nevada legislative and industry interests. The claim has been made again and again that Nevada supported this bill because they were afraid of the competition that the Indians would present to the state's casino industry. As a long time observer of the Nevada gaming industry, my reaction to this claim is that it is misdirected; Nevada is not worried about the competition from Indians. Nevada is worried about the questions of image and legitimacy for commercial gaming.

Over the years, Indians have complained about the stereotyping of Indians by non-Indians, and recently, the applications of such stereotypes to Indian gaming. During one of the Senate Select Committee hearings in 1988, for example, allegations were made that there had been organized crime infiltration into Indian gaming operations in Oklahoma, suggesting this pattern was wide-spread. Indian leaders have complained that perhaps there is a bad operation here or there, but that does not mean all Indian gaming operations are infiltrated or corrupt. Similarly, when problems of propriety among the leadership of the Navajos in Arizona recently surfaced, the question of corruption among tribal leadership in general was raised. Again, Indian leaders complained that non-Indians would look at a situation like this and conclude that this is the norm; all Indian leaders are corrupt. Indians have also been plagued by the stereotypes of the drunken Indian or the lazy Indian, even though these are likely the exception rather than the norm.

The gaming industry in Nevada is not unfamiliar with such stereotyping. The stereotyping that came from organized crime infiltration has stigmatized all gaming operations, whether correctly or not, since the 1950s. The reason the gaming industry was considered a pariah industry was not because all gaming operators were corrupt and not because organized crime was involved in every gaming operation, but rather because there were some for which the stereotype was correct. As long as there were some, the stereotyping continued.

In the past twenty years, the gaming industry and the state of Nevada have adopted a strategy of cleaning up the industry's image. But the reality of removing organized crime and corruption, which has resulted largely because of the entrance of publicly traded corporations into the gaming industry and by strengthening regulation of the ownership, game integrity, and accounting practices of casino operations, has occurred before the image has begun to move in the same direction. Image always trails reality. The casino industry, which is far better operated in the 1980s than ever before, still has the image of being somewhat suspect, especially to the casual observer. The negative image will continue to diminish over time as long the gaming industry continues to improve practices and operations, and as long as it remains free of scandal.

However, one of the main concerns of the gaming industry with respect to Indian gaming deals with the fact that the general public looks at commercial gaming operations as if they were a single entity, in the same manner that non-Indians look at Indians, as if they were just a single tribe or a single people. There is tremendous diversity within the various commercial gaming industries in the United States. But if any one of them had a significant scandal, it would taint all of the others as well. Thus, if Indian gaming were self-regulated (or unregulated) as many tribal leaders advocate under self-rule, all it would take is for just a few bad situations to create a scandal for the entire gaming industries. It would first taint all of the Indian gaming operations, but then ultimately other commercial gaming industries could be caught up in the backwash. If such a scandal did occur, commercial gaming industries are still politically vulnerable enough that there is the potential that their legal status could be changed. This is because gambling is one of those grey-area activities that always attracts the media, the moralists, and people who are damaged by compulsive gambling. Historically, legal commercial gaming has seldom existed in a stable environment. In the public policy arena, one of the major concerns about commercial gambling over the years has been the fear of infiltration by organized crime, or by undesirable characters who would skim and scam customers as well as owners of gaming establishments. If the image of commercial gaming moved strongly toward the negative pole, there is a real possibility that legislation prohibiting such gambling could once again emerge. Thus, if one wants to understand why Nevada supported the Indian Gaming Act in the form that became law, the answers lie in the issues of legitimacy and image.

Furthermore, this is not just a Nevada issue. The gaming industry interests in Nevada also have substantial presence in other jurisdictions throughout the United States and throughout the world. Their loyalty to Nevada is not that strong, but their loyalty to their own long term interests is very strong. And those interests are best served by a positive image and continuing gains in legitimacy for commercial gaming generally.

This line of argument suggests that a fundamental requirement for success for any form of commercial gaming is a strong regulatory base to provide a strong environment, both legal and economic, which has the potential of attracting long term financial capital, and which has the potential of generating a profitable environment for those operations. For Indian gaming operations, this is going to require a more sophisticated type of organization than can now be found in many of the Indian gaming operations that are currently in existence.

A parallel can be drawn between today's Indian gaming operations and the early experience of casinos and bingo halls in Las Vegas and Reno in the 1930s to the 1950s, where many of the gaming operators learned the business through trial and error. Through tough experience, they developed the techniques on how to protect the games, how to run the operation, and how to apply rudimentary marketing skills. Given the difference in competitive environments, Indian gaming operations will not have the luxury of such slow learning processes in the 1990s and beyond. They are going to have to become sophisticated and efficient operators relatively quickly because their window of opportunity, while competition remains limited, may not last very long. The gaming operations that will survive in the long term are those best able to create both the reality and the image of a strong regulatory, legal, and competitive environment.

One practical recommendation that can be made with respect to the question of regulation has to do with security of the games and the integrity of cash controls and accounting controls within a gaming facility. There are two issues that have historically dominated regulatory concerns. One is infiltration of gaming operations by undesirables, whether or not they are "organized crime" or just low-lifers. This is an issue that can be readily addressed with careful regulation, whoever is doing it, as long as the regulators are well intentioned and have enough expertise.

The second concern has to due with theft. For the most part, theft in a gaming operation is internally based, which means that money is being stolen by employees or skimmed by management. One possible compromise to the Class III gaming compact, which can preserve the dignity associated with Indian sovereignty but also preserves the spirit of the Indian Gaming Act, is that strong redundant regulatory structures be put forward both by the state through a compact agreement, and by the Indian tribe themselves. The regulatory structures offered by the state and by the tribes would effectively exist as parallel systems, and each could verify the integrity of the other. Looking to the long term, if such a system were established, at some future point the state might become convinced that Indians could indeed regulate themselves at the same level of effectiveness as the state could. In this case, the state's interest in regulation of gaming on Indian lands could shift to that of a typical outside auditor, an entity which would want to check from time to time on the validity of the system, but is otherwise not interested in having an ongoing presence in continuing regulation of such gaming regulations.

In summary, in spite of all the complaining by Indian tribes about the Indian Gaming Act passed by Congress, tribes should see this as an opportunity. This issue of commercial gambling appeared to Indian tribes almost like manna from heaven. The Seminoles discovered in the late 1970s that significant economic gains for the tribe could be found in bingo. This was at about the same time that society's views toward the acceptability of gambling and commercial gaming were changing. Thus, by the 1980s, many Indian tribes found themselves holding a piece of gambling rock that had a vein of gold in it. But then Congress came out and nicked off a portion of the rock, and as a result everyone is complaining.

Instead of seeing only the negative in this sequence of events, tribes should see it as a positive opportunity that has a relatively short window. That window will close, likely before the dawn of the 21st century. And so my prognosis with an economist's perspective rests on Indian tribes' willingness to accept fundamental realities. In ten years, if Indian gaming operations accept the premise that strong regulation is the only direction to bring about economically viable commercial gaming industries, then they may fare adequately in a competitive environment, and the promises that Indian gaming holds for economic development, for job creation, and for revenue generation, may come true. On the other hand, if self-regulation wins the day, or if the fighting over sovereignty continues without resolution, then I fear the opportunities will pass and the window will close.

VI

The Canadian Experience

1

Vina Starr
Barrister & Solicitor
British Columbia

I.   *INTRODUCTION*

In Canada, the Indian gaming controversy is about five to ten years behind the legal precedents set in the United States, where the constitutional right of Indians to regulate gaming on Indian land has been recognized. The controversy in Canada began in 1985 when the federal government entered into an agreement with all ten provinces whereby the Government of Canada agreed to withdraw from all participation in the field of gaming with the exception of horse racing.

The agreement represents a political compromise successfully negotiated by the ten provincial governments who objected to initiatives by the Government of Canada to set up sports lotteries in the early 1980s. The reciprocal federal-provincial agreement dated June 11, 1985 provides that, in return for three annual payments of $100 million to the federal Crown from each of the ten provinces over three years, the federal government would vacate the field and " . . . ensure that the rights of the Provinces in that field are not reduced or restricted." It is those provincial rights which the provinces seek to impose on Canadian Indians who conduct Bingos and other gaming activities on Indian land.

II.   REVIEW OF CANADIAN CONSTITUTIONAL LAW - DIVISION OF POWERS

At Canadian Confederation in 1867, all the powers of the British Colonial Crown to make laws were divided more or less equally between the federal government and the provincial governments. Any residual power not specifically allocated under the *British North America Act*, 1867 was vested in the federal government under the Peace, Order and Good Government clause. This constitutional arrangement represents the reverse of the United States constitutional scheme whereby the States are vested with the right to make law for any matter not specifically provided for in the United States Constitution.

The power to regulate gambling was vested in the federal government under section 91(27) of the BNA Act which is the criminal law head of power. Gambling, *per se*, is not specifically mentioned in the BNA Act because it was subsumed under the criminal law-making power of section 91(27). Hence, when the federal government agreed to vacate the field of gaming in favor of the provinces, it effectively transferred a portion of its constitutional law-making power to the provinces.

In British Columbia, the provincial government has legislated accordingly pursuant to section 190 of the *Criminal Code* which allows "Permitted Lotteries". The provincial legislation is entitled: "Terms and Conditions Respecting Licensing of Lottery Events in British Columbia."

III. LEGAL ISSUE: CAN PROVINCIAL LAW REGULATE INDIAN GAMING ACTIVITY ON INDIAN LAND?

It becomes apparent based on the foregoing brief review of Canadian constitutional law that the proper legal question to be asked is: "Can provincial law regulate Indian Gaming activity on Indian land?" To the best of my knowledge, virtually all Indian Bands and Tribes in Canada have answered that question in the negative. The constitutional position taken by Canadian Indians is that Indian gaming is an "existing aboriginal right" within the meaning of section 35(1) of the *Constitution Act*, 1982. That section provides:

> Section 35(1). "The existing aboriginal and treaty rights of the aboriginal peoples of Canada are hereby recognized and affirmed."

The problem is that, to date, no test case has come before the Canadian courts to determine whether or not provincial gaming regulations are inconsistent with the constitutional protection extended to aboriginal rights under section 35(1). More to the point, Canadian courts have not yet ruled on whether or not Indian gaming activities are indeed "aboriginal rights" within the meaning of section 35(1). Given these circumstances, it is appropriate for us to look at established Court precedents interpreting the meaning of "aboriginal rights" under the Canadian Constitution.

So far, we have only one such precedent to look to for guidance: *Sparrow v The Queen, [1987] 1 Canadian Native Law Reporter 145* (B.C. Court of Appeal) now on appeal to the Supreme Court of Canada. In that case, Mr. Sparrow of the Musqueam Indian Band successfully proved that fishing is an aboriginal right within the meaning of section 35(1). The analysis of the British Columbia Court of Appeal in their decision is instructive.

The Crown had first argued that there were no existing aboriginal rights in British Columbia, which was accepted by the lower court who thereupon convicted Mr. Sparrow of fishing without a licence. At appeal the Crown argued in the alternative that, even if there had been an aboriginal right to fish in British Columbia, it had been extinguished by successive and continuous legislation over a period of 100 years pursuant to the federal *Fisheries Act*. The Court of Appeal rejected the argument of the Crown in the following words:

> "In our view, the 'extinguished by regulation" proposition has no merit. The short answer to it is that regulation of the exercise of a right <u>presupposes the existence of the right</u>. If Indians did not have a special right in respect of the fishery, there would have been no reason to mention them in the regulations." (p.116, emphasis added)

In the present circumstances regarding the existence of Indian gaming as an aboriginal right, there are no regulations which specifically or expressly restrict the Indian right to gamble as do the Canadian fishing regulations. Rather, we have a situation where the Indian right to gamble is simply not mentioned, neither in the *Criminal Code* at any time since its inception, nor in the Federal-Provincial Agreement transferring regulatory power to the provinces, nor the "Terms and Conditions Respecting Licencing of Lottery Events in British Columbia".

Given this silence, we are compelled to look further at the analysis used by the Court of Appeal when considering whether or not a particular Indian activity falls within the meaning of an aboriginal right. In so doing, the Court looked to section 37 of the *Constitution Act*, 1982 which deals with the identification and definition of aboriginal rights. The Court said:

> "Section 37 provides for the identification and definition of aboriginal rights by the essentially political process of conventions. In so doing, it recognized what is obviously the fact - many aboriginal rights are inadequately identified and defined. It made provision for resolving those doubts by a course of compromise and negotiation rather than the "win or lose" process of litigation. <u>But it did not say or imply that no aboriginal rights can be enforced before being</u>

identified and defined by the convention process."
(p.168, emphasis added)

The quotation describes precisely the situation we have in Canada regarding the constitutional recognition of Indian gaming rights. Even though Indian gaming has not yet been ruled an aboriginal Canadian right, there is ample evidence that traditional Indian gambling games pre-existed the Canadian confederation of 1867, pre-existed the patriation of the Canadian Constitution from England to Canada in 1982, pre-existed the transfer of legislative power from the federal to the provincial governments in 1985, and certainly pre-existed the first provincial regulations on licencing of lottery events first passed in 1986. The Indian gambling game of "lahal" or "slahal" has been played since time immemorial up to and including the present day.

Our analysis has now brought us to the point where we can ask: "Are Canadian courts likely or unlikely to rule that Indian gaming is an aboriginal right within the meaning of section 35(1) of the *Constitution Act*, 1982?" Again, we look to the reasoning of the British Columbia Court of Appeal in *Sparrow* which responds to the "extinguishment by regulation" argument of the Crown by saying:

"This submission gives no meaning to section 35. If accepted, it would result in denying its clear statement that existing rights are hereby recognized and affirmed, and would turn that into a mere promise to recognize and affirm those rights sometime in the future; or perhaps never if the convention process fails to produce a final answer. To so consider section 35(1) would be to ignore its language and the principle that the constitution should be interpreted in a liberal and remedial way. We cannot accept that that principle applies less strongly to aboriginal rights than to the rights guaranteed by the Charter (of Rights and Freedoms), particularly having regard to the history and to the approach to interpreting treaties and statutes relating to Indians required by such cases as *Nowegijik v The Queen*, [1983] 2

C.N.L.R. 89 (S.C.C.)." (which was an Indian tax case).

The principle of statutory interpretation laid down by Chief Justice Brian Dickson of the Supreme Court of Canada in *Nowegijick* was that:

" . . . treaties and statutes relating to Indians should be liberally construed and doubtful expressions resolved in favour of the Indian. If the statute contains language which can reasonably be construed to confer tax exemption, that construction, in my view, is to be preferred over a more technical construction which may be available to deny exemption."

The Supreme Court of Canada, in laying down that principle of statutory construction relied directly on an old American Indian case of the United States Supreme Court: *Jones v Meehan (1899)* 175 U.S. 1 where it was held that:

"Indian treaties must be construed, not according to the technical meaning of their words, but in the sense in which they would naturally be understood by the Indians."

IV.   CONCLUSION

Given these authorities, it appears in my opinion that Indian gaming is likely to be held an aboriginal right within the meaning of section 35(1) of the *Constitution Act* of Canada. However, even if it is not, there are further constitutional arguments which Canadian Indians may rely on to prove that the provincial lottery regulations do not apply to Indian gaming activities on Indian land.

2

Judith A. Osborne

Associate Professor, School of Criminology
Simon Fraser University, Burnaby, B.C.

I.   INTRODUCTION

In the last two decades, Canada's indigenous peoples have been engaged in a rejuvenated campaign for legal recognition of aboriginal title to certain lands and for some measure of political autonomy or right to self government. Regarding the native Indian population, as distinct from the Metis and Inuit peoples, the White Paper released in 1969[1], which proposed to dismantle the apparatus of the *Indian Act*[2] and eliminate any vestiges of special status accorded to Indian peoples, is considered by many to be "the single most important catalyst[3]" in raising the political consciousness of Indian peoples.

Coincidentally, the same time span has accommodated a noticeable liberalization of that part of Canadian criminal law which prohibits gambling. Since 1969, the *Criminal Code*[4] has permitted certain forms of gambling under licence. Consequently, there has been a rapid expansion of legalized gambling in this country.

These two distinct developments have merged in the last two to three years as several Indian bands across Canada have sought to conduct organized gambling activities, particularly bingos, on reserves, without the requisite licences. This has led to criminal charges being laid, resulting in convictions in some instances albeit with symbolic penalties, with stays of proceedings being entered in others[5]. The basic issue is one of jurisdiction. The bands and the provinces are each claiming the right to regulate gambling on reserves, while the federal government maintains that it has no jurisdiction in this sphere.

The aim of this paper is to examine and evaluate the competing jurisdictional claims over Indian band-run bingos. In part, this will entail a comparative focus on the United States where state-level governments and Indian tribes have also been in conflict over gambling on Indian lands.

When compared with the magnitude and significance of Indian land claims and assertions of sovereignty, gambling may seem a relatively trivial issue. Bingo, after all, is hardly of great social consequence. The thesis to be presented here is that it is of symbolic consequence, presenting in microcosm many of the concerns at play in the larger struggle for native rights.

II.   THE LEGAL BACKGROUND[6]

(a)   Indians and the *Indian Act*

Although there was an initial semblance of willingness to treat the Indians as having some form of sovereignty, as evidenced by the treaties made with the British Crown, the European settlement of Canada ultimately meant political, legal, social and cultural subservience for her native peoples. At Confederation, the power to legislate for "Indians and Lands reserved for Indians" was assigned to the federal arm of government by section 91(24) of the *Constitution Act*, 1867[7]. As Ponting and Gibbins indicate, this allocation of Indian issues to the federal level can be traced back to an earlier concern of the Imperial government in London that the chief threat to the native population would likely come from land-hungry settlers who also controlled the local and provincial governments. In 1867, the federal government was the most distant from local government, where it existed, and the only alternative where it did not (i.e. the western territories)[8]. This is echoed by Sanders[9]:

> "[T]he decision to give responsibility to the more distant level of government removed Indian policy from direct competition with local interests."

The legislative policy of the federal government under this head of power did not, however, depart dramatically from that of pre-Confederation enactments which were designed to "civilize" the Indians and assimilate them into the dominant culture. The *Indian Act*, which was first passed in 1876 was merely a consolidation of pre-existing provincial and territorial legislation that dealt with Indians[10].

The general scheme of the *Indian Act*, operational to this day, is essentially paternalistic. It prescribes a complex system for defining and registering Indians, administering their lands and regulating their lives[11]. The ultimate responsibility rests with the federal government minster charged with Indian affairs, and this despite the fact that since the very early days powers of local government have devolved on the individual reserves. The *Act* tinkered with tribal arrangements to produce a system of band councils which possess "very modest[12]" by-lawmaking powers. As one commentator notes, this creates a fundamental inconsistency between the encouragement of local self-government on the reserves and the insistence on total control in the hands of the Minister[13].

The by-lawmaking powers, which are now found in section 81 of the *Act*, are generally confined to matters with which a rural municipality would be concerned. They are, of course, subordinate to regulations enacted pursuant to the *Indian Act* but also to the more pernicious power of disallowance vested in the Minister of Indian Affairs by virtue of section 82 of the *Act*:

> "*s.82(2)* A by-law made under section 81 comes into force forty days after a copy thereof is forwarded to the Minister pursuant to subsection (1), unless it is disallowed by the Minister within that period . . . "

As will be shown, this power of disallowance is very important in the bingo context, as many bands have attempted to enact by-laws to authorize the bingos. All except one have been disallowed by the Minister.

The *Indian Act* is undeniably extensive in its ambit. As Hogg points out, Parliament has taken the view that it may legislate for Indians on matters which otherwise would lie outside its jurisdictional competence e.g. the rules which govern the succession to the property of deceased Indians. He suggests that while there might be some question whether these enactments are in pith and substance in relation to Indians or to lands reserved for Indians, the courts would probably uphold any provision which could be rationally related to intelligible Indian policies[14].

Extensive though the *Indian Act* may be, it is certainly not exhaustive. Other federal statutes, such as the *Criminal Code* and the *Fisheries Act* apply on reserves independent of the *Indian Act*. In other words, legislation is applied to the native population that is not tailored to meet their particular needs and values[15]. Beyond that, provincial laws of general application have moved to fill in other gaps. Before 1951, however, the application of provincial legislation to Indians tended to depend on whether the incident concerned took place on or off a reserve. The courts allowed only very limited provincial jurisdiction on reserves[16].

In 1951, what is now section 88 of the *Indian Act* was introduced. It makes all provincial laws of general application applicable to Indians, subject to treaties and federal legislation, and except to the extent that they conflict with the *Act* and its regulations. This amendment has been characterized in both positive and negative terms. Hogg, for example, states that section 88 does not expand the body of provincial law that applies to Indians, but in fact limits it[17]. Bartlett, on the other hand, is of the opinion that section 88 represents a "massive intrusion of provincial jurisdiction" into the powers of government to which band councils might otherwise lay claim[18]. It unquestionably legitimated a role for provincial governments on Indian reserves which, by its own terms, is limited only by treaties, where they exist, and by the presence of federal enactments. In turn, it may preempt band by-laws. With the entrenchment of the *Constitution Act, 1982*[19], there now exists the potential for limits on provincial and federal legislative presence on the reserves by virtue of section 35(1):

> "The existing aboriginal and treaty rights of the aboriginal peoples of Canada are hereby recognized and affirmed."

Thus, to the extent that any legislative enactments conflict with an existing aboriginal or treaty right, it will be of no force or effect. In the struggle over gambling on reserves, the applicability of provincial enactments is crucial and will entail a close examination of the interplay between the legal issues mentioned briefly here.

(b)   Gambling and the *Criminal Code of Canada*

The playing of games was never illegal at common law[20]. From the late 13th century on, however, successive English monarchs placed statutory limitations on gaming and gambling. Thus, Part V of the *Criminal Code* ("Disorderly Houses, Gaming and Betting") has its origins in English statute law rather than in common law. Its genesis was legislative rather than judicial.

Canadian legislation has its deepest roots in a 1388 statute[21] passed when the monarch feared losing all his skilled archers to "idle" games of dice. As a result, all games, except for archery, were prohibited. As one commentator notes, it is that blanket prohibition, eroded by centuries of amendment and repeal, which is with us today, "a patchwork of fossilized law"[22].

In the colonial fashion, English anti-gambling legislation was extended to Canada. After Confederation, when jurisdiction over criminal law and procedure was vested in the federal government, the various betting and gaming laws were reduced to three general statutes: *An Act Respecting Gaming Houses*[23]; *An Act Respecting Lotteries, Betting and Pool Selling*[24] and *An Act Respecting Gambling in Public Conveyances*[25]. These were substantially re-enacted in the first *Criminal Code* in 1892[26]. Keeping common gaming houses, conducting lotteries (except where very minor sums of money were involved), cheating at play, and gambling in public conveyances were prohibited under criminal sanction. The *Code* did provide an exemption which would be used to accomodate pari-mutuel, on-track betting on horse races[27].

More than a decade after a joint committee of both chambers of Parliament had recommended a remodelling of the criminal law on gambling along the lines of the provincial liquor control model[28], major changes to Part V of the *Code* were enacted in 1969[29]. The law was relaxed but in a rather unusual way. Section 190, as amended, permitted the Government of Canada to conduct "lottery schemes", a term which encompasses true lotteries and quasi-lotteries[30].   More significantly, it also allowed the provinces to conduct or authorize such lottery schemes. For example, it became lawful for a charitable or religious organization "under the authority of a licence issued by the Lieutenant Governor-in- Council of a province" to conduct and manage a lottery scheme in that province.

This paved the way for lotteries, bingo and casino- style games of chance to become common-place in Canada and a source of revenue, not only for charities and community groups, but also for government treasuries.

True lotteries in particular also became a bone of contention and a source of litigation between the federal and provincial governments. This dispute was resolved in 1985 when an agreement was struck between the federal Minster of Sport and the provincial ministers responsible for lotteries that, in exchange for a joint provincial contribution of one hundred million dollars to the Calgary Winter Olympic Games, the *Criminal Code* would be amended to divest the federal government of any capacity to conduct lottery schemes. Parliament co-operated and the amendment took effect in January 1986[31].   Thus, as the law now stands, gambling is still prohibited by the *Criminal Code* unless it has been licensed by the appropriate provincial authority, or unless it is being conducted by the province itself. The two principal provisions of section 190 of the *Criminal Code*, which creates the exemptions from criminal prohibition, now read as follows:

"**s.190.** (1)Notwithstanding any of the provisions of this Part relating to gaming and betting, it is lawful

(a) for the government of a province, either alone or in conjunction with the government of another province, to conduct and manage a lottery scheme in that province, or in that and the other province, in accordance with any law enacted by the legislature of that province;

> (b) for a charitable or religious organization, pursuant to a licence issued by the Lieutenant Governor in Council of a province or by such other person or authority in the province as may be specified by the Lieutenant Governor in Council thereof, to conduct or manage a lottery scheme in that province if the proceeds from the lottery scheme are used for a charitable or religious object or purpose;" .

The federal and provincial governments who negotiated this arrangement seem eminently satisfied with it. Indian bands are clearly dissatisfied with it. They were certainly not a party to the federal-provincial negotiations, nor were they consulted by the Senate Committee on Legal and Constitutional Affairs when it was examining the *Criminal Code (Lotteries) Amendment Bill*[32]. None of the exemptions laid out in section 190 of the *Code* allow for Indian band councils to operate permitted lottery schemes. Their interests were, at best, overlooked and, at worst, ignored. It seems to have been taken for granted that they should be treated exactly the same as each provincial population concerned, subject to provincial regulatory schemes, regardless of whether they were appropriate to band needs and aspirations.

Given the experience in the United States in the past 15 to 20 years, this statutory silence and assumption of identical regulatory treatment was extremely short-sighted. When legalized gambling, particularly lotteries, began to spread through the American states in the late 1960s and early 1970s, some American Indian bands began running so-called "monster" bingo games, card rooms and other gambling enterprises, generating substantial revenues, without state sanction. State and county governments then instigated legal action against the bands concerned. In 1987, the United States Supreme Court rendered a decision in one of these cases which endorsed the right of Indian tribes to conduct gambling operations on their lands in certain situations[33].

If Canadian Indian bands continue their current bingo practices, there is an extreme likelihood that the Supreme Court of Canada will be called upon to decide the legal merits of these actions. Accordingly, before analysing these merits, the American experience will be examined as it offers some enlightening comparisons.

III. U.S. EXPERIENCE WITH GAMBLING ON INDIAN TRIBAL LANDS

(a) The American Situation

What Rose has termed the "third wave" of legalized gambling in the United States[34] began in the mid-1960s with state lotteries and has grown to encompass the transformation of New Jersey into a destination casino resort, video gambling, off-track betting, legal card rooms, charity bingos and Indian bingos:

> "Legalized gambling has become the biggest growth industry of the 1980s on the nation's Indian reservations. At least 100 of the 283 Indian tribes in the United States are considering setting up bingo games on tribal land. The Rincon Indian Tribe is the third tribe in San Diego County to set up high-stakes gambling. The tribe, with only 500 members,is building a bingo hall that will seat 1,000. The Seminole Tribe in Florida reported that its bingo operation grossed more than $20 million in 1982, resulting in a net profit of $2.7 million for the tribe's 1,500 members. Similar operations have been set up in Maine, Minnesota and Washington[35]."

This has provoked vehement state opposition. As one observer notes, to the states, counties and cities involved, it seems to signify an appropriation of their right to govern, "a menacing intrusion on local control and on state plenary powers[36]".

At the federal level, however, the response has been more positive. For example, the Department of the Interior, which has the primary responsibility for Indian Affairs in the U.S., has made grants and has guaranteed loans for the purpose of constructing bingo facilities[37]. The Secretary of the Interior has approved tribal ordinances establishing and regulating gaming activities[38]. The federal government is on record as being opposed to a proposal mooted in the early 1980s to give the states control of gambling activities on reservations[39]:

> "Such a proposal is inconsistent with the President's Indian Policy Statement of January 24, 1983[40] . . . A number of tribes have begun to engage in bingo and similar gambling operations on their reservations for the very purpose enunciated in the President's Message. Given the often limited resources which tribes have for revenue producing activities, it is believed that this kind of revenue producing possibility should be protected and enhanced."

Consequently, Indian bingos are at the centre of a struggle between the states to assert their jurisdiction and the Indian tribes to reject it. This struggle is a recurring one and requires some elucidation.

(b)   Jurisdiction over Indian Affairs

Canada and the United States have adopted largely parallel policies vis-a-vis their Indian populations, vacillating between assimilation and separation, but always exerting paternalistic control[41]. American courts have, however, been more prepared than their Canadian counterparts to play at least lip service to the notion of Indian sovereignty.

The constitutional arrangements in the United States are somewhat different from those in Canada. Indian affairs are only peripherally referred to in the Constitution:

> "Congress is authorized to regulate Commerce . . . with the Indian Tribes[42]."

This is the only express grant of federal power over Indians. There is no direct American equivalent to section 91(24) of the *Constitution Act, 1867*. Since the decision of the U.S. Supreme Court in *United States v. Kagama*[43] this constitutional gap has been irrelevant. While the Court recognized that there was no explicit constitutional justification for federal assertions of jurisdiction over Indians and Indian land, it decided that that power <u>must</u> rest with either the states or with the federal government. The Court opted for an inherent power over Indian affairs vested in the federal level of government. Indian autonomy over Indian affairs beyond a narrow range was not given any consideration[44].

The exclusion of state interests on Indian reserves, characterized by one source as being "an insurmountable wall" from 1831 to 1882[45], has, however, been eroded by the courts over the last century. As Kronowitz et al., note, many states have extended their legal controls over Indians and Indian lands situated within state borders, and have been supported in this by the Supreme Court[46]. The Court now subscribes to a view that Indian reservations are a part of the surrounding state[47]. State laws will therefore apply unless they have been preempted by federal legislation[48]. This expansion of state interests has been achieved, not at the cost of federal power, but at the expense of Indian interests:

> "[Recent Supreme Court] decisions . . . reverse the long- standing presumption of the exclusion of state jurisdiction over Indians and establish a presumption of state jurisdiction unless Congress has specifically pre-empted state law. Taken together, they potentialy leave no area of tribal jurisdiction untouched by

the states. The Court's decisions necessitate Indian challenges to state action through expensive and time-consuming litigation, and provide strong incentives for states to assert their jurisdiction over Indians and Indian territory within their borders[49]."

Putting aside this discussion of the expansion of state controls on Indian reserves temporarily, it should also be noted that, unlike its Canadian counterpart, the United States constitution vests the criminal law power in the states. Consequently, the federal government preserved its jurisdiction over Indian affairs by creating a separate system of criminal laws for the reserves.

The *General Crimes Act*[50] sets out the powers of the federal government to punish offences by non-Indians against the person or property of Indians, and offences by Indians against the person or property of non-Indians. The *Major Crimes Act*[51] also gives the central government jurisdiction over fourteen specific offences committed by Indians on reserves. These serious offences aside, tribal governments have exclusive jurisdiction over crimes committed by Indians against Indians occurring on tribal lands. The states, on the other hand, have exclusive power over all off- reservation crimes involving non-Indians and Indians.

This arrangement begs the question of who has jurisdiction over crimes committed by non-Indians on reservations. In *Oliphant v. Suquamish Indian Tribe*[52] the Supreme Court held that the states had that power, rejecting the Indian claim that the tribal courts had jurisdiction.

The final component of this jurisdictional scheme regarding criminal law, is the federal enactment *Public Law 280*[53], which has proved to be the most significant legislative factor in Indian gambling litigation. Enacted in 1953, this statute delegates to the states some of the federal government's power to regulate activities on reservations[54]. Congress had expressed some concern regarding apparent lawlessness on some reservations and in response granted the six states with the largest Indian populations (Alaska, California, Minnesota, Nebraska, Oregon and Wisconsin) complete criminal jurisdiction and more limited civil jurisdiction over reservations within their borders[55]. Any other state could assume such jurisdiction by statute or state constitutional amendment, which has added another nine states to the list[56]. Since 1968, however, tribal consent to state jurisdiction is required[57].

The Supreme Court first considered *Public Law 280* in *Bryan v. Itasca County*[58], which focussed on the application to Indians of the rather ambiguous grant of civil jurisdiction which was also included in the Law. The Court held that the states were only granted civil jurisdiction over private civil suits between Indians and Indians and between Indians and non-Indians. The Court reasoned that tribal governments would be rendered toothless if they were subject to the full spectrum of state and county civil regulations. The Court created a careful distinction between the criminal and civil sections of *Public Law 280* which was to become crucial in the Indian gambling decisions.

Turning specifically to gambling, the federal government enacted prohibitory legislation in 1951 which provides that it is illegal to operate a gambling device within the boundaries of an Indian reservation[59]. The term "gambling device" encompasses slot machines, roulette wheels and similar devices. It would not necessarily affect bingo games[60]. The *Organized Crime Control Act of 1970*[61], which makes illegal gambling a federal offence also applies on reservations, but only if they are situated in states where gambling is a violation of state law. As was mentioned earlier, gambling has been legalized in the majority of states in the Union.

(c)   Indian Gambling Before the Courts

Prior to the Supreme Court's decision in *California v. Cabazon Band of Mission Indians*[62], the Indian gambling cases fell into two categories: those based on Public Law 280 (PL 280) and those invoking the *Organized Crime Control Act* (OCCA). The former comprise the larger group and will be considered first.

As has been noted above, PL 280 contains a grant of power from the federal to the state level of criminal and civil law jurisdiction on Indian reservations and the Supreme Court had been careful to limit the scope of the civil powers. In *Seminole Tribe of Florida v. Butterworth*[63], the Fifth Circuit considered whether PL 280 acted to make Florida's bingo statute applicable to the Seminole tribe's bingo operations. The Florida statute permitted small scale, charitable bingos. The Seminoles operated a permanent, commercial facility.

Relying on the Supreme Court's decision in *Bryan v. Itasca*, the Court determined that, if the statute was classified as "prohibitory" or criminal, it would apply; if it were designated "regulatory" or civil, however, it would not. It was observed that one could not simply point to the inclusion of penal sanctions in the Florida statute and conclude that it was prohibitory. A much more sophisticated analysis was required, focussing on the public policy of the state on the issue of bingo and the intent of the legislature in enacting the bingo statute. This analysis produced a determination that the bingo statute was "civil- regulatory" in nature and hence not applicable to the Seminole operations[64]:

> "Bingo appears to fall in a category of gambling that the state has chosen to regulate by imposing certain limitations to avoid abuses. Where the state regulates the operation of bingo halls to prevent the game of bingo from becoming a money-making business, the Seminole Indian tribe is not subject to that regulation and cannot be prosecuted for violating the limitations imposed . . . Legislative intent determines whether the statute is regulatory or prohibitory, and although the state of Florida prohibits lotteries in general, exceptions are made for certain forms of gambling including bingo."

In other words, as long as the state permits bingo to some degree, then the Indians are free to operate bingos without state constraint. It is not clear whether the Court was going so far as to say, that as long as the state permitted some forms of gambling that the Indian tribes could operate any and all forms of gambling operations. What is more important, though, is that the Court took as its reference point the state's legislative policy. That, not Indian interests, was to be the decisive factor.

A similar case, *Oneida v. Wisconsin*[65], reached a similar conclusion. The State of Wisconsin permitted the playing of bingo, but regulated the conduct of games by licensing, control and taxation. Again, the Court was faced with the task of categorizing the nature of these bingo laws in order to determine whether they would apply to Indian-run operations. Employing the analysis used in *Seminole Indians*, it concluded that they were civil rather than criminal.

The Wisconsin Chief Judge was, however, reluctant simply to leave it at that, finding it "too mechanical" an approach[66]. He chose to buttress his finding by presenting it against a so-called "back-drop" of tribal sovereignty. He recognized the continued existence of sovereign rights inhering in the Indian tribes, though in a much more restricted form than they did 150 years ago, and the historically limited role for state intervention on tribal lands[67]. These deliberations produced the following conclusion[68]:

"Keeping in mind the backdrop of Indian sovereignty against which Public Law 280 must be measured, as well as that 'eminently sound and vital canon . . . that statutes passed for the benefit of dependent tribes . . . are to be liberally construed, doubtful expressions being resolved in favour of the Indians', . . . I conclude that when Congress conferred jurisdiction on the State of Wisconsin to enforce its criminal laws on the Oneida Reservation, Congress intended to limit the exercise of that jurisdiction to enforcement

of laws generally prohibiting activities that the state
determined are too dangerous, unhealthy, or otherwise detrimental to the well-being of the state's
citizens . . . [This] conclusion . . . appears to be in
keeping with present federal policy encouraging tribal
self-government."

With its concern to respect tribal sovereignty by limiting state
jurisdiction, *Oneida*, in moving away from the narrow classification
issue, is overall the most favourable of the cases for Indian interests.

In *Barona Group of Capitan Grand Band v. Duffy*[69], the
Southern District Court of California rendered a decision consistent
with the Florida and Wisconsin cases. California permitted some
bingo games albeit under strict regulation. Indian tribes were not
bound by those civil enactments. Although not as dismissive of
Indian interests as the court in *Seminole Tribe v. Butterworth*, the
court in *Barona* focussed mainly on the classification issue, noting
that it was a close question and "not susceptible of easy application[70]".

This difficulty was acknowledged by the U.S. Supreme Court
in *California v. Cabazon Band of Mission Indians*[71]. In a 6 to 3
decision, the Court endorsed the classification scheme adopted in the
lower courts for determining whether state laws applied to Indian
reservations by virtue of PL 280. This ratification was, however,
rather lukewarm[72]:

"It is not a bright-line rule, however; and . . . and
argument of some weight may be made that the bingo
statute is prohibitory rather than regulatory. But in
the present case, the court [of Appeals] reexamined
the state law and reaffirmed its holding in *Barona*,
and we are reluctant to disagree with that court's
view of the nature and intent of the state law at issue
here."

The Court was careful to point out that each state law must be examined in detail before they can be characterized as regulatory or prohibitory[73].

If the decision had rested there, it would merely have been subject to the criticism levied against *Seminole Tribe v. Butterworth*, i.e. that state policy is the determining factor. But, like the Wisconsin court in *Oneida*, the Supreme Court was compelled to place the classification scheme for PL 280 in a larger context. In this instance, however, it was not a back-drop of tribal sovereignty, but the general issue of state jurisdiction on reserves.

From the outset, the Court underlined that it had not, in previous decisions, established "an inflexible per se rule" precluding state jurisdiction over tribes and tribal members in the absence of congressional consent[74]. Indeed, the Court recognized a role for the state regardless of the federal position "if the state interests at stake are sufficient to justify the assertion of state authority[75]". Accordingly, there was to be a balancing of federal, state and Indian interests in determining the applicability of state laws to Indian lands. The state interest asserted in *Cabazon* was the prevention of organized crime. The legitimacy of this concern was recognized, but, in the absence of any evidence of organized criminal involvement in the Cabazon gambling operations, the Supreme Court was not prepared to override "compelling" federal and tribal interests of encouraging tribal self-sufficiency and economic development[76]. What this implies is that if there is some degree of evidence of organized crime (however that might be defined) on Indian reservations, then state legislation, whether or not it is merely "regulatory" will apply.

To summarize the *Cabazon* decision: the Supreme Court constructed a two-pronged test for determining state jurisdiction on Indian lands under PL 280. First, should the state legislation be characterized as criminal-prohibitory or civil-regulatory? Secondly, even if it is designated a civil enactment, are state interests sufficiently important to make it applicable nonetheless?

Regarding the first aspect of this test, Turner criticizes it as assimilationist, because tribal interests are held in abeyance while the policy interests of the state are assessed. This, he argues will produce non-uniform and incongruous results due to policies which vary dramatically from state to state[77]. This criticism pales beside the one offered by Kronowitz et al., which is directed at the second aspect of the *Cabazon* test. It deserves to be quoted in full[78]:

> "Even more dangerous to the future of tribal self-government, however, was the Court's deference to state interests. . . . The Court refused to recognize that the critical interest at stake is the sovereign right of the tribes to govern reservation affairs free from state intrusion. In failing to do so, *Cabazon* illustrates the modern Court's continuing willingness to use unique factual situations to render general, open-ended opinions in Indian law. The rationale used by the Court, although granting a short-term victory for the Indian plaintiffs in *Cabazon*, may easily be applied to the detriment of other tribes seeking protection from state jurisdictional intrusion in the future."

It is fair to say that the Supreme Court's decision is perhaps not as benign as it may first appear to be.

In *Cabazon*, the applicability of the *Organized Crime Control Act* (OCCA) to Indian gambling operations was also considered. The Court recognized that there was a conflict between the decisions of the lower courts on this issue. In *U.S. v. Farris*[79], for example, the Puyallup Indians in Washington were running casinos without any approval or licence from the State Gambling Commission. Although PL 280 had been adopted by the state, it covered only eight specific subject areas, and gambling was not included in them. Having acknowledged this, the court then considered whether the casino operations violated OCCA's prohibition of illegal gambling. As was indicated earlier, there must therefore be a violation of state law for OCCA to apply. The state of Washington allowed some forms of gambling, but it had strict regulations against professional gambling. These regulations did not, however, apply to Indians on Indian land. Nonetheless, it was held that OCCA was applicable because the casino operations contravened the state's public policy against professional gambling. The judge who dissented in this case summed up the logical difficulties with this view[80]:

> "It exceeds the limits of reasonable construction to hold that conduct which could not be punished under the state law is nonetheless "a violation of the law of [the] State" within the meaning of 18 U.S.C. # 155. Conduct to which the law is inapplicable does not violate the law in the ordinary meaning of those words. The idea that a person can transgress state law by conduct not punishable under that state law is inconsistent with minimum notions of notice and fairness."

Farris was applied to the OCCA argument raised in *Barona*[81]. The California court explained that whether a tribal activity is "a violation of the law of a state" within the meaning of OCCA depends on whether it violates the "public policy" of the state, the same test for application of state law under PL 280. Hence, it concluded that the Barona's bingo operations were not contrary to the public policy of California. This merging of the tests for OCCA and PL 280 would appear to limit the applicability of the federal enactment to those states in which gambling is completely prohibited.

Compare this interpretation with the decision in *U.S. v. Dakota*[82], where the Michigan court stated that although the state legislation was not applicable to Indians on Indian land, it could be incorporated by reference into OCCA to determine whether the gambling was illegal. There was no need, therefore to divine state "public policy" on the issue; if Indians engage in gambling operations above statutorily defined levels which are illegal off the reserve under state law, this is a violation of OCCA. This approach was justified on the basis that OCCA is a federal statute and raises no danger of encroachment on Indian sovereignty by the states[83]. There is certainly no <u>direct</u> state encroachment, but the incorporation of state statutory standards in federal legislation has exactly the same impact on Indian autonomy as if they were applied directly.

The Supreme Court in *Cabazon* chose not to resolve this inconsistency, but it did make an observation which will likely limit the use of OCCA against Indian gambling operations[84]:

> "There is nothing in OCCA indicating that the States are to have any part in enforcing federal crimes or are authorized to make arrests on Indian reservations that in the absence of OCCA they could not effect. We are not informed of any federal efforts to employ OCCA to prosecute the playing of bingo on Indian reservations, although there are more than 100 such enterprises currently in operation, many of which have been in existence for several years, for the most part with the encouragement of the Federal Government."

In the wake of the Supreme Court's decision in *Cabazon*, the federal government reactivated earlier, failed efforts to legislate a regulatory scheme for gambling operations in Indian country. In 1983 a bill known as the *Indian Gambling and Control Act* had been introduced in Congress[85]. Designed to meet concerns regarding the supervision of tribal gambling activities, it proposed to establish minimum federal standards by requiring the adoption of tribal ordinances to regulate gambling operations and by requiring background checks on individuals and management firms involved in the tribal gaming operations. Further, the Secretary of the Interior would have to approve all tribal gambling ordinances and management contracts entered into by an Indian tribe for the operation and management of the gambling operations. This bill failed to pass that session of Congress and was reintroduced in identical form in 1985[86]. In addition a Senate version was also introduced which provided for the creation of Indian-controlled Gaming Commissions to supervise Indian gambling enterprises.[87] Neither of these were passed into law.

Late in 1988, however, in the dying days of the Reagan Administration, the *Indian Gaming Regulatory Act* became law[88]. This Act establishes an National Indian Gaming Commission and a tri-partite regulatory scheme. Traditional forms of Indian gambling are within the exclusive control of the tribes; bingo games will be supervised by the Commission; every other form of gambling (e.g. casino games, lotteries, pari-mutuel betting) requires the Indians to enter into a "compact" with the state in which the reservation is situated. Inevitably, this latter provision has provoked extensive criticism and opposition from the tribes, who perceive it as an unjustified encroachment on their sovereignty. Several court challenges have been launched.

(d)   The Lessons of U.S. Experience

The first is that Indian tribes or bands are capable of operating lucrative gambling businesses which have direct economic benefits. This is not unimportant given the prevailing paternalistic approach taken to native peoples and scepticism regarding their abilities.

The second lesson is one that must be taken to heart: that major objectives such as the goal of Indian sovereignty may be damaged by more immediate successes such as the right to run gambling enterprises. As the situation now stands in the U.S., there is the potential for great irony. Indians now have a means to achieve greater economic independence from the federal government, but it may ultimately cost them their autonomy from state control. Good federal intentions to enhance tribal sovereignty (even if they are fuelled more by fiscal concerns than anything else) will be meaningless and even counter-productive if the state, or the province, simply takes the federal government's place.

IV. THE CANADIAN CONTEXT

(a) The Significance of Gambling on Reserves

Indian bands view the right to control gambling on the reserves as important for several reasons. Gambling has cultural significance for native Indians. For example, Maranda in her ethnological/historical study of the Coast Salish Indians, found that gambling had deep, historic roots in their culture[89]. It served as a form of social expression and as a forum in their polytheistic religion for supernatural power. The gambling games of dice, disc and bone, hand or slahal were seen to be an expression of man's power affiliations. Power was an element which could affect the outcome of each gambling event, and the games would themselves be an endorsement of the "power favour", as they gave tangible and observable verification of the influence of power[90]. The hand, bone or slahal game is the only Coast Salish gambling game of aboriginal origin still being played today. Modern forms of gambling, such as bingo and pull tickets, have taken the place of the others. The continued significance of the bone game is noted by Starr who observes that the Gitksan on the Skeena River still observe and maintain a traditional chieftain position whose Indian name is "Gambling Chief[91]":

> "He derives his power and position of Chief as a result of his skill and cunning in the bone game. The Chief participates equally with other Gitksan chiefs of high rank in their potlach . . . Traditionally, the Gitksans gambled for the right to win spoils of war which then became the common property of the house (or clan) of the chief who won it. The communal ownership of gambling winnings is in keeping with the fundamental and unique Indian philosophy of communal ownership of property."

Gambling has always been a socially acceptable activity in Indian communities and remains so. As in other communities, bingo and other forms of gambling play an important social function. Increasingly, however, band councils are coming to appreciate the revenue generating potential that gambling has for the reserves. The Gitksan is one of the bands running its own bingo operations, the proceeds from which are kept in the community for projects such as community and treatment centres and funding court challenges.

In recent years, there has been increasing attention given to economic development on reserves. In part, this stems from the federal government which doubtless wants to reduce the Indian dependence on federal funding. But it also reflects a determination on the part of the bands to reassert control over their own affairs.

Economic dependency stems directly from the structure of the *Indian Act* and its underlying philosophy of paternalism. Under the terms of the legislation, Indian land is protected by provisions which exclude Indian people from taxes, liens, mortgages or other charges on their lands. These provisions have, however, made it difficult for Indians to enter the modern debtor society. Ponting and Gibbins observe that they have made it next to impossible for Indians to raise outside investment capital, for potentially valuable Indian land cannot be mortgaged so that there is reliance on the federal government for the capital needed to promote economic development. The ostensibly protective provisions of the *Act* "now serve as a shackle on Indian self-reliance[92]".

Section 87 of the *Indian Act* exempts from taxation the interests of an Indian or a band in reserve or surrendered lands and the personal property of the same situated on a reserve. As Bartlett points out, the denial of the ability of other governments to tax a community may secure the autonomy of that community[93]. He further comments that, regardless of the powers of government possessed by a community, an exemption from taxation will encourage economic development of that community[94]. That only holds true, however, if the community has resources of its own to finance such development. Political power is, to a large extent, dependent on economic power.

The legislation which protects Indians from external taxation also largely prevents them from developing their own tax base. Section 83 of the *Indian Act* provides that where a band "has reached an advanced state of development, the council of the band may, subject to the approval of the minister make by-laws for" inter alia "the raising of money by the assessment and taxation of interests in land in the reserve of persons lawfully in possession thereof". A government task force recently concluded that band taxation powers are underdeveloped due to the limitations set out in section 83 and that this is incompatible with the basic need of bands for tax revenue to pay for the infrastructure required to attract and support business[95].

Even if more liberal taxation powers were given to the bands there is a real question of whether, given the socio-demographic profile of many Indian bands, they would have much impact. A study of Indian lands in British Columbia and the Yukon in the late 1970s found that the vast majority have a population of 300 or less and that this small size creates problems. They lack the minimum population, especially in the labour force age group, to sustain viable economic development enterprises, and their populations are too small to permit the band to realize economies of scale in the delivery of services[96]. Limited business opportunities and high unemployment are hardly factors conducive to the nourishment of a healthy tax base. A recent government review of gaming on reserves offered the following assessment[97]:

"Most Indian communities are on the periphery of the Canadian economic system regardless of their geographic location. This is especially so in the remote areas where there tend to be few economic opportunities. There is a limit to the number of jobs, even low-skill jobs, in the primary resources sector. Moreover, given the existing fiscal restraint, government funds cannot be expected to meet all economic development requirements.

Many bands do not have an adequate tax base on which to raise significant funds additional to what is provided by federal budgeting which must concentrate first on critical areas of need such as housing. In these circumstances, gaming provides a rare opportunity for the bands to raise revenues for community purposes by "voluntary taxation[98]". "

The Task Force might also have mentioned that federal provincial conflict over the provision of social services on reserves has compounded the situation. The provinces acknowledge that the federal government has the right to legislate regarding Indians and the lands reserved for them. Some go further to assert that the federal govenment has the total responsibility to legislate and provide services for Indians on reserves. The federal government's position is that while it has the constitutional right to legislate on (and provide services to) Indians, where it chooses not to exercise that right, the normal division of powers set out in the constitution prevails[99]. In the area of social services, therefore, the provinces would, in the absence of federal action, be responsible for the provision of these costly services. In many instances, the provincial governments have chosen not to assume this responsibility, resulting in the social impoverishment of the reserves. In the words of one observer, reserve Indians "are caught in a financial squeeze and a jurisdictional conflict[100]".

Gambling revenues offer the opportunity to loosen this vise. As Starr indicates, the general objective of Indian bands in conducting bingos etc. on reserves is to supplement the annual operating budget that it receives from the federal government. The aim is to draw natives and non-natives onto the reserves to gamble. The profits are used to provide band members with community programs not otherwise affordable under the core funding[101]. It is a way of improving the immediate conditions of life on reserves while at the same time furthering economic autonomy to some degree. Indian peoples recognize that self-government is intertwined with economic development. Without the latter, self-government is a meaningless phrase[102]. Gambling means money and money equates with power. Even if, as the Task Force on Gaming on Reserves suggests, the revenue from gambling is often fairly modest[103], band-run bingos still represent an affirmation of Indian control over their own lands, that the band councils are the ones to make the decisions as to whether or not any type of activity can be carried out on their lands.

The fundamental issue to be resolved here is whether they are legally entitled to conduct gambling operations on reserves without a provincial license. There are several possibilities to consider: whether the transfer of power over gambling from the federal to the provincial governments was valid; whether B.C. gambling enactments are legally effective and are applicable on the reserves; and whether Indians on reserves have an inherent right to regulate their own affairs, including gambling.

(b) Federal Jurisdiction

Osborne and Campbell argue that the amendments made to the *Criminal Code* in 1969 and 1985, which have the cumulative effect of giving the provinces exclusive jurisdiction to permit various forms of gambling (pari-mutuel betting excepted) are an invalid transfer of power between the federal and provincial governments[104].

The constitution of Canada contains no express power of interdelegation of jurisdiction between federal and provincial authorities. The inclusion of the term "exclusively" in s.91 of the *Constitution Act, 1867*, which defines the scope of the federal government, arguably precludes the authorization of a delegation of legislative power to any body, including a provincial legislature[105]. In the so-called *Nova Scotia Interdelegation* case, the Supreme Court rejected as unconstitutional an interdelegation of powers between

Parliament and a provincial legislature[106], which is what is attempted in s.190(1)(a) of the *Code*:

"Notwithstanding any of the provisions of this Part relating to gaming and betting, it is lawful

(a) for the government of a province ... to conduct and manage a lottery scheme in that province, in accordance with any law enacted by the legislature of that province;" (emphasis added).

By comparison, subs. 190(1)(b), which relates to charity gaming, refers merely to the Lieutenant Governor in Council having the power to license charitable or religious organizations "to conduct and manage a lottery scheme". There is no explicit power bestowed on the provincial government to legislate in this regard, but some form of legislative action is implied. For example, in British Columbia, the provincial legislature enacted a *Lotteries Act*, and promulgated regulations thereunder. These regulations were repealed in 1986 and replaced by something called policy directives, which, in turn, were replaced by terms and conditions respecting licensing of lottery events in the province in 1987[107].

Although the Supreme Court of Canada has, since the *Nova Scotia Interdelegation* case, relaxed its approach to permit the delegation of powers between the federal government and provincial boards or commissions such as a marketing board[108], the scheme set out in s.190 of the *Code* does not fit easily into the recognized exceptions to the prohibition against interdelegation. In neither subs. 190(1)(a) or (b) is there a delegation to a body comparable to a provincial board or commission. Subsection 190(1)(a) delegates power to the provincial legislature; subs. 190(1)(b) delegates it to the Lieutenant Governor in Council, i.e. the provincial Cabinet.

Nor can it be convincingly argued that the federal- provincial co-operative effort vis-a-vis lotteries and gaming constitutes valid referential and conditional legislation. These are two techniques of legislative co-operation that have been frequently used in the past and which, in principle at least, were not affected by the *Nova Scotia Interdelegation* case. As defined by Russell, referential legislation incorporates the <u>valid</u> enactments of another legislative body; conditional legislation makes the carrying out of the policy stated in a statute conditional upon the act of another government agency[109].

The key cases in this area concern the federal *Lord's Day Act*[110] which was enacted in 1906 after the Privy Council struck down provincial Sunday observance legislation as an encroachment on the federal criminal law power[111]. The *Act* prohibited certain activities on Sundays unless they were otherwise permitted under provincial legislation "now or hereafter in force". The validity of this scheme was litigated in *Lord's Day Alliance of Canada v. Attorney General for Canada*[112]. The Privy Council deemed it relevant to ask "whether or not it would have been within the competence of the [provincial] Legislature . . . effectively to enact it had there been on this subject of Sunday excursions no previous Dominion legislation at all" in order to determine if this was a statute "in force" within the meaning of the exemption[113]. The Privy Council, which just over 20 years earlier had categorized provincial Sunday observance enactments as criminal law, this time concluded that they came within the provinces' powers regarding civil rights in the province or matters of a local nature[114]:

> "Legislative permission to do on Sunday things or acts which persons of stricter sabbatarian views might regard as Sabbath breaking is no part of the criminal law where the acts or things permitted had not previously been prohibited . . . [W]hat the Parliament of Canada may do in this manner it may also forbear to do, and permissive provincial legislation effective for its purpose, because the Parliament of Canada has not previously intervened at all, can be no less effective after such intervention if by its very terms the previous liberty of the Provinces in this matter remains unaffected. In each case, the Provincial

Legislature is exercising a power which, in the one
case by silence and in the other case in words, the
Parliament of Canada has left intact."

What the Privy Council seemed to be saying here is that,
because Sunday activities were not criminal until the federal legislation was passed in 1906, and because that statute preserved provincial powers in this sphere, the federal Act did not expand provincial
jurisdiction as a true interdelegation would, and it therefore con-
situted valid referential legislation.

As Driedger indicates, the decision has inherent weaknesses[115], not the least being that the form of the statutory exemption was delegation in the form of an express invitation to the
legislatures to make exceptions to criminal offences. Even if the
judgement in the *Lord's Day Alliance* were to be taken at face value,
its rationale is hardly supportive of the validity of s.190 of the *Code*.
In that provision, there is no question of Parliament coming fresh to
the field of prohibiting lotteries and gaming and preserving "intact"
a valid provincial power. The prohibition of gambling has been part
of Canadian criminal law since the colonial era. The *Criminal Code*
does not simply incorporate or "borrow" valid provincial legislation;
it enables the provincial legislatures to act in this sphere.

In a more recent examination of the *Lord's Day Act* by the
Supreme Court of Canada, *Lord's Day Alliance of Canada v.
Attorney General of British Columbia*[116], it was adjudged to be a
"misconception" of the operation of the *Act* to say that its effect was
to create a delegation of federal powers to the provinces. In Mr
Justice Rand's view, it could not be open to serious debate that
Parliament may limit the operation of its own legislation and may do
so upon any event or condition[117].

Two eminent constitutional scholars are independently critical
of this decision in ways that are appliacble to the validity of s.190 of
the *Code*. Hogg, for example, comments that, if the making of a
Sunday observance law is a matter of criminal law outside provincial

competence, as was decided in *Hamilton Street Railway*, then the repeal of a Sunday observance law is equally a matter of criminal law outside provincial competence. He concludes that the decision is inconsistent with the *Nova Scotia Interdelegation* case[118]. Similarly, Weiler characterizes the opting-out clause in the *Lord's Day Act* as amounting, functionally, to Parliament delegating to provincial legislatures the power to amend its criminal law in accordance with different and changing sentiments in the respective provinces[119].

In true referential legislation, where Parliament adopts a particular piece of existing provincial legislation for its own use, it is easy enough to distinguish it from an interdelegation. It is, in Lysyk's words, "a legislative short-cut[120]". Where future provincial enactments are involved, however, the incorporation is, in reality, delegation by another name. Judicial ingenuity has, however, confined the prohibition against interdelegation to a narrow range, although that could change.

Regarding s.190 of the *Code*, there has been remarkably little judicial attention given to its constitutional validity, arguably because the federal-provincial arrangements have found widespread favour with virtually all parties involved. The only reported case to date has been resolved at a relatively low level – the Ontario Supreme Court – and it will not be proceeding any further.

In *R. v. Furtney et al.*[121], the Crown appealed the respondents' acquittals on charges of counselling the conduct of bingo operations in a manner not authorized pursuant to s.190, i.e. in violation of the terms and conditions issued by the Ontario Ministry of Consumer and Corporate Relations. At trial, the provincial court judge acquitted them on the basis inter alia that Parliament in s.190 improperly delegated criminal law power to the provinces. On appeal, Mr Justice Campbell of the Supreme Court of Ontario reversed this finding based on the argument that the scheme provided by s.190 is analogous to that set up under the federal *Fisheries Act*, which had been upheld by the Ontario Court of

Appeal in 1985 in *Re Peralta et al., and the Queen in right of Ontario et al.*[122]:

> "[It] upheld the delegation in the federal Fisheries Regulations of power to a provincial minister to issue fishing licences and to impose terms and conditions. The court held that the effect of the federal regulations was to set general policy and in setting individual fishing quotas within those policy guidelines the provincial Minister was acting in a manner consistent with the regulations."

This, in fact, is a misreading of *Re Peralta* and other decisions dealing with the nature of the *Fisheries Act* and the regulations made thereunder. *Re Peralta* actually confirmed that the fishing quotas were inserted by the provincial Minister pursuant to federal legislation, not provincial enactments[123]. This deserves further examination of the legislative scheme set up under the federal *Fisheries Act* and of how it differs from that set up under s.190 of the *Code*.

The regulation of fisheries is clearly a matter of federal competence under s.91(12) of the *Constitution Act, 1867* which gives the federal Parliament exclusive jurisdiction to legislate regarding "Sea Coast and Inland Fisheries". Accordingly, the *Fisheries Act* was enacted. The power to do so was confirmed by the Privy Council in *Fisheries Reference*[124], but it was pointed out that the s.91(12) head of power did not confer proprietary rights over fisheries. Thus, where fishing rights are owned by the province, the province may legislate in relation to fisheries under the power to manage and sell public lands[125]. As one observer notes, this overlapping of authority has been resolved in practice by the delegation of <u>administrative</u> (as opposed to legislative) powers from the federal to the provincial governments: Parliament enacts fisheries legislation - including the delegation to the Governor in Council (not the Lieutenant Governor in Council) to make regulations for carrying out the purposes and provisions of the *Act*[126] - and then, in conjunction with each province, enacts regulations which are administered by the officers of a provincial ministry[127]. Thus, the *Ontario Fishery Regulations*, for example, are actually federal regulations administered by a provincial body. They are provincial regulations in name only, but federal enactments in law[128], and cannot be assailed as being ultra vires the provinces[129].

The constitutionality of this arrangement was upheld in *Re Shoal Lake Band*[130], which was cited approvingly in *Re Peralta* and also in a more recent decision of the Ontario Court of Appeal, *R. v. Agawa*[131], in which it was stated,

> "the learned summary conviction appeal court judge treated the *Ontario Fishery Regulations* as if they were provincial laws subject to Indian treaty rights because they are administered by provincial officials. The delegation of administrative authority over the *Ontario Fishery Regulations* is a proper exercise of Parliament's legislative authority and does not alter their status as federal laws".

The regulations and other subordinate legislation enacted pursuant to s.190 of the *Criminal Code* are not in the same mode. They are provincial enactments administered by the provinces. Accordingly, the analogy drawn between the legislative scheme in the *Fisheries Act* and provincial gambling provisions is not a valid one, and the constitutionality of the latter remains suspect[132].

If the transfer of power over gambling and lotteries were to be struck down as being invalid, gambling would once more be firmly within federal jurisdiction, and any gambling on Indian reserves would, absent any other legally compelling argument, require federal legislative action. This would at least restore the traditional constitutional arrangements regarding Indian affairs by precluding provincial involvement. As the Task Force on Gaming on Reserves notes, some bands would be willing to accept federal regulation, but for others such an arrangement would be an unacceptable compromising of inherent aboriginal rights over gaming on reserves[133]. This position will be examined shortly after the applicability of provincial enactments on reserve lands has been scrutinized. The constitutional validity of those provincial laws will be assumed, without prejudice to the foregoing discussion.

(c)   *Provincial Jurisdiction*

Although the federal government has exclusive jurisdiction over "Indians and Lands reserved for Indians[134]", provincial legislation may apply on reserves if it conforms to s.88 of the *Indian Act*:

> "Subject to the terms of any treaty and any other Act of the Parliament of Canada, all laws of general application from time to time in force in any province are applicable to and in respect of Indians in the province, except to the extent that such laws are inconsistent with this Act or any order, rule, regulation or by-law made thereunder, and except to the extent that such laws make provision for any matter for which provision is made by or under the Act."

The first issue to be examined is whether provincial lottery and gambling enactments are "laws of general application". As was mentioned above[135], starting early in 1970, the British Columbia Legislature enacted regulations pertaining to the licensing of gambling activities[136]. These were repealed in 1986[137], and replaced by Policy Directives which in turn were replaced inferentially by Terms and Conditions Respecting Licensing of Lottery Events in B.C. There is some question regarding the legal status of these provisions which, in addition to purportedly regulating gaming in the province, also create the B.C. Gaming Commission as the responsible government body[138]. Both the policy directives and the terms and conditions are clearly intended to be regulatory in nature, but, as Starr indicates, it is questionable whether they have any force in law[139]. They are not supported by Orders in Council, nor have they been gazetted.

A similar scheme operates in Ontario, although there the terms and conditions are supported by orders in council. Its legal validity was questioned in *R. v. Furtney et al.*[140], where it was argued that the charges of counselling bingo operations in violation of the terms and conditions issued by the provincial ministry did not disclose an offence known to law by reference to the fact that the terms and conditions of the licence had not been gazetted. The appeal court judge found that neither the orders in council nor the terms and conditions are regulations or statutory instruments and there is therefore no requirement that they be gazetted. Further, even if there is a constitutional requirement in the *Canadian Charter of Rights and Freedoms* that the content of criminal sanctions should be reasonably accessible to the public, that requirement was met here as the licensing conditions are printed up and given to each licensee when the licence is issued.

What this decision ignores is the formalization process that generally precedes legally binding enactments. As Mr Justice Dickson, as he then was, noted in *Attorney General of B.C. v. Parklane Private Hospital et al.*[141], "one does not establish statutory regulations by circulars." In this case, the province was attempting to rely on the rates set out in government circulars sent to private hospitals to limit their indebtedness to those institutions for providing services to social assistance patients. The Court classified the circulars as "mere notifications" which were not legally binding.

In the case of the B.C. lottery licence terms and conditions, they are unsupported by any statutory infra-structure, void of any formal characteristics of the legal process and come perilously close to law-making by fiat. Their status as "laws of general application" is questionable. Assuming that they are valid, however, the other specifications of s.88 of the *Indian Act* must be met for them to be applicable to Indians, including those who live on reserves[142].

One of the key cases on the applicability of provincial legislation "to and in respect of Indians in the province" is *Cardinal v. Attorney General of Alberta*[143], in which it was stated that "[n]o statute of the provincial legislature dealing with Indians or their lands as such would be valid and effective, but there is no reason why general legislation may not affect them.[144]" Within Cardinal one of the main issues in contention was whether or not such provincial laws apply through referential incorporation in s.88 of the *Indian Act* i.e. its terms become federal law and apply to Indians as such, or whether they apply independently as long as the subject matter comes within provincial jurisdiction[145]. The former view, often referred to as the "enclave theory" - that Indian reserves are federal enclaves from which provincial laws are excluded – was rejected by the majority. It supported the view that s.88 simply declares that, within its terms, provincial laws apply of their own force[146].

Accordingly, provincial gambling legislation, to be applicable "in respect of Indians" must at the very least come within one the enumerated heads of s.92 of the *Constitution Act, 1867*. There are several which could encompass a provincial lottery and gambling licensing scheme: s.92(9) authorizes the provinces to impose "Shop, Saloon, Tavern, Auctioneer and other Licences in order to the raising of a Revenue for Provincial, Local or Municipal Purposes"; the provinces have power over property and civil rights (s.92(13)) and also over matters of a local or private nature (s.92(16)).

Three Supreme Court of Canada decisions in recent years have considered the extent to which Indians enjoy immunity from otherwise valid provincial legislation, In *Four B Manufacturing Ltd. v. United Garment Workers of America,*[147] the Court established that a law which is within provincial jurisdiction under s.92 applies to Indians of its own force unless it affects "an integral part of primary federal jurisdiction over Indians and Lands reserved for the Indians". It would be virtually impossible to sustain such an argument in relation to provincial gambling legislation in the fact of the un-qualified, explicit, federal divestment of control over the area found in the *Criminal Code*.

In *Kruger and Manuel v. The Queen*[148], the Supreme Court held that the term "laws of general application" in s.88 excluded any law that, "by its effect, impairs the status or capacity of a particular group" (emphasis added). More recently, however, the Court limited the scope of this exemption by defining as a law of general application one which impairs Indian status, provided that it does not "overtly or colourably . . . single out Indians for special treatment and impair their status as Indians[149]." Consequently, as Monachan and Petter observe, it is the purpose of the law, rather than its effect, that determines whether it is a "law of general application" within the meaning of s.88[150].

Provincial gambling laws would not be excluded from this definition of a "law of general application". The gambling regulations do not preclude native groups which have a charitable or religious purpose from applying for and being granted licenses to conduct bingos and other lottery schemes. Indeed, in 1986 the Federal Court of Appeal overruled the Minister of National Revenue and granted a native Indian organization charitable status under the *Income Tax Act*[151]. Nonetheless, as Starr comments, although most Indians and Indian bands are poor, they are neither charitable nor religious organizations[152].

Even if a provincial enactment qualifies as a "law of general application" its application to Indians will be precluded if it is inconsistent with the *Indian Act* "or any order, rule, regulation or by-law made thereunder". As was noted above,[153] s.87 of the *Indian Act* provides an exemption from taxation for the property interests of Indians on reserves as follows:

> ". . . the following property is exempt from taxation, namely:
> (a)   the interest of an Indian or a band in reserve or surrendered lands; and
> (b)   the personal property of an Indian or band situated on a reserve;
>   and no Indian or band is subject to taxation in respect of the ownership, occupation or use of any property mentioned in paragraph

(a) or (b) or is otherwise subject to taxation
in respect of any such property;" .

For the purposes of s.88, it must be determined whether or
not the licensing of gambling activities can be categorized as a form
of taxation from which reserve Indians are exempt. As Bartlett
points out, s.87 will afford an exemption only in respect of taxation;
it affords not protection to financial levies which are otherwise
classified[154]. The courts have distinguished between taxes and
licences in the application of s.87 of the *Indian Act*. For example,
in *Attorney General for Quebec v. Williams,*[155] the Court, in considering the nature of a one dollar licensing fee under provincial tobacco
tax legislation, drew a distinction between a license which is merely
a permit and one which is a form of taxation[156]:

> ". . . tax is a general word which includes any con-
> tribution imposed by a competent authority to assure
> the services of the State. License would be a
> permission to do any act whatsoever. Although
> demanded with a view to regulation, it could never-
> theless incidentally comprise an amount of money
> capable of assuring the services of the State. From
> this it may be realized that if a license seems to be
> imposed solely to assure revenue for the state, such
> permit is not longer a license but a tax, whatever may
> be the word used in the text of the Act."

In British Columbia, the terms and Conditions Respecting
Licensing of Lottery Events impose licence fees of $15 or one per
cent of gross receipts, whichever is greater, for bingos with prizes
exceeding $500 and of $10 for those bingos offering prizes of less
than $500. These relatively minor licence fees would seem to be in
the category of a permit rather than a tax.

There is, however, another argument which might be made:
that the proceeds of gambling events (which go to charitable or
religious organizations) are a substitute for tax dollars. In other

words, if the province did not allow these groups to raise revenues for themselves, the province itself would have to provide the social services and community amenities funded by those organizations through tax revenues. Provincially licensed gambling, from this perspective, is a form of surrogate taxation. The concept of true lotteries as a form of indirect taxation is quite widely accepted and well-documented[157]. Regarding quasi-lotteries, however, this argument is more speculative and would require fairly minute analysis of provincial social services spending patterns before and after the expansion of gambling that has occurred particularly in the past decade. Just as the Indian bands who are interested in promoting gambling are using it as a substitute for powers of taxation, the provincial governments are also using gambling revenues as an alternative to direct taxation.

One final issue regarding the applicability of s.88 of the *Indian Act* which must be examined is the impact of band by-laws which purport to authorize and regulate gaming on reserves. Section 88 provides that provincial legislation which duplicates or conflicts with a by-law will not apply "in respect of Indians".

As was discussed above, s.81 of the *Act* provides band councils with rather limited powers to enact by-laws[158]. In a 1981 decision of the Quebec Court of Appeal they were categorized as follows[159]:

> "The powers conferred by s.81 are first of all, powers to regulate, and to regulate only "administrative statutes". In other words, a band council has, in this area, the same sort of legislative powers as those possessed by the council of a municipal corporation. The poser to give effect to regulations cannot extend beyond these administrative statutes; they are accessory and nothing more."

The band councils are, according to this determination, a third-rate, rather than a third order of government.

There have been attempts by more than 220 band councils to enact by-laws enabling bingo and other lottery schemes on Indian reserves pursuant to s.81(m).[160] All but one, passed in 1979, were disallowed by the Minister of Indian Affairs under the power contained in s.82.[161] The reason given for this action is that the *Criminal Code* takes precedence over the *Indian Act*. Starr reveals that, in an open letter to all Chiefs and Councils in British Columbia dated October 23, 1986, the Regional Director of Economic Development offered to following justification[162]:

"As you probably know, the *Criminal Code* takes precedence over the *Indian Act*. Thus the Department has had no choice but to disallow the by-laws, notwithstanding or recognition of the economic benefits that can be generated by gaming activities."

In other words, the federal government considers itself bound by the agreement it made with the provinces in 1985 to vacate the field of regulating lottery schemes. And, despite the fact that the *Criminal Code* and the *Indian Act* are both federal statutes, the former is ranked above, and is deemed to prevail over the latter. The federal government is thus unprepared to recognize that Indian bands have the power under the by-law provision, or otherwise, to remedy the failure to address Indian interest in the 1985 federal-provincial agreement regarding jurisdiction over permitted gambling. As Lyon indicates, the practice of ignoring Indian enactments which purport to remedy such deficiencies, stems from the enactment of s.88 of the *Indian Act* which induces the belief that provincial laws fill all legislative gaps[163].

Starr argues in the strongest terms that this represents an unnecessarily narrow approach to band by-law making powers and one which is at odds with the federal government's own view of the role that this power will play in realizing the future aspirations of Indian peoples regarding self-government[164]. She refers to two court decisions in which there is judicial acknowledgement of the intention of the Canadian government to expand the power over local band affairs in the pursuit of Indian self-government through economic self-reliance.[165] Her arguments are bolstered by recent amendments made to the *Indian Act* which expand the taxation powers of band councils.[166]

This situation underscores what to Indians is an uncontrovertible political fact: that provinces have far more power over federal policies, even those regarding Indians, than do the aboriginal peoples themselves. As long as the Minister of Indian Affairs continues to exercise his veto power over band by-laws authorizing gambling activities on the reserves, there is limited opportunity to test their validity before the courts.

A case was recently brought before the Federal Court by a band for a declaration that two by-laws, unrelated to gaming, adopted by the band council were in force notwithstanding the disallowance by the Minister.[167] The federal trial judge dismissed the action on the grounds that there was no requirement of fairness in the exercise of the power of disallowance and that the purpose of empowering the Minister to disallow by-laws is in part to allow him/her to take into account larger interest going beyond those of the band itself.[168] Regarding gambling by-laws, these larger interest would be those of the provinces and of maintaining federal-provincial harmony. The judge did recognize, however, that it was at least arguable that the power of disallowance has some implied limitation in that "it may not be used to frustrate completely the purposes of the *Indian Act*."[169] It could be argued that the blanket disallowance of gambling by-laws is frustrating federal policy to secure the economic independence of Indians. If band councils cannot get their by-laws before the courts for a judicial assessment of the vires the perhaps a challenge to the power of the Minister under s.82 might be pursued.

The foregoing discussion illustrates that section 190 of the *Criminal Code* and section 88 of the *Indian Act* have combined to constitute a significant area of provincial control over activities on reserves. The arguments put forward, however, indicate that the provincial seal around the authorization and regulation of lottery schemes is not watertight. But these arguments can be criticized on the basis that they define Indian power to control gambling by reference to federal and provincial jurisdiction. They proceed on the basis that those powers, rather than those of Indians, are the crucial determinants. As was stated earlier, even if provincial jurisdiction were to be rejected and replaced by federal regulation of gambling, this would be unacceptable to those who favor Indian control[170]. The final section of this paper will be directed to an examination of these assertions of Indian jurisdiction.

(d)   *Indian Jurisdiction*

The authorization, operation and regulation of gaming on reserves is one aspect of a much larger issue requiring resolution by the Canadian polity: the allocation or division of power between federal, provincial governments and Canada's indigenous peoples.

During the past few decades, the claims of the latter to certain inalienable rights, particularly to land, but also to a significant measure of self-government, have been asserted in the strongest terms. They stem from the fundamental proposition that native peoples are sovereign nations rather than dependents of the state. While that sovereignty may have been ignored or denied in the past, it was not extinguished. As Flanagan observes, "[a] sovereign nation retains its right of self-determination even when it is under external domination[171]." Acceptance of this position involves a redefinition of established views. Thus, for example, Venne offers the following re-evaluation of the powers and functions of band councils[172]:

"Bands and band councils are often described as 'creatures of statute', created as federal municipalities and exercising delegated powers. Indian Chiefs and Councils have rejected this analysis and are asserting a contrary proposition: Indian governments have extensive powers of self-government, including taxation, which are not delegated from the federal government. The source of Indian government jurisdiction is not the *Indian Act*, but rather a pre-existing or "aboriginal" right of self-government that has not been extinguished."

There is a growing body of literature which examines the historical roots and legal status of these claims[173]. To some extent, their existence, at least on a symbolic level, is now beyond dispute with the enactment of s.35 of the *Constitution Act, 1982*, which recognizes and affirms the "existing aboriginal and treaty rights of the aboriginal peoples of Canada".[174]

The doctrine of aboriginal rights is, as Slattery indicates, a basic principle of Canadian common law that defines the constitutional links between the Crown and Aboriginal peoples and regulates the interaction between the Canadian legal system and native rights, laws and institutions.[175] The precise content of "aboriginal rights" as enshrined in the Constitution is, however, unclear.

Mason describes s.35 as, at a minimum, setting a floor for native rights.[176] In Lyon's view, there is a range of possibilities encompassed by this provision which go beyond title to land and hunting and fishing rights to include the right to live under traditional forms of government and to be governed by customary laws.[177] There is increasing recognition being given to the position that s.35 recognizes the existence of a right to self-government, often described as a "third order of government" with powers parallel to those of the federal and provincial governments.[178] The concepts of aboriginal rights and of native self-government have evolved rapidly in recent years and have become inextricably connected. One observer has characterized the relationship in symbiotic terms: self-government is advocated as an aboriginal right, and a variety of aboriginal rights are advanced as aspects of native self-government.[179] Certainly, to have some constitutional status and protection, the right to self-government must be anchored to some source in the Constitution.[180]

The recognition of the right of self-government as an aboriginal right was advocated strongly by the special committee of the House of Commons which examined Indian self-government in the early 1980s. It recommended that section 91(24) of the *Constitution Act, 1867* should be interpreted to allow parliament to enact laws in all fields (including those reserved to the provinces in Section 92) insofar as they relate to "Indians and lands reserved for the Indians". Parliament should then proceed to vacate these areas of jurisdiction to recognized Indian governments. Consequently, virtually the entire range of law-making, policy, program delivery, law enforcement and adjudication powers would be available to a native government within its territory.[181] In the committee's view, native governments would derive their legitimacy not from parliament, nor from the constitution itself, but from the pre-existing rights of aboriginal peoples which the constitution does not create, but merely recognizes.[182]

The precise nature of the aboriginal rights that are recognized by Section 35 is the subject of considerable debate, mostly stemming from the inclusion of the phrase "existing aboriginal and treaty rights" within its terms. In addition, there has been no legislative action to implement the recommendations of the House of Commons Subcommittee, nor have the constitutional conferences attended by federal, provincial and native leaders with the aim of fleshing out the precise scope of this provision met with any success.

There is a measure of consensus among academic writers that an aboriginal or treaty right which has not been extinguished, but simply restricted or limited by legislation, is an existing right within Section 35. A representative statement of this view is provided by McNeil, who propounds this test for determining "existing" rights[183]:

"A workable test that might be applied to determine whether a particular right has been extinguished or merely rendered unexercisable would be to ask whether the right would be restored if the legislation affecting it was repealed. If the answer is no, then the right must have been extinguished; if yes, it must still exist and therefore is entitled to constitutional protection under section 35(1)."

The criminal law is one area in which Indian peoples are claiming their right to self-determination. Venne offers this assessment[184]:

"The criminal code is a law of general application that does not specify as applying to Indians. It no doubt was assumed that Indians, being considered British subjects, were to be covered by the Code. How does the Criminal Code relate, if at all, to the continuance of Indian customary "criminal" law? There has been no specific statute terminating the Indian law, thus it continues to "exist". Indian criminal jurisdiction has been removed by federal and provincial policy, but these policies cannot be defined as an extinguishment."

If, to use McNeil's test, the *Criminal Code* were to be repealed vis-a-vis its applicability to native peoples on their lands, the right to self-determination on this issue could quite easily be revived. According to this scenario, inherent aboriginal rights would, according to the Task Force on Gaming on Reserves, take precedence over the *Criminal Code* and the *Indian Act*[185].

To focus specifically on the gambling provisions of the *Code*, it can be argued quite strongly that they have, in effect, already been repealed by federal evacuation of the area, leaving the way clear for a re-activation of Indian jurisdiction over the field. As was illustrated above, there is ample evidence that gambling is a traditional Indian activity, an essential part of native culture, although not in the form it assumes today[186]. As one native leader notes, it would be unrealistic to expect that an aboriginal right exercised in the late 1980s would still take its ancient form[187].

This is, in fact, the basis on which several Indian bands are claiming the power to conduct gambling operations on reserves. In British Columbia, for example, the Gitksan and Kitimaat tribal councils assert that gambling is an existing aboriginal right within the meaning of Section 35 of the *Constitution Act, 1982*[188]. In the face of provincial opposition to these assertions and counter-claims of exclusive provincial jurisdiction regarding gambling, the conflict will have to be resolved sooner or later.

As experience in the United States has shown, it is important, from the native perspective, that it be done in a manner which does not create or enhance provincial control over Indian affairs. One solution which might be pursued is the amendment of the *Criminal Code* and of the *Indian Act* to indicate clearly that neither federal nor provincial gambling enactments apply to lottery schemes conducted on reserves by band councils. It is unlikely that this would be done unilaterally by the federal government without extensive consultation with the provinces. It is equally unlikely that the provinces would concede to such changes without considerable concessions being made to them, by the federal government. In order to ensure that these concessions are not exacted at a greater cost to Indian interests than the benefits gained from a grant of control over gambling, native leaders should be key players in the federal-provincial negotiation process. This would entail a radical re-alignment of the policy-making process in Canada.

A more satisfactory, long-term solution would be an amendment to the Constitution to provide, within a right of aboriginal self-government, jurisdiction over gambling on Indian lands. The immediate prospects for this kind of solution are not favourable in view of the failure of the constitutional conferences mandated by Section 35.1 of the *Constitution Act, 1981* to reach any agreement regarding the issue.

The other alternative is adjudication: asking the courts to determine jurisdiction over gambling on Indian lands in light of Section 35 of the *Constitution Act, 1981*. There is not, as yet, a large body of case law on the impact of this constitutional provision. A recent decision of the Ontario court of appeal, however, sounds a cautionary note. In *R. v. Agawa*[189], the Court was asked to decide whether the right to fish without a licence was an "existing treaty right" within the terms of Section 35. In the appellant's case, the Court found that his treaty fishing rights had not been extinguished, but merely restricted by a licensing requirement. It went on to say that hunting and fishing rights could not be divorced from the realities of life in present-day Canada, which required the conservation and management of fish stocks. Accordingly, Indian treaty rights were held to be subject to reasonable limitations, such as licensing requirements, despite the fact the Section 1 of the *Charter of Rights and Freedoms* does not apply to Section 35 of the *Constitution Act*. The exercise of Indian treaty rights, it was said, involved <u>a balancing of the interests and values of the rights of others.</u>

The Court of Appeal did not specify the entire range of interests that might be taken into account in determining the scope of "existing aboriginal and treaty rights". It could potentially include provincial interests. If it does, then this test bears more than a passing similarity to that enunciated by the U.S. Supreme Court in *California v. Cabazon Band of Mission Indians*[190], that tribal jurisdiction can be limited by state legislation if state interests are adjudged to be sufficiently compelling. It remains to be seen whether the Supreme Court of Canada will endorse such an approach to aboriginal and treaty rights and allow provincial interests a critical role.

V.   CONCLUSION

The purpose of this paper was to examine and evaluate the competing juridictional claims regarding gambling on reserves. An issue which, twenty years ago, would have been a matter between band councils and the federal government, which has exclusive jurisdiction over both Indian affairs and criminal law and procedure, was, as a result of a federal-provincial agreement on which Indians were not consulted, transformed into a dispute between band councils and provincial governments.   There is a struggle over the power to gamble on Indian lands.

There are arguments which can be made to challenge the validity of the initial transfer of power between the federal and provincial levels of government and to question the applicability of provincial laws on reserves.   Some Indian bands have, however, couched their jurisdictional assertions in terms which reject the division of powers set out in Sections 91 and 92 of the *Consitution Act, 1867*.   Instead, they claim the right to gamble on Indian lands as part their inherent power of self-determination.   They are staking a claim to, and gambling on real political power.

Progress towards official recognition of self-government as a constitutionally protected aboriginal right is painfully slow.   The resolution of the dispute over gambling through negotiation, legislation or adjudication is likely to occur much faster because it is an issue of much more immediate concern for the provinces.   As long as it is seen and treated as a small, yet important aspect of the larger issue, then the outcome could signify a real advance for aboriginal rights.

[1]D.I.A.N.D.,*Statement of the Government of Canada on Indian Policy*, 1969 (Ottawa: Queen's Printer, 1969).

[2]R.S.C.1970, c.I-6.

[3]Boldt and Long (eds.), *The Quest for Justice:Aboriginal Peoples and Aboriginal Rights* (Toronto:University of Toronto Press,1985) at 7 and Mason "Canadian and United States Approaches to Indian Sovereignty", (1983) 21 *Osgoode Hall Law Journal* 422 at 433.

[4] R.S.C. 1970, c.C-34.

[5] Indian and Northern Affairs Canada (INAC), *Gaming on Reserves* (Ottawa:INAC,1987) Annex J, details some of the charges and confrontations which have arisen in the last few years.

[6] It is hoped that what follows will be read both by those who are interested in native issues as well as those whose major interest is gambling. Given the widely different nature of this two areas, this section will provide some basic background materials on the law in these areas in order to provide a context for the discussion which will follow in Section IV.

[7]30-31 Vict., c.3 as amended.

[8] Ponting and Gibbins, *Out of Irrelevance* (Toronto: Butterworths, 1980) at 7.

[9]Sanders, "The Friendly Care and Directing Hand of the Government: A Study of Government Trusteeship of Indians in Canada" (Unpublished paper, 1977) at 6.

[10]Bartlett, "The Indian Act of Canada", (1978) 27 *Buffalo Law Review* 581; Ponting and Gibbins supra fn.8 at 8.

[11]Morse, "Aboriginal Peoples and the Law" in Morse (ed.) *Aboriginal Peoples and the Law etc.* (Ottawa:Carleton University Press, 1985) 1-15 at 1.

[12]Nakaratsu, "A Constitutional Right of Indian Self-Government", (1985), 43 *University of Toronto Faculty of Law Review* 72 at 75.

[13]Bartlett, supra fn.10 at 584.

[14]Hogg, *Consitutional Law of Canada* (2d ed.) (Toronto: Carswell,1985) at 554.

[15]Morse, supra fn.11 at 8.

[16]Bartlett, supra fn.10 at 603.

[17]Hogg, supra fn.14 at 561.

[18]Bartlett, supra fn.10 at 607.

[19]Enacted by the *Canada Act*, 1982 (U.K.) c. 11, Schedule B.

[20]*The Case of Monopolies*, (1603) 11 Co.Rep. 84, 77 Eng.Rep. 1260.

[21]12 Rich.II, c.6 (1388)

[22]Glickman, "Our gaming laws: conditions dicey to say the least", (March, 1979) *Canadian Lawyer* 11.

[23]S.C. 1886, c.158.

[24]S.C. 1886, c.159.

[25]S.C. 1886, c.160.

[26]55-56 Vict. c.29.

[27]Ibid section 204(2).

[28]Canada, *Reports of the Joint Committee on Capital and Corporal Punishment and Lotteries* (Ottawa: Queen's Printer, 1956).

[29]S.C. 1968-69, c.38.

[30]True lotteries are games such as "Lotto 649" and "The Provincial"; quasi-lotteries are other games of chance such as bingo, blackjack and roulette, although dice games are not included.

[31]*The Criminal Code (Lotteries) Amendment Act*, S.C. 1985, c.52. For a more detailed commentary on these changes see Osborne and Campbell, "Recent Amendments to Canadian Lottery and Gaming Laws etc.", (1988) *Osgoode Hall Law Journal* (forthcoming).

[32]Bill C-81, 1st Sess. 33rd Parl, 1984-85.

[33]*Cabazon Band of Mission Indians v. California*, 107 S.Ct. 1083 (1987); 55 *Law Week* 4225.

[34]Rose, *Gambling and the Law* (Hollywood: Gambling Times, 1986) at 1.

[35]Ibid at 210.

[36]DeDomenicis, "Betting on Indian Rights" (1983) 3 *California Lawyer* 29.

[37]U.S. *Senate Report*, (1986)No.99-493, p.5.

[38]U.S. *House of Representatives Report*, (1986)No.99-488, p.10.

[39]These statements were relied on in *California v. Cabazon Band of Mission Indians* at the Court of Appeals level. 783 F.2d 900 at 904-5 (1986).

[40]"It is important to the concept of self-government that tribes reduce their dependence on Federal funds by providing a greater percentage of the cost of their self-government." Quoted in *California v. Cabazon Band of Mission Indians*, (1987) 55 Law Week 4225 at 4229 (U.S.S.C.).

[41]Mason, supra fn.3 at 423.

[42]*United States Constitution*, article 1, paragraph 8, clause 18 (Indian Commerce Clause).

[43]118 U.S. 375 (1886).

[44]For a trenchant criticism of this decision as well as of U.S. Indian policy as a whole, see Kronowitz et al., "Towards Consent and Cooperation: Reconsidering the political Status of Indian Nations", (1987) 22 *Harvard Civil Rights-Civil Liberties Law Review* 507.

[45]Haslam, "Indian Sovereignty: Confusion Prevails", (1988) 63 *Washington Law Review* 169 170.

[46]Kronowitz et al., supra fn. 44 at 561.

[47]*Organized Village of Kake v. Egan*, 369 U.S. 60 (1962); *Rice v. Renner*, 463 U.S. 713 (1983). In the latter decision, Madam Justice O'Connor stated (at 723) that "'absolute' federal jurisdiction was not always exclusive jurisdiction".

[48]*McClanahan v. Arizona*, 411 U.S. 164 (1973).

[49]Kronowitz et al., supra fn.44 at 569-70.

[50]18 U.S.C. # 1152 (1982)

[51]18 U.S.C. # 1153 (1982)

[52]435 U.S. 191 (1978).

[53]18 U.S.C. #1162, 28 U.S.C. #1360 (1982 and Supp. III).

[54]McDonnell, "Federal and State Regulation of Gambling and Liquor Sales Within Indian Country", (1985) 8 *Hamline Law Review* 599 at 606.

[55]DeDomenicis, supra fn.36 at 31.

[56]Arizona, Florida, Idaho, Iowa, Montana, Nevada, North Dakota, Utah and Washington.

[57]*Indian Civil Rights Act*, 25 U.S.C. ##1321-1322,1326 (1982).

[58]426 U.S. 373 (1975).

[59]15 U.S.C. #1175 (1982)

[60]Indeed, in *United States v. Farris*, 624 F.2d 890 (1980), a prosecution brought against the Puyallup Indians who were operating a casino, the limited range of this enactment was noted as was "the conspicuous caution" of the casinos to avoid the use of gambling devices which would be caught by it (at 896).

[61]18 U.S.C. #155 (1982).

[62]Supra fn.40.

[63]658 F.2d 310 (1981).

[64]Ibid at 314-15.

[65]518 F.Supp. 712 (1981).

[66]Ibid at 719, per Crabb, Chief Judge.

[67]Ibid at 715.

[68]Ibid at 720.

[69]694 F.2d 1185 (1982).

[70]Ibid at 1189.

[71]Supra fn.40.

[72]Ibid at 4227.

[73]Ibid.

[74]Ibid at 4228.

[75]Ibid at 4229, quoting from *New Mexico v. Mescalero Apache Tribe*, 462 U.S. at 334.

[76]*California v. Cabazon*, ibid at 4230.

[77]Turner, "Evolution, Assimilation and State Control of Gambling in Indian Country: etc.", (1988) 24 *Idaho Law Review* 317 at 335.

[78]Kronowitz et al., supra fn. 44 at 583.

[79]624 F.2d 890 (1980).

[80]Ibid at 898 per Browning, Circuit J.

[81]Supra fn.69 at 1190.

[82]796 F.2d 186 (1986).

[83]Ibid at 188.

[84]*California v. Cabazon*, supra fn. 40 at 4228.

[85]H.R. 4566, 98th Cong., 1st Sess. (1983).

[86]H.R. 1920, 99th Cong., 1st Sess. (1985).

[87]S. 902, 99th Cong., 1st Sess. (1985).

[88]Public Law 100-497, 100th Cong.(Oct. 1988).

[89]Maranda, *Coast Salish Gambling Games*, Canadian Ethnology Service Paper # 93 (Ottawa: National Museums of Canada, 1984).

[90]Ibid at (vi).

[91]"Submission to the Task Force on Gaming on Reserves", in INAC, *Gaming on Reserves*, supra fn.5 at 35.

[92]Supra fn.8 at 10.

[93]"Taxation" in Morse (ed.) supra fn. 11 at 579.

[94]Ibid.

[95]INAC. Task Force on Indian Economic Development. *Summary of the report to the Deputy Minister, INAC* (Ottawa: Supply and Services Canada, 1986) at 21.

[96]Ponting and Gibbins, supra fn. 8 at 36. The recent task force on Indian economic development also concluded that small markets on Indian reserves have stunted the growth of the retail and manufacturing sectors of the native business community - INAC. Task Force on Indian Economic Development, supra fn 94 at 11.

[97]INAC, supra fn. 5 at 13.

[98]By attracting non-natives onto the reserves to play bingo etc. the bands would not be wholly reliant on their own members to generate revenues. Such enterprises would also perhaps stem the flow of native gambling expenditures off the reserve.

[99]Ponting and Gibbins, supra fn.8 at 182.

[100]Morse, supra fn. 11 at 8.

[101]Supra fn. 90 at 2.

[102]See the comments made by Chief Gabriel Gopher of the North Battleford District Chiefs to the Task Force on Indian Economic Development, supra fn. 94 at 46.

[103]Supra fn.5 at 13-18.

[104]Osborne and Campbell, supra fn.30.

[105]Driedger, "The Interaction of Federal and Provincial Law", (1976) 54 *Canadian Bar Review* 695 at 698.

[106]*Attorney General for Nova Scotia v. Attorney General for Canada*, [1952] 2 S.C.R. 31.

[107]R.S.B.C. 1979 c. 249; B.C. Regs. 108/70 - 123/86; "Policy Directives Respecting Licensing of Lottery Events in B.C." issed 3/6/86; "Terms and Conditions Respecting Licensing of Lottery Events in B.C." issued by the B.C. Gaming Commission, 13/7/87. More will be said about these enactments infra.

[108]*P.E.I. Marketing Board v. H.B. Willis Inc.*, [1952] 2 S.C.R. 392.

[109]Russell, *Leading Constitutional Decisions*, (3d ed.) (Ottawa: Carleton University Press, 1984) at 471.

[110]S.C. 1906 c. 27.

[111]*Attorney General of Ontario v. Hamilton Street Railway,* [1903] A.C. 524.

[112][1925] A.C. 384 (P.C.).

[113]Ibid at 392, per Lord Blanesburgh speaking for the unanimous five member bench.

[114]Ibid.

[115]Supra fn. 104 at 706.

[116][1959] S.C.R. 497.

[117]Ibid at 509-10.

[118]Supra fn. 14 at 306-07.

[119]Weiler, "The Supreme Court and the Law of Canadian Federalism", (1973) 23 *University of Toronto Law Journal* 307 at 315.

[120]Lysyk, "The Interdelegation Doctrine: A Constitutional Paper Tiger?", (1969) 47 *Canadian Bar Review* 271 at 274.

[121]Unreported decision, Supreme Court of Ontario, 13/9/88.

[122](1985) 49 O.R. (2d) 705.

[123]Ibid at 716, per MacKinnon A.C.J.O.

[124][1898] A.C. 700.

[125]*Constitution Act, 1867, s.92(5).*

[126]*Fisheries Act* R.S.C. 1970, c.F-14, s.34.

[127]Pibus, "The Fisheries Act and Native Fishing Rights in Canada: 1970-1980", (1981) 39 *University of Torornto Faculty of Law Review* 43 at 44.

[128]Consolidated Regulations of Canada 1978 c.849.

[129]Ibid.

[130](1978) 25 O.R.(2d) 334 (Ont. H.C.). Cory J. held that the federal *Fisheries Act* adopted the machinery provided by the provincial *Game and Fish Act* by means of the regulations and that this was a valid adoption of administrative authority.

[131][1988] 3 C.N.L.R. 73.

[132]Interestingly, if the parallel were to be upheld, it would mean that provincial gambling enactments are in fact federal provisions, and that the federal government could not maintain its inability to act in this sphere, based on the 1985 federal-provincial agreement.

[133]Supra fn. 5 at 19.

[134]*Constitution Act, 1867, s.91(24).*

[135]See fn.106 and surrounding text.

[136]B.C. Reg. 108/70, amended and consolidated as B.C.Reg 17/73; amended by B.C. Reg. 436/74; B.C. Reg 651/76; B.C. Reg. 265/78; B.C. Reg. 362/84.

[137]B.C. Reg. 123/86.

[138]Murray, "Gambling is Illegal in Canada: Casino and Bingo Gaming in British Columbia - The Legal Framework", *Bingo Caller News* 15/8/88 p. 24.

[139]Supra fn.90 at 9.

[140]Supra fn. 120.

[141][1975] 2 S.C.R. 47 at 56-57. My attention was drawn to these remarks by Starr, supra fn.90 at 9.

[142]Sanders notes that s.88, by its terms, only refers to the application of provincial laws to "Indians": "The Application of Provincial Laws" in Morse (ed), supra fn.11 at 456. It does not purport to deal specifically with the application of provincial laws on Indian reserves, nor does it explicitly preclude it.

[143][1974] 2 S.C.R.695.

[144]Ibid at 706 per Martland J.

[145]Hogg, supra fn. 14 at 558.

[146]For a more detailed discussion of the enclave theory and of provincial jurisdiction over Indians and reserve lands see Hughes, "Indians and Lands Reserved for the Indians: Off-Limits to the Provinces", (1983) 21 *Osgoode Hall Law Journal* 82.

[147][1980] 1 S.C.R. 1031

[148][1978] 1 S.C.R. 104.

[149]*R. v. Dick*, [1985] 2 S.C.R. 309.

[150]Monachan and Petter, "Developments in Constitutional Law: The 1985-86 Term", (1987) 9 *Supreme Court Law Review* 69 at 162.

[151]*Native Communications Society of B.C. v. The Minister of National Revenue*, (1986) 11(8) *Canadian Human Rights Advocate* 7.

[152]Supra fn. 90 at 10.

[153]See fn. 92 and surrounding text.

[154]Bartlett, *Indians and Taxation* (Saskatoon: Native Law Centre, 1980).

[155](1944) 82 C.C.C. 166 (Queb. Ct. Sess.).

[156]Ibid at 169 per Guerin J.Sess.

[157]See e.g. Johnson, "An Economic Analysis of Lotteries", (1976) 24 *Canadian Tax Journal* 639; Livernois, "The Redistibutive Effects of Lotteries: Evidence from Canada", (1987) 15 *Public Finance Quarterly* 339; McLoughlin, "The Lotteries Tax", (1979) 1 *Canadian Taxation* 16 and Vaillancourt and Grignon, "Canadian Lotteries as Taxes: Revenues and Incidence", (1988) 36 *Canadian Tax Journal* 369.

[158]See fn. 12 and surrounding text.

[159]*Re Stacey and Montour and the Queen*, (1981 63 C.C.C. (2d) 61, per Bernier J.A.

[160]"The council of a band by make by-laws . . . for any or all of the following purposes, namely: . . . (m) the control and prohibition of public games, sports, races, athletic contests, and other amusements".

[161]Starr, supra fn. 90 at 2-3.

[162]Ibid at 4-5.

[163]Lyon, "Constitutional Issues in Native Law", in Morse (ed.), supra fn. 11 at 421.

[164]Starr, supra fn. 90 at 10-15.

[165]Ibid. See *Whitebear Band Council v. Carpenters Provincial Council*, [1982] 3 C.N.L.R. 181 (Sask.C.A.) and *Waskaganish Band V. Blackned*, [1986] 3 C.N.L.R. 168 (Que.Prov.Ct.)

[166]*An Act to amend the Indian Act (designated lands)*, Bill c-115, S.C. 1986-87-88.

[167]*Twin et al. v. Canada (M.I.A.N.D.)*, (1987) 6 F.T.R. 41.

[168]Ibid at 45.

[169]Ibid at 44 per Strayer J.

[170]Supra fn. 132 and surrounding text.

[171]"From Indian Title to Aboriginal Rights" in Knafla (ed.) Law and Justice in a New Land: Essays in Western Canadian Legal History , (Toronto: Carswell, 1986) at 99.

[172]Venne, "Indian Jurisdiction" in INAC, *Gaming on Reserves*, supra fn. 5 at 2.

[173]e.g. Boldt and Long (eds.), supra fn. 3; Flanagan, supra fn. 170; Morse, supra fn. 11 and Slattery, "Understanding Aboriginal Rights", (1987) 66 *Canadian Bar Review* 725.

[174]Because of the broad definition given to "aboriginal peoples" in s.35 - it includes the Indian, Inuit and Metis peoples - the potential impact of this provision extends beyond native Indians.

[175]Slattery, supra fn. 172 at 732.

[176]Mason, supra fn. 3 at 438.

[177]Lyon, supra fn. 161 at 419.

[178]Slattery, "The Hidden Constitution: Aboriginal Rights in Canada", in Boldt and Long (eds.), supra fn. 3 at 137.

[179]Tennant, "Aboriginal Rights and the Penner Report on Indian Self Government" in Boldt and Long (eds.), supra fn. 3 at 321.

[180]Nakaratsu, supra fn. 12 at 81.

[181]Canada House of Commons, *Report of the Special Committee on Indian Self-Government* (Penner Report) (Ottawa: Supply and Services, 1983) at 329.

[182]Ibid at 328.

[183]McNeil, "The Constitutional Rights of the Aboriginal Peoples of Canada", (1982) 4 *Supreme Court Law Reporter* 255 at 258. See also Slattery, "The Constitutional Guarantee of Aboriginal and Treaty Rights", (1983) 8 *Queen's Law Journal* 232.

[184]Venne, supra fn. 171 at 25.

[185]Supra fn. 5 at 28.

[186]See fn. 88 and surrounding text.

[187]Ahenakew, "Aboriginal Title and Aboriginal Rights: The Impossible Task of Identification and Definition", in Boldt and Long (eds.), supra fn. 3 at 27.

[188]Starr, supra fn. 90 at 35. The Gitksan position is set out in more detail in an interview with tribal president, Don Ryans reported in *Kahtou*, vol. 6(11), 6/6/88.

[189]Supra fn. 130.

[190]Supra fn. 40.

APPENDICES

California v. Cabazon
Indian Gaming Regulatory Act
California Tribal Compact (1999)
Federally Recognized Gaming Tribes

CALIFORNIA ET AL
v.
CABAZON BAND OF
MISSION INDIANS ET AL.

No. 85-1708

SUPREME COURT OF THE UNITED STATES

480 U.S. 202; 107 S. Ct. 1083; 1987 U.S. LEXIS 935; 94 L.
Ed. 2d. 244; 55 U.S.L.W. 4225

Argued December 9, 1986

February 25, 1987

SYLLABUS:

Appellee Indian Tribes (the Cabazon and Morongo Bands of Mission Indians) occupy reservations in Riverside County, Cal. Each Band, pursuant to its federally approved ordinance, conducts on its reservation bingo games that are open to the public. The Cabazon Band also operates a card club for playing draw poker and other card games. The gambling games are open to the public and are played predominantly by non-Indians coming onto the reservations. California sought to apply to the Tribes its statute governing the operation of bingo games. Riverside County also sought to apply its ordinance regulating bingo, as well as its ordinance prohibiting the playing of draw poker and other card games. The Tribes instituted an action for declaratory relief in Federal District Court, which entered summary judgment for the Tribes, holding that neither the State nor the county had any authority to enforce its gambling laws within the reservations. The Court of Appeals affirmed.

Held:

1. Although state laws may be applied to tribal Indians on their reservations if Congress has expressly consented, Congress has not done so here either by Pub. L. 280 or by the Organized Crime Control Act of 1970 (OCCA). Pp. 207-214.

(a) In Pub. L. 280, the primary concern of which was combating lawlessness on reservations, California was granted broad criminal jurisdiction over offenses committed by or against Indians within all Indian country within the State but more limited, nonregulatory civil jurisdiction. When a State seeks to enforce a law within an Indian reservation under the authority of Pub. L. 280, it must be determined whether the state law is criminal in nature and thus fully applicable to the reservation, or civil in nature and applicable only as it may be relevant to private civil litigation in state court. There is a fair basis for the Court of Appeals' conclusion that California's statute, which permits bingo games to be conducted only by certain types of organizations under certain restrictions, is not a "criminal/prohibitory" statute falling within Pub. L. 280's grant of criminal jurisdiction, but instead is a "civil/regulatory" statute not authorized by Pub. L. 280 to be enforced on Indian reservations. That an otherwise regulatory law is enforceable (as here) by criminal as well as civil means does not necessarily convert it into a criminal law within Pub. L. 280's meaning. Pp. 207-212.

(b) Enforcement of OCCA, which makes certain violations of state and local gambling laws violations of federal criminal law, is an exercise of federal rather than state authority. There is nothing in OCCA indicating that the States are to have any part in enforcing the federal laws or are authorized to make arrests on Indian reservations that in the absence of OCCA they could not effect. California may not make arrests on reservations and thus, through OCCA, enforce its gambling laws against Indian tribes. Pp. 212-214.

2. Even though not expressly authorized by Congress, state and local laws may be applied to on-reservation activities of tribes and tribal members under certain circumstances. The decision in this case turns on whether state authority is pre-empted by the operation of federal law. State jurisdiction is pre-empted if it interferes or is incompatible with federal and tribal interests reflected in federal law, unless the state interests at stake are sufficient to justify the assertion of state authority. The federal interests in Indian self-government, including the goal of encouraging tribal self-sufficiency and economic development, are important, and federal agencies, acting under federal laws, have sought to implement them by promoting and overseeing tribal bingo and gambling enterprises. Such policies and actions are of particular relevance in this case since the tribal games provide the sole source of revenues for the operation of the tribal governments and are the major sources of employment for tribal members. To the extent that the State seeks to prevent all bingo games on tribal lands while permitting regulated off-reservation games, the asserted state interest in preventing the infiltration of

the tribal games by organized crime is irrelevant, and the state and county laws are pre-empted. Even to the extent that the State and county seek to regulate short of prohibition, the laws are pre-empted since the asserted state interest is not sufficient to escape the pre-emptive force of the federal and tribal interests apparent in this case. Pp. 214-222.

783 F. 2d 900, affirmed and remanded.

WHITE, J., delivered the opinion of the Court, in which REHNQUIST, C.J., and BRENNAN, MARSHALL, BLACKMUN, and POWELL, JJ., joined. STEVENS, J., filed a dissenting opinion, in which O'CONNOR and SCALIA, JJ., joined, *post*, p. 222.

APPEAL-STATEMENT:
APPEAL FROM THE UNITED STATES COURT OF APPEALS FOR THE NINTH CIRCUIT

JUDGES:
Rehnquist, Brennan, White, Marshall, Blackmun, Powell, Stevens, O'Connor, Scalia

COUNSEL:
Roderick E. Walston, Supervising Deputy Attorney General of California, argued the cause for appellants. With him on the briefs were *John K. Van de Kamp*, Attorney General, *Steve White*, Chief Assistant Attorney General, *Frederick R. Millar, Jr.*, Supervising Deputy Attorney General, *Rudolph Corona, Jr.*, Deputy Attorney General, *Gerald J. Geerlings, Peter H. Lyons*, and *Glenn R. Salter.*

Glenn M. Feldman argued the cause for appellees. With him on the brief were *Barbara A. Karshmer* and *George Forman.*[*]

---

[*]Briefs of *amici curiae* urging reversal were filed for the State of Arizona et al. by *Robert K. Corbin*, Attorney General of Arizona, *Anthony B. Ching*, Solicitor General, *Ian A. Macpherson, Brian McKay*, Attorney General of Nevada, and *Paul*
(continued...)

OPINION BY: WHITE

OPINION:
JUSTICE WHITE delivered the opinion of the Court.

The Cabazon and Morongo Bands of Mission Indians, federally recognized Indian tribes, occupy reservations in Riverside County, California[1]. Each Band, pursuant to an ordinance approved by the

---

Bardacke, Attorney General of New Mexico; and for the State of Washington et al. by *Kenneth O. Eikenberry*, Attorney General of Washington, *Timothy R. Malone*, Assistant Attorney General, *Bronson C. La Follette*, Attorney General of Wisconsin, and *John J. Kelly*, Chief State's Attorney of Connecticut.

Briefs of *amici curiae* urging affirmance were filed for the Chehalis Indian Tribe et al. by *Henry J. Sockbeson* and *Stephen V. Quesenberry*; for the Jicarilla Apache Tribe et al. by *Alan R. Taradash*; for the Oneida Indian Nation of New York by *William W. Taylor III* and *Christine Nicholson*; for the Pueblo of Sandia et al. by *L. Lamar Parrish, Theodore W. Barudin, Michael D. Bustamante*, and *Scott E. Borg*; for the San Manuel Band of Mission Indians by *Jerome L. Levine* and *David A. Lash*; and for the Seminole Tribe of Florida et al. by *Bruce S. Rogow*.

Briefs of *amici curiae* were filed for the State of Minnesota by *Hubert H. Humphrey III*, Attorney General, and *James M. Schoessler*, Assistant Attorney General; for the Pueblo of Laguna et al. by *W. Richard West, Jr., Thomas W. Fredericks, Rodney B. Lewis, Carol L. Barbero, John Bell, Rodney J. Edwards*, and *Art Bunce*; and for the Tulalip Tribes of Washington et al. by *Allen H. Sanders*.

[1]The Cabazon Reservation was originally set apart for the "permanent use and occupancy" of the Cabazon Indians by Executive Order of May 15, 1876. The Morongo Reservation also was first established by Executive Order. In 1891, in the Mission Indian Relief Act, 26 Stat. 712, Congress declared reservations "for the sole use and benefit" of the Cabazon and Morongo Bands. The United States holds the land in trust for the Tribes. The governing bodies of both Tribes have been recognized by the Secretary of the Interior. The Cabazon Band has 25 enrolled members and the Morongo Band has approximately 730 enrolled members.

Secretary of the Interior, conducts bingo games on its reservation[2]. The Cabazon Band has also opened a card club at which draw poker and other card games are played. The games are open to the public and are played predominantly by non-Indians coming onto the reservations. The games are a major source of employment for tribal members, and the profits are the Tribes' sole source of income. The State of California seeks to apply to the two Tribes Cal. Penal Code Ann. § 326.5 (West Supp. 1987). That statute does not entirely prohibit the playing of bingo but permits it when the games are operated and staffed by members of designated charitable organizations who may not be paid for their services. Profits must be kept in special accounts and used only for charitable purposes; prizes may not exceed $ 250 per game. Asserting that the bingo games on the two reservations violated each of these restrictions, California insisted that the Tribes comply with state law[3]. Riverside

---

[2]The Cabazon ordinance authorizes the Band to sponsor bingo games within the reservation "[i]n order to promote economic development of the Cabazon Indian Reservation and to generate tribal revenues" and provides that net revenues from the games shall be kept in a separate fund to be used "for the purpose of promoting the health, education, welfare and well being of the Cabazon Indian Reservation and for other tribal purposes." App. to Brief for Appellees 1b-3b. The ordinance further provides that no one other than the Band is authorized to sponsor a bingo game within the reservation, and that the games shall be open to the public, except that no one under 18 years old may play. The Morongo ordinance similarly authorizes the establishment of a tribal bingo enterprise and dedicates revenues to programs to promote the health, education, and general welfare of tribal members. *Id.*, at 1a-6a. It additionally provides that the games may be conducted at any time but must be conducted at least three days per week, that there shall be no prize limit for any single game or session, that no person under 18 years old shall be allowed to play, and that all employees shall wear identification.

[3]The Tribes admit that their games violate the provision governing staffing and the provision setting a limit on jackpots. They dispute the State's assertion that they do not maintain separate funds for the bingo operations. At oral argument, counsel for the State asserted, contrary to the position taken in the merits brief and contrary to the stipulated facts in this case, App. 65, ¶24, 82-83, ¶15, that the Tribes are among the charitable organizations authorized to sponsor bingo games under the

(continued...)

County also sought to apply its local Ordinance No. 558, regulating bingo, as well as its Ordinance No. 331, prohibiting the playing of draw poker and the other card games.

The Tribes sued the county in Federal District Court seeking a declaratory judgment that the county had no authority to apply its ordinances inside the reservations and an injunction against their enforcement. The State intervened, the facts were stipulated, and the District Court granted the Tribes' motion for summary judgment, holding that neither the State nor the county had any authority to enforce its gambling laws within the reservations. The Court of Appeals for the Ninth Circuit affirmed, 783 F. 2d 900 (1986), the State and the county appealed, and we postponed jurisdiction to the hearing on the merits. 476 U.S. 1168.[4]

---

[3](...continued)

statute. It is therefore unclear whether the State intends to put the tribal bingo enterprises out of business or only to impose on them the staffing, jackpot limit, and separate fund requirements. The tribal bingo enterprises are apparently consistent with other provisions of the statute: minors are not allowed to participate, the games are conducted in buildings owned by the Tribes on tribal property, the games are open to the public, and persons must be physically present to participate.

[4]The Court of Appeals "affirm[ed] the summary judgment and the permanent injunction restraining the County and the State from applying their gambling laws on the reservations." 783 F. 2d, at 906. The judgment of the District Court declared that the state statute and county ordinance were of no force and effect within the two reservations, that the State and the county were without jurisdiction to enforce them, and that they were therefore enjoined from doing so. Since it is now sufficiently clear that the state and county laws at issue were held, as applied to the gambling activities on the two reservations, to be "invalid as repugnant to the Constitution, treaties or laws of the United States" within the meaning of 28 U.S.C. § 1254(2), the case is within our appellate jurisdiction.

I

The Court has consistently recognized that Indian tribes retain "attributes of sovereignty over both their members and their territory," *United States* v. *Mazurie*, 419 U.S. 544, 557 (1975), and that "tribal sovereignty is dependent on, and subordinate to, only the Federal Government, not the States," *Washington* v. *Confederated Tribes of the Colville Indian Reservation*, 447 U.S. 134, 154 (1980). It is clear, however, that state laws may be applied to tribal Indians on their reservations if Congress has expressly so provided. Here, the State insists that Congress has twice given its express consent: first in Pub. L. 280 in 1953, 67 Stat. 588, as amended, 18 U.S.C. § 1162, 28 U.S.C. § 1360 (1982 ed. and Supp. III), and second in the Organized Crime Control Act in 1970, 84 Stat. 937, 18 U.S.C. § 1955. We disagree in both respects.

In Pub. L. 280, Congress expressly granted six States, including California, jurisdiction over specified areas of Indian country[5] within the States and provided for the assumption of jurisdiction by other States. In § 2, California was granted broad criminal jurisdiction over offenses committed by or against Indians within all Indian country within the State.[6] Section 4's grant of civil jurisdiction was

---

[5]"Indian country," as defined at 18 U.S.C. § 1151, includes "all land within the limits of any Indian reservation under the jurisdiction of the United States Government, notwithstanding the issuance of any patent, and, including rights-of-way running through the reservation." This definition applies to questions of both criminal and civil jurisdiction. *DeCoteau* v. *District County Court*, 420 U.S. 425, 427, n. 2 (1975). The Cabazon and Morongo Reservations are thus Indian country.

[6]Section 2(a), codified at 18 U.S.C. § 1162(a), provides:

"Each of the States . . . listed in the following table shall have jurisdiction over offenses committed by or against Indians in the areas of Indian country listed . . . to the same extent that such State . . . has jurisdiction over offenses committed elsewhere within the State . . ., and the criminal laws of such State . . . shall have the same force and effect within such Indian country as they have elsewhere within the State . . . :

(continued...)

234

more limited.[7] In *Bryan* v. *Itasca County*, 426 U.S. 373 (1976), we interpreted § 4 to grant States jurisdiction over private civil litigation involving reservation Indians in state court, but not to grant general civil regulatory authority. *Id.*, at 385, 388-390. We held, therefore, that Minnesota could not apply its personal property tax within the reservation. Congress' primary concern in enacting Pub. L. 280 was combating lawlessness on reservations. *Id.*, at 379-380. The Act plainly was not intended to effect total assimilation of Indian tribes into mainstream American society. *Id.*, at 387. We recognized that a grant to States of general civil regulatory power over Indian reservations would result in the destruction of tribal institutions and values. Accordingly, when a State seeks to enforce a law within an Indian reservation under the authority of Pub. L. 280, it must be determined whether the law is criminal in nature, and thus fully applicable to the reservation under § 2, or civil in nature, and applicable only as it may be relevant to private civil litigation in state court.

The Minnesota personal property tax at issue in *Bryan* was unquestionably civil in nature. The California bingo statute is not so easily categorized. California law permits bingo games to be conducted only by charitable and other specified organizations, and

---

[6](...continued)

"California..............All Indian country within the State."

[7]Section 4(a), codified at 28 U.S.C. § 1360(a) (1982 ed. and Supp. III) provides:

"Each of the States listed in the following table shall have jurisdiction over civil causes of action between Indians or to which Indians are parties which arise in the areas of Indian country listed . . . to the same extent that such State has jurisdiction over other civil causes of action, and those civil laws of such State that are of general application to private persons or private property shall have the same force and effect within such Indian country as they have elsewhere within the State:

"California..............All Indian country within the State."

then only by their members who may not receive any wage or profit for doing so; prizes are limited and receipts are to be segregated and used only for charitable purposes. Violation of any of these provisions is a misdemeanor. California insists that these are criminal laws which Pub. L. 280 permits it to enforce on the reservations.

Following its earlier decision in *Barona Group of the Capitan Grande Band of Mission Indians, San Diego County, Cal. v. Duffy*, 694 F. 2d 1185 (1982), cert. denied, 461 U.S. 929 (1983), which also involved the applicability of § 326.5 of the California Penal Code to Indian reservations, the Court of Appeals rejected this submission. 783 F. 2d, at 901-903. In *Barona*, applying what it thought to be the civil/criminal dichtomy drawn in *Bryan* v. *Itasca County*, the Court of Appeals drew a distinction between state "criminal/prohibitory" laws and state "civil/regulatory" laws: if the intent of a state law is generally to prohibit certain conduct, it falls within Pub. L. 280's grant of criminal jurisdiction, but if the state law generally permits the conduct at issue, subject to regulation, it must be classified as civil/regulatory and Pub. L. 280 does not authorize its enforcement on an Indian reservation. The shorthand test is whether the conduct at issue violates the State's public policy. Inquiring into the nature of § 326.5, the Court of Appeals held that it was regulatory rather than prohibitory.[8] This was the analysis employed, with similar

---

[8]The Court of Appeals questioned whether we indicated disapproval of the prohibitory/regulatory distinction in *Rice* v. *Rehner*, 463 U.S. 713 (1983). We did not. We rejected in that case an asserted distinction between state "substantive" law and state "regulatory" law in the context of 18 U.S.C. § 1161, which provides that certain federal statutory provisions prohibiting the sale and possession of liquor within Indian country do not apply "provided such act or transaction is in conformity both with the laws of the State in which such act or transaction occurs and with an ordinance duly adopted by the tribe having jurisdiction over such area of Indian country. . . ." We noted that nothing in the text or legislative history of § 1161 supported the asserted distinction, and then contrasted that statute with Pub. L. 280. "In the absence of a context that might possibly require it, we are reluctant to make such a distinction. Cf. *Bryan* v. *Itasca County*, 426 U.S. 373, 390 (1976) (grant of civil jurisdiction in 28 U.S.C. § 1360 does not include regulatory jurisdiction to tax in light of tradition of immunity from taxation)." 463 U.S., at 734, n. 18.

results, by the Court of Appeals for the Fifth Circuit in Seminole Tribe of Florida v. Butterworth, 658 F. 2d 310 (1981), cert. denied, 455 U.S. 1020 (1982), which the Ninth Circuit found persuasive.[9]

We are persuaded that the prohibitory/regulatory distinction is consistent with *Bryan's* construction of Pub. L. 280. It is not a bright-line rule, however; and as the Ninth Circuit itself observed, an argument of some weight may be made that the bingo statute is prohibitory rather than regulatory. But in the present case, the court reexamined the state law and reaffirmed its holding in *Barona*, and we are reluctant to disagree with that court's view of the nature and intent of the state law at issue here.

There is surely a fair basis for its conclusion. California does not prohibit all forms of gambling. California itself operates a state lottery, Cal. Gov't Code Ann. § 8880 *et seq.* (West Supp. 1987), and daily encourages its citizens to participate in this state-run gambling. California also permits parimutuel horse-race betting. Cal. Bus. & Prof. Code Ann. §§ 19400-19667 (West 1964 and Supp. 1987). Although certain enumerated gambling games are prohibited under Cal. Penal Code Ann. § 330 (West Supp. 1987), games not enumerated, including the card games played in the Cabazon card club, are permissible. The Tribes assert that more than 400 card rooms similar to the Cabazon card club flourish in California, and the State does not dispute this fact. Brief for Appellees 47-48. Also, as the Court of Appeals noted, bingo is legally sponsored by many different organizations and is widely played in California. There is no effort to forbid the playing of bingo by any member of the public over the age of 18. Indeed, the permitted bingo games *must* be open to the general public. Nor is there any limit on the number of games which eligible organizations may operate, the

---

[9]*Seminole Tribe* v. *Butterworth* was an action by the Seminole Tribe for a declaratory judgment that the Florida bingo statute did not apply to its operation of a bingo hall on its reservation. See also *Mashantucket Pequot Tribe* v. *McGuigan,* 626 F. Supp. 245 (Conn. 1986); *Oneida Tribe of Indians of Wisconsin* v. *Wisconsin,* 518 F. Supp. 712 (WD Wis. 1981).

receipts which they may obtain from the games, the number of games which a participant may play, or the amount of money which a participant may spend, either per game or in total. In light of the fact that California permits a substantial amount of gambling activity, including bingo, and actually promotes gambling through its state lottery, we must conclude that California regulates rather than prohibits gambling in general and bingo in particular.[10]

California argues, however, that high stakes, *unregulated* bingo, the conduct which attracts organized crime, is a misdemeanor in California and may be prohibited on Indian reservations. But that an otherwise regulatory law is enforceable by criminal as well as civil means does not necessarily convert it into a criminal law within the meaning of Pub. L. 280. Otherwise, the distinction between § 2 and § 4 of that law could easily be avoided and total assimilation permitted. This view, adopted here and by the Fifth Circuit in the *Butterworth* case, we find persuasive. Accordingly, we conclude that Pub. L. 280 does not authorize California to enforce Cal. Penal Code Ann. § 326.5 (West Supp. 1987) within the Cabazon and Morongo Reservations.[11]   California and Riverside County also

---

[10]Nothing in this opinion suggests that cockfighting, tattoo parlors, nude dancing, and prostitution are permissible on Indian reservations within California. See *post*, at 222. The applicable state laws governing an activity must be examined in detail before they can be characterized as regulatory or prohibitory. The lower courts have not demonstrated an inability to identify prohibitory laws. For example, in *United States* v. *Marcyes*, 557 F. 2d 1361, 1363-1365 (CA9 1977), the Court of Appeals adopted and applied the prohibitory/regulatory distinction in determining whether a state law governing the possession of fireworks was made applicable to Indian reservations by the Assimilative Crimes Statute, 62 Stat. 686, 18 U.S.C. § 13. The court concluded that, despite limited exceptions to the statute's prohibition, the fireworks law was prohibitory in nature. See also *United States* v. *Farris*, 624 F. 2d 890 (CA9 1980), cert. denied, 449 U.S. 1111 (1981), discussed *infra*, at 213.

[11]Nor does Pub. L. 280 authorize the county to apply its gambling ordinances to the reservations. We note initially that it is doubtful that Pub. L. 280 authorizes the application of any local laws to Indian reservations. Section 2 of Pub. L. 280 provides that the criminal laws of the "State" shall have the same force and effect
(continued...)

argue that the Organized Crime Control Act (OCCA) authorizes the application of their gambling laws to the tribal bingo enterprises. The OCCA makes certain violations of state and local gambling laws violations of federal law.[12]   The Court of Appeals rejected appellants' argument, relying on its earlier decisions in *United States v. Farris*, 624 F. 2d 890 (CA9 1980), cert. denied, 449 U.S. 1111 (1981), and *Barona Group of the Capitan Grande Band of Mission Indians, San Diego County, Cal. v. Duffy*, 694 F. 2d 1185 (1982). 783 F. 2d, at 903. The court explained that whether a tribal activity is "a violation of the law of a state" within the meaning of OCCA depends on whether it violates the "public policy" of the State, the same test for application of state law under Pub. L. 280, and

---

[11](...continued)

within Indian country as they have elsewhere. This language seems clearly to exclude local laws. We need not decide this issue, however, because even if Pub. L. 280 does make local criminal/prohibitory laws applicable on Indian reservations, the ordinances in question here do not apply. Consistent with our analysis of Cal. Penal Code Ann. § 326.5 (West Supp. 1987) above, we conclude that Ordinance No. 558, the bingo ordinance, is regulatory in nature. Although Ordinance No. 331 prohibits gambling on all card games, including the games played in the Cabazon card club, the county does not prohibit municipalities within the county from enacting municipal ordinances permitting these card games, and two municipalities have in fact done so. It is clear, therefore, that Ordinance No. 331 does not prohibit these card games for purposes of Pub. L. 280.

[12]OCCA, 18 U.S.C. § 1955, provides in pertinent part:

"(a) Whoever conducts, finances, manages, supervises, directs, or owns all or part of an illegal gambling business shall be fined not more that $ 20,000 or imprisoned not more than five years, or both.

"(b) As used in this section –

"(1) 'illegal gambling business' means a gambling business which –

"(i) is a *violation of the law of a State or political subdivision* in which it is conducted;

"(ii) involves five or more persons who conduct, finance, manage, supervise, direct, or own all or part of such business; and

"(iii) has been or remains in substantially continuous operation for a period in excess of thirty days or has a gross revenue of $ 2,000 in any single day." (Emphasis added.)

---

similarly concluded that bingo is not contrary to the public policy of California.[13]

The Court of Appeals for the Sixth Circuit has rejected this view. *United States* v. *Dakota*, 796 F. 2d 186 (1986).[14] Since the OCCA standard is simply whether the gambling business is being operated in "violation of the law of a State," there is no basis for the regulatory/prohibitory distinction that it agreed is suitable in construing and applying Pub. L. 280. 796 F. 2d, at 188. And because enforcement of OCCA is an exercise of federal rather than state authority, there is no danger of state encroachment on Indian tribal sovereignty. *Ibid.* This latter observation exposes the flaw in appellants' reliance on OCCA. That enactment is indeed a federal law that, among other things, defines certain federal crimes over which the district courts have exclusive jurisdiction.[15] There is nothing in OCCA indicating that the States are to have any part in enforcing federal crimes or are authorized to make arrests on Indian reservations that in the absence of OCCA they could not effect. We are not informed of any federal efforts to employ OCCA to prosecute the playing of bingo on Indian reservations, although there are more than 100 such enterprises currently in operation, many of which have been in existence for several years, for the most part

---

[13]In *Farris*, in contrast, the court had concluded that a gambling business, featuring blackjack, poker, and dice, operated by tribal members on the Puyallup Reservation violated the public policy of Washington; the United States, therefore, could enforce OCCA against the Indians.

[14]In *Dakota*, the United States sought a declaratory judgment that a gambling business, also featuring the playing of blackjack, poker, and dice, operated by two members of the Keweenaw Bay Indian Community on land controlled by the community, and under a license issued by the community, violated OCCA. The Court of Appeals held that the gambling business violated Michigan law and OCCA.

[15]Title 18 U.S.C. § 3231 provides: "The district courts of the United States shall have original jurisdiction, exclusive of the courts of the States, of all offenses against the laws of the United States."

with the encouragement of the Federal Government.[16] Whether or not, then, the Sixth Circuit is right and the Ninth Circuit wrong about the coverage of OCCA, a matter that we do not decide, there is no warrant for California to make arrests on reservations and thus, through OCCA, enforce its gambling laws against Indian tribes.

II

Because the state and county laws at issue here are imposed directly on the Tribes that operate the games, and are not expressly permitted by Congress, the Tribes argue that the judgment below should be affirmed without more. They rely on the statement in *McClanahan* v. *Arizona State Tax Comm'n*, 411 U.S. 164, 170-171 (1973), that "'[s]tate laws generally are not applicable to tribal Indians on an Indian reservation except where Congress has expressly provided that State laws shall apply'" (quoting United States Dept. of the Interior, Federal Indian Law 845 (1958)). Our cases, however, have not established an inflexible *per se* rule precluding state jurisdiction over tribes and tribal members in the absence of express congressional consent.[17] "[U]nder certain circumstances a

---

[16]See S. Rep. No. 99-493, p. 2 (1986). Federal law enforcement officers have the capability to respond to violations of OCCA on Indian reservations, as is apparent from *Farris* and *Dakota*. This is not a situation where the unavailability of a federal officer at a particular moment would likely result in nonenforcement. OCCA is directed at large-scale gambling enterprises. If state officers discover a gambling business unknown to federal authorities while performing their duties authorized by Pub. L. 280, there should be ample time for them to inform federal authorities, who would then determine whether investigation or other enforcement action was appropriate. A federal police officer is assigned by the Department of the Interior to patrol the Indian reservations in southern California. App. to Brief for Appellees 1d-7d.

[17]In the special area of state taxation of Indian tribes and tribal members, we have adopted a *per se* rule. In *Montana* v. *Blackfeet Tribe*, 471 U.S. 759 (1985), we held that Montana could not tax the Tribe's royalty interests in oil and gas leases issued to non-Indian lessees under the Indian Mineral Leasing Act of 1938. We
(continued...)

State may validly assert authority over the activities of nonmembers on a reservation, and . . . in exceptional circumstances a State may assert jurisdiction over the on-reservation activities of tribal members." *New Mexico* v. *Mescalero Apache Tribe*, 462 U.S. 324, 331-332 (1983) (footnotes omitted). Both *Moe* v. *Confederated Salish and Kootenai Tribes*, 425 U.S. 463 (1976), and *Washington* v. *Confederated Tribes of the Colville Indian Reservation*, 447 U.S. 134 (1980), are illustrative. In those decisions we held that, in the absence of express congressional permission, a State could require tribal smokeshops on Indian reservations to collect state sales tax from their non-Indian customers. Both cases involved nonmembers entering and purchasing tobacco products on the reservations involved. The State's interest in assuring the collection of sales taxes from non-Indians enjoying the off-reservation services of the State

---

17(...continued)

stated: "In keeping with its plenary authority over Indian affairs, Congress can authorize the imposition of state taxes on Indian tribes and individual Indians. It has not done so often, and the Court consistently has held that it will find the Indians' exemption from state taxes lifted only when Congress has made its intention to do so unmistakably clear." *Id.*, at 765. We have repeatedly addressed the issue of state taxation of tribes and tribal members and the state, federal, and tribal interests which it implicates. We have recognized that the federal tradition of Indian immunity from state taxation is very strong and that the state interest in taxation is correspondingly weak. Accordingly, it is unnecessary to rebalance these interests in every case. In *Mescalero Apache Tribe* v. *Jones*, 411 U.S. 145, 148 (1973), we distinguished state taxation from other assertions of state jurisdiction. We acknowledged that we had made repeated statements "to the effect that, even on reservations, state laws may be applied unless such application would interfere with reservation self-government or would impair a right granted or reserved by federal law. . . . Even so, *in the special area of state taxation*, absent cession of jurisdiction or other federal statutes permitting it, there has been no satisfactory authority for taxing Indian reservation lands or Indian income from activities carried on within the boundaries of the reservation, and *McClanahan* v. *Arizona State Tax Comm'n*, [411 U.S. 164 (1973)], lays to rest any doubt in this respect by holding that such taxation is not permissible absent congressional consent." *Ibid.* (emphasis added).

was sufficient to warrant the minimal burden imposed on the tribal smokeshop operators.[18]

This case also involves a state burden on tribal Indians in the context of their dealings with non-Indians since the question is whether the State may prevent the Tribes from making available high stakes bingo games to non-Indians coming from outside the reservations. Decision in this case turns on whether state authority is pre-empted by the operation of federal law; and "[s]tate jurisdiction is pre-empted . . . if it interferes or is incompatible with federal and tribal interests reflected in federal law, unless the state interests at stake are sufficient to justify the assertion of state authority." *Mescalero*, 462 U.S., at 333, 334. The inquiry is to proceed in light of traditional notions of Indian sovereignty and the congressional goal of Indian self-government, including its "overriding goal" of encouraging tribal self-sufficiency and economic development. *Id.*, at 334-335.[19] See also, *Iowa Mutual Insurance Co.*

---

[18]JUSTICE STEVENS appears to embrace the opposite presumption – that state laws apply on Indian reservations absent an express congressional statement to the contrary. But, as we stated in *White Mountain Apache Tribe* v. *Bracker*, 448 U.S. 136, 151 (1980), in the context of an assertion of state authority over the activities of non-Indians within a reservation, "[t]hat is simply not the law." It is even less correct when applied to the activities of tribes and tribal members within reservations.

[19]In *New Mexico* v. *Mescalero Apache Tribe*, 462 U.S., at 335, n. 17, we discussed a number of the statutes Congress enacted to promote tribal self-government. The congressional declarations of policy in the Indian Financing Act of 1974, as amended, 25 U.S.C. § 1451 *et seq.* (1982 ed. and Supp. III), and in the Indian Self-Determination and Education Assistance Act of 1975, as amended, 25 U.S.C. 450 et seq. (1982 ed. and Supp. III), are particularly significant in this case: "It is hereby declared to be the policy of Congress . . . to help develop and utilize Indian resources, both physical and human, to a point where the Indians will fully exercise responsibility for the utilization and management of their own resources and where they will enjoy a standard of living from their own productive efforts comparable to that enjoyed by non-Indians in neighboring communities." 25 U.S.C. § 1451. Similarly, "[t]he Congress declares its commitment to the maintenance of the Federal Government's unique and continuing relationship with and responsibility to

(continued...)

---

v. *LaPlante, ante*, p. 9; *White Mountain Apache Tribe* v. *Bracker*, 448 U.S. 136, 143 (1980).

These are important federal interests. They were reaffirmed by the President's 1983 Statement on Indian Policy.[20] More specifically, the Department of the Interior, which has the primary responsibility for carrying out the Federal Government's trust obligations to Indian tribes, has sought to implement these policies by promoting tribal bingo enterprises.[21] Under the Indian Financing Act of 1974, 25 U.S.C. § 1451 *et seq.* (1982 ed. and Supp. III), the Secretary of the Interior has made grants and has guaranteed loans for the purpose

---

[19](...continued)
the Indian people through the establishment of a meaningful Indian self-determination policy which will permit an orderly transition from Federal domination of programs for and services to Indians to effective and meaningful participation by the Indian people in the planning, conduct, and administration of those programs and services." 25 U.S.C. § 450a(b).

[20]"It is important to the concept of self-government that tribes reduce their dependence on Federal funds by providing a greater percentage of the cost of their self-government." 19 Weekly Comp. Pres. Doc. 99 (1983).

[21]The Court of Appeals relied on the following official declarations. 783 F. 2d, at 904-905. A policy directive issued by the Assistant Secretary of the Interior on March 2, 1983, stated that the Department would "strongly oppose" any proposed legislation that would subject tribes or tribal members to state gambling regulation. "Such a proposal is inconsistent with the President's Indian Policy Statement of January 24, 1983. . . . A number of tribes have begun to engage in bingo and similar gambling operations on their reservations for the very purpose enunciated in the President's Message. Given the often limited resources which tribes have for revenue-producing activities, it is believed that this kind of revenue-producing possibility should be protected and enhanced." The court also relied on an affidavit submitted by the Director of Indian Services, Bureau of Indian Affairs, on behalf of the Tribes' position:
"It is the department's position that tribal bingo enterprises are an appropriate means by which tribes can further their economic self-sufficiency, the economic development of reservations and tribal self-determination. All of these are federal goals for the tribes. Furthermore, it is the Department's position that the development of tribal bingo enterprises is consistent with and in furtherance of President Reagan's Indian Policy Statement of January 24, 1983."

---

of constructing bingo facilities. See S. Rep. No. 99-493, p. 5 (1986); *Mashantucket Pequot Tribe* v. *McGuigan*, 626 F. Supp. 245, 246 (Conn. 1986). The Department of Housing and Urban Development and the Department of Health and Human Services have also provided financial assistance to develop tribal gaming enterprises. See S. Rep. No. 99-493, *supra*, at 5. Here, the Secretary of the Interior has approved tribal ordinances establishing and regulating the gaming activities involved. See H.R. Rep. No. 99-488, p. 10 (1986). The Secretary has also exercised his authority to review tribal bingo management contracts under 25 U.S.C. § 81, and has issued detailed guidelines governing that review.[22] App. to Motion to Dismiss Appeal or Affirm Judgment 63a-70a.

These policies and actions, which demonstrate the Government's approval and active promotion of tribal bingo enterprises, are of particular relevance in this case. The Cabazon and Morongo Reservations contain no natural resources which can be exploited. The tribal games at present provide the sole source of revenues for the operation of the tribal governments and the provision of tribal services. They are also the major sources of employment on the reservations. Self-determination and economic development are not within reach if the Tribes cannot raise revenues and provide employment for their members. The Tribes' interests obviously parallel the federal interests.

California seeks to diminish the weight of these seemingly important tribal interests by asserting that the Tribes are merely

---

[22]Among other things, the guidelines require that the contract state that no payments have been made or will be made to any elected member of the tribal government or relative of such member for the purpose of obtaining or maintaining the contract. The contractor is required to disclose information on all parties in interest to the contract and all employees who will have day-to-day management responsibility for the gambling operation, including names, home and business addresses, occupations, dates of birth, and Social Security numbers. The Federal Bureau of Investigation must conduct a name-and-record check on these persons before a contract may be approved. The guidelines also specify accounting procedures and cash management procedures which the contractor must follow.

marketing an exemption from state gambling laws. In *Washington* v. *Confederated Tribes of the Colville Indian Reservation*, 447 U.S., at 155, we held that the State could tax cigarettes sold by tribal smokeshops to non-Indians, even though it would eliminate their competitive advantage and substantially reduce revenues used to provide tribal services, because the Tribes had no right "to market an exemption from state taxation to persons who would normally do their business elsewhere." We stated that "[i]t is painfully apparent that the value marketed by the smokeshops to persons coming from outside is not generated on the reservations by activities in which the Tribes have a significant interest." *Ibid.* Here, however, the Tribes are not merely importing a product onto the reservations for immediate resale to non-Indians. They have built modern facilities which provide recreational opportunities and ancillary services to their patrons, who do not simply drive onto the reservations, make purchases and depart, but spend extended periods of time there enjoying the services the Tribes provide. The Tribes have strong incentive to provide comfortable, clean, and attractive facilities and well-run games in order to increase attendance at the games.[23] The tribal bingo enterprises are similar to the resort complex, featuring hunting and fishing, that the Mescalero Apache Tribe operates on its reservation through the "concerted and sustained" management of reservation land and wildlife resources. *New Mexico* v. *Mescalero Apache Tribe*, 462 U.S., at 341. The Mescalero project generates

---

[23]An agent of the California Bureau of Investigation visited the Cabazon bingo parlor as part of an investigation of tribal bingo enterprises. The agent described the clientele as follows:

"In attendance for the Monday evening bingo session were about 300 players. . . . On row 5, on the front left side were a middle-aged latin couple, who were later joined by two young latin males. These men had to have the game explained to them. The middle table was shared with a senior citizen couple. The aisle table had 2 elderly women, 1 in a wheelchair, and a middle-aged woman. . . . A goodly portion of the crowd were retired age to senior citizens." App. 176. We are unwilling to assume that these patrons would be indifferent to the services offered by the Tribes.

funds for essential tribal services and provides employment for tribal members. We there rejected the notion that the tribe is merely marketing an exemption from state hunting and fishing regulations and concluded that New Mexico could not regulate on-reservation fishing and hunting by non-Indians. *Ibid.* Similarly, the Cabazon and Morongo Bands are generating value on the reservations through activities in which they have a substantial interest.

The State also relies on *Rice* v. *Rehner*, 463 U.S. 713 (1983), in which we held that California could require a tribal member and a federally licensed Indian trader operating a general store on a reservation to obtain a state license in order to sell liquor for off-premises consumption. But our decision there rested on the grounds that Congress had never recognized any sovereign tribal interest in regulating liquor traffic and that Congress, historically, had plainly anticipated that the States would exercise concurrent authority to regulate the use and distribution of liquor on Indian reservations. There is no such traditional federal view governing the outcome of this case, since, as we have explained, the current federal policy is to promote precisely what California seeks to prevent.

The sole interest asserted by the State to justify the imposition of its bingo laws on the Tribes is in preventing the infiltration of the tribal games by organized crime. To the extent that the State seeks to prevent any and all bingo games from being played on tribal lands while permitting regulated, off-reservation games, this asserted interest is irrelevant and the state and county laws are pre-empted. See n. 3, *supra.* Even to the extent that the State and county seek to regulate short of prohibition, the laws are preempted. The State insists that the high stakes offered at tribal games are attractive to organized crime, whereas the controlled games authorized under California law are not. This is surely a legitimate concern, but we are unconvinced that it is sufficient to escape the pre-emptive force of federal and tribal interests apparent in this case. California does not allege any present criminal involvement in the Cabazon and Morongo enterprises, and the Ninth Circuit discerned none. 783 F. 2d, at 904. An official of the Department of Justice has expressed some concern about tribal bingo operations,[24] but far from any action being taken evidencing this concern -- and surely the Federal Government has the authority to forbid Indian gambling enterprises -- the prevailing federal policy continues to support these tribal enterprises, including those of the Tribes involved in this case.[25]

We conclude that the State's interest in preventing the infiltration of the tribal bingo enterprises by organized crime does not justify state regulation of the tribal bingo enterprises in light of the compelling federal and tribal interests supporting them. State regulation would impermissibly infringe on tribal government, and this conclusion applies equally to the county's attempted regulation of the Cabazon card club. We therefore affirm the judgment of the Court of Appeals and remand the case for further proceedings consistent with this opinion.

It is so ordered.

DISSENT BY: STEVENS

DISSENT:

---

[24]Hearings on H.R. 4566 before the House Committee on Interior and Insular Affairs, 98th Cong., 2d Sess., 15-39, 66-75 (1984); App. 197-205.

[25]JUSTICE STEVENS' assertion, *post*, at 226, that the State's interest in restricting the proceeds of gambling to itself, and the charities it favors, justifies the prohibition or regulation of tribal bingo games is indeed strange. The State asserted no such discriminatory economic interest; and it is pure speculation that, in the absence of tribal bingo games, would-be patrons would purchase lottery tickets or would attend state-approved bingo games instead. In any event, certainly California has no legitimate interest in allowing potential lottery dollars to be diverted to non-Indian owners of card clubs and horse tracks while denying Indian tribes the opportunity to profit from gambling activities. Nor is California necessarily entitled to prefer the funding needs of state-approved charities over the funding needs of the Tribes, who dedicate bingo revenues to promoting the health, education, and general welfare of tribal members.

JUSTICE STEVENS, with whom JUSTICE O'CONNOR and JUSTICE SCALIA join, dissenting.

Unless and until Congress exempts Indian-managed gambling from state law and subjects it to federal supervision, I believe that a State may enforce its laws prohibiting high-stakes gambling on Indian reservations within its borders. Congress has not pre-empted California's prohibition against high-stakes bingo games and the Secretary of the Interior plainly has no authority to do so. While gambling provides needed employment and income for Indian tribes, these benefits do not, in my opinion, justify tribal operation of currently unlawful commercial activities. Accepting the majority's reasoning would require exemptions for cockfighting, tattoo parlors, nude dancing, houses of prostitution, and other illegal but profitable enterprises. As the law now stands, I believe tribal entrepreneurs, like others who might derive profits from catering to non-Indian customers, must obey applicable state laws.

In my opinion the plain language of Pub. L. 280, 67 Stat. 588, as amended, 18 U.S.C. § 1162, 28 U.S.C. § 1360 (1982 ed. and Supp. III), authorizes California to enforce its prohibition against commercial gambling on Indian reservations. The State prohibits bingo games that are not operated by members of designated charitable organizations or which offer prizes in excess of $ 250 per game. Cal. Penal Code Ann. § 326.5 (West Supp. 1987). In § 2 of Pub. L. 280, Congress expressly provided that the criminal laws of the State of California "shall have the same force and effect within such Indian country as they have elsewhere within the State." 18 U.S.C. § 1162(a). Moreover, it provided in § 4(a) that the civil laws of California "that are of general application to private persons or private property shall have the same force and effect within such Indian country as they have elsewhere within the State." 28 U.S.C. § 1360(a) (1982 ed., Supp. III).

It is true that in *Bryan* v. *Atasca County*, 426 U.S. 373 (1976), we held that Pub. L. 280 did not confer civil jurisdiction on a State to impose a personal property tax on a mobile home that was owned by a reservation Indian and located within the reservation. Moreover, the reasoning of that decision recognizes the importance of preserving the traditional aspects of tribal sovereignty over the relationships among reservation Indians. Our more recent cases have made it clear, however, that commercial transactions between Indians and non-Indians – even when conducted on a reservation – do not enjoy any blanket immunity from state regulation. In *Rice* v. *Rehner*, 463 U.S. 713 (1983), respondent, a federally licensed Indian trader, was a tribal member operating a general store on an Indian reservation. We held that the State could require Rehner to obtain a state license to sell liquor for off-premises consumption. The Court attempts to distinguish *Rice* v. *Rehner* as resting on the absence of a sovereign tribal interest in the regulation of liquor traffic to the exclusion of the States. But as a necessary step on our way to deciding that the State could regulate all tribal liquor sales in Indian country, we recognized the State's authority over transactions, whether they be liquor sales or gambling, between Indians and non-Indians: "If there is any interest in tribal sovereignty implicated by imposition of California's alcoholic beverage regulation, it exists only insofar as the State attempts to regulate Rehner's sale of liquor to other members of the Pala Tribe on the Pala Reservation." Id., at 721. Similarly, in *Washington* v. *Confederated Tribes of the Colville Indian Reservation*, 447 U.S. 134 (1980), we held that a State could impose its sales and cigarette taxes on non-Indian customers of smokeshops on Indian reservations.

Today the Court seems prepared to acknowledge that an Indian tribe's commercial transactions with non-Indians may violate "the State's public policy." *Ante*, at 209. The Court reasons, however, that the operation of high-stakes bingo games does not run afoul of California's public policy because the State permits some forms of gambling and, specifically, some forms of bingo. I find this approach to "public policy" curious, to say the least. The State's policy concerning gambling is to authorize certain specific gambling activities that comply with carefully defined regulation and that provide revenues either for the State itself or for certain charitable purposes, and to prohibit all unregulated commercial lotteries that are operated for private profit.[1] To argue that the tribal bingo games comply with the public policy of California because the State permits some other gambling is tantamount to arguing that driving over 60 miles an hour is consistent with public policy because the State allows driving at speeds of up to 55 miles an hour.

In my view, Congress has permitted the State to apply its prohibitions against commercial gambling to Indian Tribes. Even if Congress had not done so, however, the State has the authority to assert jurisdiction over appellees' gambling activities. We recognized this authority in *Washington v. Confederated Tribes, supra*; the Court's attempt to distinguish the reasoning of our decision in that case is unpersuasive. In *Washington v. Confederated Tribes*, the Tribes contended that the State had no power to tax on-reservation sales of cigarettes to non-Indians. The argument that we rejected there has a familiar ring:

"The Tribes contend that their involvement in the operation and taxation of cigarette marketing on the reservation ousts the State from any power to exact its sales and cigarette taxes from nonmembers purchasing cigarettes at tribal smokeshops. The primary argument is economic. It is asserted that smokeshop cigarette sales generate substantial revenues for the Tribes which they expend for essential governmental services, including programs to combat severe poverty and underdevelopment at the

---

[1]The Court holds that Pub. L. 280 does not authorize California to enforce its prohibition against commercial gambling within the Cabazon and Morongo Reservations. *Ante*, at 212. The Court reaches this conclusion by determining that § 4(a) of Pub. L. 280, 28 U.S.C. § 1360(a), withholds from the States general civil regulatory authority over Indian tribes, and that the State's rules concerning gambling are regulatory rather than prohibitory. In its opinion, the Court dismisses the State's argument that high-stakes, unregulated bingo is prohibited with the contention that an otherwise regulatory law does not become a prohibition simply because it "is enforceable by criminal as well as civil means." *Ante*, at 211. Aside from the questionable merit of this proposition, it does not even address the meaning of § 2(a) of Pub. L. 280, 18 U.S.C. 1162(a) (1982 ed., Supp. III), a provision which is sufficient to control the disposition of this case. See *supra*, at 222.

reservations. Most cigarette purchasers are outsiders attracted onto the reservations by the bargain prices the smokeshops charge by virtue of their claimed exemption from state taxation. If the State is permitted to impose its taxes, the Tribes will no longer enjoy any competitive advantage vis-à-vis businesses in surrounding areas." *Id.*, at 154.

"What the smokeshops offer these customers, and what is not available elsewhere, is solely an exemption from state taxation." *Id.*, at 155.I

In *Confederated Tribes*, the tribal smokeshops offered their customers the same products, services, and facilities that other tobacconists offered to their customers. Although the smokeshops were more modest than the bingo palaces involved in this case, presumably they were equally the product of tribal labor and tribal capital. What made them successful, however, was the value of the exemption that was offered to non-Indians "who would normally do their business elsewhere." *Id.*, at 155.

Similarly, it is painfully obvious that the value of the Tribe's asserted exemption from California's gambling laws is the primary attraction to customers who would normally do their gambling elsewhere. The Cabazon Band of Mission Indians has no tradition or special expertise in the operation of large bingo parlors. See Declaration of William J. Wallace, ¶2, App. 153, 171. Indeed, the entire membership of the Cabazon Tribe – it has only 25 enrolled members – is barely adequate to operate a bingo game that is patronized by hundreds of non-Indians nightly. How this small and formerly impoverished band of Indians could have attracted the investment capital for its enterprise without benefit of the claimed exemption is certainly a mystery to me.

I am entirely unpersuaded by the Court's view that the State of California has no legitimate interest in requiring appellees' gambling business to comply with the same standards that the operators of other bingo games must observe. The State's interest is both economic and protective. Presumably the State has determined that its interest in generating revenues for the public fisc and for certain charities outweighs the benefits from a total prohibition against publicly sponsored games of chance. Whatever revenues the Tribes receive from their unregulated bingo games drain funds from the state-approved recipients of lottery revenues – just as the tax-free cigarette sales in the *Confederated Tribes* case diminished the receipts that the tax collector would otherwise have received.

Moreover, I am unwilling to dismiss as readily as the Court does the State's concern that these unregulated high-stakes bingo games may attract organized criminal infiltration. Brief for Appellants 25-26, 29; Reply Brief for Appellants 12. Comprehensive regulation of the commercial gambling ventures that a State elects to license is obviously justified as a prophylactic measure even if there is presently no criminal activity associated with casino gambling in the State. Indeed, California regulates charitable bingo, horseracing, and its own lottery. The State of California requires that charitable bingo games may only be operated and staffed by members of designated charitable organizations, and that proceeds from the games may only be used for charitable purposes. Cal. Penal Code Ann. § 326.5 (West Supp. 1987). These requirements for staffing and for dispersal of profits provide bulwarks against criminal activity; neither safeguard exists for bingo games on Indian reservations.[2] In my judgment, unless Congress authorizes and regulates these commercial gambling ventures catering to non-Indians, the State has a legitimate law enforcement interest in proscribing them.

Appellants and the Secretary of the Interior may well be correct, in the abstract, that gambling facilities are a sensible way to generate revenues that are badly needed by reservation Indians. But the

---

[2]The Cabazon Band's bingo room was operated under a management agreement with an outside firm until 1986; the Morongo Band operates its bingo room under a similar management agreement. App. to Brief for Appellees, C-1 to C-3; Morongo Band of Mission Indians Tribal Bingo Enterprise Management Agreement, ¶4B, App. 97-98.

---

decision to adopt, to reject, or to define the precise contours of such a course of action, and thereby to set aside the substantial public policy concerns of a sovereign State, should be made by the Congress of the United States. It should not be made by this Court, by the temporary occupant of the Office of the Secretary of the Interior, or by non-Indian entrepreneurs who are experts in gambling management but not necessarily dedicated to serving the future well-being of Indian tribes.

I respectfully dissent.

> Text was obtained from LEXIS courtesy of Mead Data Control.

B

PUBLIC LAW 100-497
OCTOBER 17, 1988

100th Congress

An Act

To regulate gaming on Indian Lands.

Be it enacted by the Senate and House of Representatives of the United States of America in Congress assembled,
That this Act may be cited as the "Indian Gaming Regulatory Act.

FINDINGS

Sec. 2. The Congress finds that–

(1)   numerous Indian tribes have become engaged in or have licensed gaming activities on Indian lands as a means of generating tribal governmental revenue;

(2)   Federal courts have held that section 2103 of the Revised Statues (25 U.S.C. 81) requires Secretarial review of management contracts dealing with Indian gaming, but does not provide standards for approval of such contracts;

(3)   existing Federal law does not provide clear standards or regulations for the conduct of gaming on Indian lands:

(4)   a principal goal of Federal Indian policy is to promote tribal economic development, tribal self-sufficiency, and strong tribal government; and

(5)   Indian tribes have the exclusive right to regulate gaming activity on Indian lands if the gaming activity is not specifically prohibited by federal law and is conducted within a State which does not, as a matter of criminal law and public policy, prohibit such gaming activity.

DECLARATION OF POLICY

Sec. 3. The purpose of the Act is–

(1)   to provide a statutory basis for the operation of gaming by Indian tribes as a means of promoting tribal economic development, self-sufficiency, and strong tribal governments;

(2)   to provide a statutory basis for the regulation of gaming by an Indian tribe adequate to shield it from organized crime and other corrupting influences, to ensure that the Indian tribe is the primary

beneficiary of the gaming operation, and to assure that gaming is conducted fairly and honestly by both the operator and players;   and

(3)   to declare that the establishment of independent Federal regulatory authority for gaming on Indian lands, the establishment of Federal standards for gaming on Indian lands, and the establishment of a National Indian Gaming commission are necessary to meet congressional concerns regarding gaming and to protect such gaming as a means of generating tribal revenue.

DEFINITIONS

Sec. 4.   For purposes of this Act–

(1)   The term "Attorney General" means the Attorney General of the United States.

(2)   The term "Chairman means the Chairman of the National Indian Gaming Commission.

(3)   The term "Commission" means the National Indian Gaming Commission established pursuant to section 5 of this Act.

(4)   The term "Indian lands" means–

(A) all lands within the limits of any Indian reservation; and

(B) any lands title to which is either held in trust by the United States for the benefit of any Indian tribe or individual or held by any Indian tribe or individual subject to restriction by the United States against alienation and over which an Indian tribe exercises governmental power.

(5)   The term "Indian tribe" means any indian tribe, band, nation, or other organized group or community of Indians which–

(A) is recognized as eligible by the Secretary for the special programs and services provided by the United States to Indians because of their status as Indians, and

(B) is recognized as possessing powers of self-government.

(6)   The term "class I gaming" means social games solely for prizes of minimal value or traditional forms of Indian gaming engaged in by individuals as a part of, or in connection with, tribal ceremonies or celebrations.

(7)(A)The term "class II gaming" means–

(i)   the game of chance commonly known as bingo (whether or not electronics, computer, or other technologic aids are used in connection therewith)–

(I)   which is played for prizes, including monetary prizes, with cards bearing numbers or other designations,

(II)   in which the holder of the card covers such numbers or designations when objects, similarly numbered or designated, are drawn or electronically determined, and

(III)   in which the game is won by the first person covering a previously designated arrangement of numbers or designations on such cards,

including (if played in the same location) pull-tabs, lotto, punch boards, tip jars, instant bingo, and other games similar to bingo, and

(ii)   card games that–

(I)   are explicitly authorized by the laws of the State, or

(II)   are not explicitly prohibited by the laws of the state and are played at any location in the State,

but only if such card games are played in conformity with those laws and regulations (if any) of the State regarding hours or periods of operation of such card games or limitations on wagers or pot sizes in such card games.

(B)   The term "class II gaming" does note include–

(i)   any banking card games, including baccarat, chemin de fer, or blackjack (21), or

(ii)   electronic or electromechanical facsimiles of any game of chance or slot machines of any kind.

(C)   Notwithstanding any other provision of this paragraph, the term "class II gaming" includes those card games played in the State of Michigan, the State of North Dakota, the State of South Dakota, or the State of Washington, that were actually operated in such State by an Indian tribe on or before May 1, 1988, but only to the extent of the nature and scope of the card games that were actually operated by an Indian tribe in such State on or before such date, as determined by the Chairman.

(D) Notwithstanding any other provision of this paragraph, the term "class II gaming" includes, during the 1-year period beginning on the date of enactment of this Act, any gaming described in subparagraph (B)(ii) that was legally operated on Indian lands on or before May 1, 1988, if the Indian tribe having jurisdiction over the lands on which such gaming was operated requests the State, by no later than the date that is 30 days after the date of enactment of this Act, to negotiate a Tribal-state compact under section 11(d)(3).

(8) The term "class III gaming" means all forms of gaming that are not class I gaming or class II gaming.

(9) The term "net revenues" means gross revenues of an Indian gaming activity less amounts paid out as, or paid for, prizes and total operating expenses, excluding management fees.

(10) The term "Secretary" means the Secretary of the Interior.

NATIONAL INDIAN GAMING COMMISSION

Sec.5.(a) There is established within the Department of the Interior a Commission to be known as the National Indian Gaming Commission.

(b)(1) The Commission shall be composed of three full-time members who shall be appointed as follows:

(A) a Chairman, who shall be appointed by the President with the advice and consent of the Senate; and

(B) two associate members who shall be appointed by the Secretary of the Interior.

(2) (A) The Attorney General shall conduct a background investigation on any person considered for appointment to the Commission.

(B) The secretary shall publish in the federal Register the name and other information the Secretary deems pertinent regarding a nominee for membership on the Commission and shall allow a period of not less than thirty days for receipt of public comment.

(3) Not more than two members of the Commission shall be of the same political party. At least two members of the Commission shall be enrolled members of any Indian tribe.

(4)(A) Except as provided in subparagraph (B), the term of office of the members of the commission shall be three years.

(B) Of the Initial members of the Commission–

(i) two members, including the Chairman, shall have a term of office of three years; and

(ii) one member shall have a term of office of one year.

(5) No individual shall be eligible for any appointment to, or to continue service on, the Commission, who–

(A) has been convicted of a felony or gaming offense;

(B) has any financial interest in, or management responsibility for, any gaming activity; or

(C) has a financial interest in, or management responsibility for, any management contract approved pursuant to section 12 of this Act.

(6) A Commissioner may only be removed from office before the expiration of the term of office of the member by the President (or, in the case of associate member, by the Secretary) for neglect of duty, or malfeasance in office, or for other good cause shown.

(c) Vacancies occurring on the Commission shall be filled in the same manner as the original appointment. A member may serve after the expiration of his term of office until his successor has been appointed, unless the member has been removed for cause under subsection (b)(6).

(d) Two members of the Commission, at least one of which is the Chairman or Vice Chairman, shall constitute a quorum.

(e) The Commission shall select, by majority vote, one of the members of the Commission to serve as Vice Chairman. The Vice Chairman shall serve as Chairman during meetings of the Commission in the absence of the Chairman.

(f) The Commission shall meet at the Call of the Chairman or a majority of its members, but shall meet at least once every 4 months.

(g)(1) The Chairman of the Commission shall be paid at a rate equal to that of level IV of the Executive Schedule under section 5315 of title 5, United States Code.

(2) The associate members of the Commission shall each be paid at a rate equal to that of level V of the Executive Schedule under section 5316 of title 5, United States Code.

(3) All members of the Commission shall be reimbursed in accordance with title 5, United States Code, for travel, subsistence, and other necessary expenses incurred by them in the performance of their duties.

POWERS OF THE CHAIRMAN

Sec. 6. (A) The Chairman, on behalf of the Commission, shall have power, subject to an appeal to the Commission, to–

(1) issue orders of temporary closure of gaming activities as provided in section 14(b).

(2) levy and collect civil fines as provided in section 14(a);

(3) approve tribal ordinances or resolutions regulating class II gaming and class III gaming as provided in section 11; and

(4) approve management contracts for class II gaming and class III gaming as provided sections 11(d)(9) and 12.

(b) The Chairman shall have such other powers as may be delegated by the Commission.

POWERS OF THE COMMISSION

Sec. 7. (a) The Commission shall have the power, not subject to delegation–

(1) upon the recommendation of the Chairman, to approve the annual budget of the Commission as provided in section 18;

(2) to adopt regulations for the assessment and collection of civil fines as provided in section 14(a);

(3) by an affirmative vote of not less that 2 members, to establish the rate of fees as provided in section 18;

(4) by an affirmative vote of not less than 2 members, to authorize the Chairman to issue subpoenas as provided in section 16; and

(5) by an affirmative vote of not less than 2 members and after a full hearing, to make permanent a temporary order of the Chairman closing a gaming activity as provided in section 14(b)(2).

(b) The Commission–

(1) shall monitor class II gaming conducted on Indian lands on a continuing basis;

(2) shall inspect and examine all premises located on Indian lands on which class II gaming is conducted,

(3) shall conduct or cause to be conducted such background investigations as may be necessary;

(4) may demand access to and inspect, examine, photocopy, and audit all papers, books and records respecting gross revenues of class II gaming conducted on Indian lands and any other matters necessary to carry out the duties of the Commission under this Act;

(5) may use the United States mail in the same manner and under the same conditions as any department or agency of the United States;

(6) may procure supplies, services, and property by contract in accordance with applicable Federal laws and regulations;

(7) may enter into contracts with Federal, State, tribal and private entities for activities necessary to the discharge of the duties of the Commission and, to the extent feasible, contract the enforcement of the Commission's regulations with the Indian tribes;

(8) may hold such hearings, sit and act at such times and places, take such testimony, and receive such evidence as the Commission deems appropriate;

(9) may administer oaths or affirmations to witnesses appearing before the Commission; and

(10) shall promulgate such regulations and guidelines as it deems appropriate to implement the provisions of this Act.

(c) The Commission shall submit a report with minority views, if any, to the Congress on December 31, 1989, and every two years thereafter. The report shall include information on–

(1) whether the associate commissioners should continue as full or part-time officials;

(2) funding, including income and expenses, of the Commission;

(3) recommendations for amendments to the Act; and

(4) any other matter considered appropriate by the Commission.

COMMISSION STAFFING

Sec. 8. (a) The Chairman shall appoint a General Counsel to the Commission who shall be paid at the annual rate of basic pay payable for GS-18 of the General Schedule under section 5332 of title 5, United States Code.

(b) The Chairman shall appoint and supervise other staff of the Commission without regard to the provisions of title 5, United States Code, governing appointments in the competitive service. Such staff shall be paid without regard to the provisions of chapter 51 and subchapter III of chapter 53 of such title relating to classification and General Schedule pay rates, except that no individual so appointed may receive pay in excess of the annual rate of basic pay payable for GS-17 of the General Schedule under section 5332 of that title.

(c) The Chairman may procure temporary and intermittent services under section 3109(b) of title 5, United States Code, but at rates for individuals not to exceed the daily equivalent of the maximum annual rate of basic pay payable for GS-18 of the General Schedule.

(d) Upon the request of the Chairman, the head of any Federal agency is authorized to detail any of the personnel of such agency to the Commission to assist the Commission in carrying out its duties under this Act, unless otherwise prohibited by law.

(e) The Secretary or Administrator of General Services shall provide to the Commission on a reimbursable basis such administrative support services as the Commission may request.

COMMISSION-ACCESS TO INFORMATION

Sec. 9. The Commission may secure from any department or agency of the United States information necessary to enable it to carry out this Act. Upon the request of the Chairman, the head of such department or agency shall furnish such information to the Commission, unless otherwise prohibited by law.

INTERIM AUTHORITY TO REGULATE GAMING

Sec. 10. Notwithstanding any other provision of this Act, the Secretary shall continue to exercise those authorities vested in the Secretary on the day before the date of enactment of this Act relating to supervision of Indian gaming until such time as the Commission is organized and prescribes regulations. The Secretary shall provide staff and support assistance to facilitate an orderly transition to regulation of Indian gaming by the Commission.

TRIBAL GAMING ORDINANCES

Sec. 11. (a)(1) Class I gaming on Indian lands is within the exclusive jurisdiction of the Indian tribes and shall not be subject to the provisions of this Act.

(2) Any class II gaming on Indian lands shall continue to be within the jurisdiction of the Indian tribes, but shall be subject to the provisions of this Act.

(b)(1) An Indian tribe may engage in, or license and regulate, class II gaming on Indian lands within such tribe's jurisdiction, if–

(A) such Indian gaming is located within a State that permits such gaming for any purpose by any person, organization or entity (and such gaming is not otherwise specifically prohibited on Indian lands by Federal law), and

(B) the governing body of the Indian tribe adopts an ordinance or resolution which is approved by the Chairman.

A separate license issued by the Indian tribe shall be required for each place, facility, or location on Indian lands at which class II gaming is conducted.

(2) The Chairman shall approve any tribal ordinance or resolution concerning the conduct, or regulation of class II gaming on the Indian lands within the tribe's jurisdiction if such ordinance or resolution provides that–

(A) except as provided in paragraph (4), the Indian tribe will have the sole proprietary interest and responsibility for the conduct of any gaming activity;

(B) net revenues from any tribal gaming are not to be used for purposes other than–

(i)   to fund tribal government operations or programs;

(ii)   to provide for the general welfare of the Indian tribe and its members,

(iii) to promote tribal economic development;

(iv)   to donate to charitable organizations; or

(v)   to help fund operations of local government agencies;

(C) annual outside audits of the gaming, which may be encompassed within existing independent tribal audit systems, will be provided by the Indian tribe to the Commission;

(D) all contracts for supplies, services, or concessions for a contract amount in excess of $25,000 annually (except contracts for professional legal or accounting services) relating to such gaming shall be subject to such independent audits;

(E) the construction and maintenance of the gaming facility, and the operation of that gaming is conducted in a manner which adequately protects the environment and the public health and safety; and

(F) there is an adequate system which–

(i) ensures that background investigations are conducted on the primary management officials and key employees of the gaming enterprise and that oversight of such officials and their management is conducted on an ongoing basis; and

(ii) includes–

(I) tribal licenses for primary management officials and key employees of the gaming enterprise with prompt notification to the Commission of the issuance of such licenses;

(II) a standard whereby any person whose prior activities, criminal record, if any, or reputation, habits and associations pose a threat to the public interest or to the effective regulation of gaming, or create or enhance the dangers of unsuitable, unfair, or illegal practices and methods and activities in the conduct of gaming shall not be eligible for employment; and

(III) notification by the Indian tribe to the Commission of the results of such background check before the issuance of any of such licenses.

(3) Net revenues from any class II gaming activities conducted or licensed by any Indian tribe may be used to make per capita payments to members of the Indian tribe only if–

(A) the Indian tribe has prepared a plan to allocate revenues to uses authorized by paragraph (2)(B);

(B) the plan is approved by the Secretary as adequate, particularly with respect to uses described in clause (i) or (iii) of paragraph (2)(B);

(C) the interests of minors and other legally incompetent persons who are entitled to receive any of the per capita payments are protected and preserved and the per capita payments are disbursed to the parents or legal guardian of such minors or legal incompetents in such amounts as may be necessary for the health, education, or welfare, of the minor or other legally incompetent person under a plan approved by the Secretary and the governing body of the Indian tribe; and

(D) the per capita payments are subject to Federal taxation and tribes notify members of such tax liability when payments are made.

(4)(A) A tribal ordinance or resolution may provide for the licensing or regulation of class II gaming activities owned by any person or entity other than the Indian tribe and conducted on Indian lands, only if the tribal licensing requirements include the requirements described in subclauses of subparagraph (B)(i) and are at least as restrictive as those established by State law governing similar gaming with the jurisdiction of the State within which such Indian lands are located. No person or entity, other than the Indian tribe, shall be eligible to receive a tribal license to own a class II gaming activity conducted on Indian lands within the jurisdiction of the Indian tribe if such person or entity would not be eligible to receive a State license to conduct the same activity within the jurisdiction of the State.

(B)(i) The provisions of subparagraph (A) of this paragraph and the provisions of subparagraphs (A) and (B) of paragraph (2) shall not bar the continued operation of an individually owned class II gaming operation that was operating on September 1, 1986, if-

(I) such gaming operation is licensed and regulated by and Indian tribe pursuant to an ordinance reviewed and approved by the Commission in accordance with section 13 of the Act,

(II) income to the Indian tribe from such gaming is used only for the purposes described in paragraph (2)(B) of this subsection,

(III) not less than 60 percent of the net revenues is income to the Indian tribe, and

(IV) the owner of such gaming operation pays an appropriate assessment to the National Indian Gaming

Commission under section 18(a)(1) for regulation of such gaming.

(ii) The exemption from the application of this subsection provided under this subparagraph may not be transferred to any person or entity and shall remain in effect only so long as the gaming activity remains within the same nature and scope as operated on the date of enactment of this Act.

(iii) Within sixty days of the date of enactment of this Act, the Secretary shall prepare a list of each individually owned gaming operation to which clause (i) applies and shall publish such list in the Federal Register.

(c)(1) The Commission may consult with appropriate law enforcement officials concerning gaming licenses issued by an Indian tribe and shall have thirty days to notify the Indian tribe of any objections to issuance of such license.

(2) If, after the issuance of a gaming license by an Indian tribe, reliable information is received from the Commission indicating that a primary management official or key employee does not meet the standard established under subsection (b)(2)(F)(ii)(II), the Indian tribe shall suspend such license and, after notice and hearing, may revoke such license.

(3) Any Indian tribe which operates a class II gaming activity and which–

(A) has continuously conducted such activity for a period of not less than three years, including at least on year after the date of the enactment of this Act; and

(B) has otherwise complied with the provisions of this section may petition the Commission for a certificate of self-regulation.

(4) The Commission shall issue a certificate of self-regulation if it determines from available information, and after a hearing if requested by the tribe, that the tribe has–

(A) conducted its gaming activity in a manner which–

(i) has resulted in an effective and honest accounting of all revenues;

(ii)   has resulted in a reputation for safe, fair, and honest operation of the activity; and

(iii)   has been generally free of evidence of criminal or dishonest activity;

(B)   adopted and is implementing adequate systems for–

(i)   accounting for all revenues from the activity;

(ii)   investigation, licensing, and monitoring of all employees of the gaming activity; and

(iii)   investigation, enforcement and prosecution of violations of its gaming ordinance and regulations; and

(C)   conducted the operation on a fiscally and economically sound basis.

(5)   During any year in which a tribe has a certificate for self-regulation–

(A)   the tribe shall not be subject to the provisions of paragraphs (1), (2), (3), and (4) of section 7(b);

(B)   the tribe shall continue to submit an annual independent audit as required by section 11(b)(2)(C) and shall submit to the Commission a complete resume on all employees hired and licensed by the tribe subsequent to the issuance of a certificate of self-regulation; and

(C)   the Commission may not assess a fee on such activity pursuant to section 18 in excess of one quarter of 1 per centum of the gross revenue.

(6)   The Commission may, for just cause and after an opportunity for a hearing, remove a certificate of self-regulation by majority vote of its members.

(d)(1) Class III gaming activities shall be lawful on Indian lands only if such activities are–

(A)   authorized by an ordinance or resolution that–

(i)   is adopted by the governing body of the Indian tribe having jurisdiction over such lands,

(ii)   meets the requirements of subsection (b), and

(iii)   is approved by the Chairman,

(B)   located in a State that permits such gaming for any purpose by any person, organization, or entity, and

(C)   conducted in conformance with a Tribal-State compact entered into by the Indian tribe and the State under paragraph (3) that is in effect.

(2)(A)   If any Indian tribe proposes to engage in, or to authorize any person or entity to engage in, a class III gaming activity on Indian lands of the Indian tribe, the governing body of the Indian tribe shall adopt and submit to the Chairman an ordinance or resolution that meets the requirements of subsection (b).

(B) The Chairman shall approve any ordinance or resolution described in subparagraph (A), unless the chairman specifically determines that–

(i)   the ordinance or resolution was not adopted in compliance with the governing documents of the Indian tribe, or

(ii)   the tribal governing body was significantly and unduly influenced in the adoption of such ordinance or resolution by any person identified in section 12(e)(1)(D).

Upon the approval of such an ordinance or resolution, the Chairman shall publish in the Federal Register such ordinance or resolution and the order of approval.

(C) Effective with the publication under subparagraph (B) of an ordinance or resolution adopted by the governing body of an Indian tribe that has been approved by the Chairman under subparagraph (B), class III gaming activity on the Indian lands of the Indian tribe shall be fully subject to the terms and conditions of the tribal-State compact entered into under paragraph (3) by the Indian tribe that is in effect.

(D)(i) The governing body of an Indian tribe, in its sole discretion and without the approval of the Chairman, may adopt an ordinance or resolution revoking any prior ordinance or resolution that authorized class III gaming on the Indian Lands of the Indian tribe. Such revocation shall render class III gaming illegal on the Indian lands of such Indian tribe.

(ii) The Indian tribe shall submit any revocation ordinance or resolution describe in clause (i) to the Chairman. The Chairman shall publish such ordinance or resolution in the Federal Register and the revocation provided by such ordinance or resolution shall take effect on the date of such publication.

(iii) Notwithstanding any other provision of this subsection–

(I) any person or entity operating a class III gaming activity pursuant to this paragraph on the date on which an ordinance or resolution described in clause (i) that revokes authorization for such class III gaming activity is published in the Federal Register may, during the 1-year period beginning on the date on which such revocation ordinance or resolution is published under clause (ii), continue to operate such activity in conformance with the Tribal-State compact entered into under paragraph (3) that is in effect, and

(II) any civil action that arises before, and any crime that is committed before, the close of such 1-year period shall not be affected by such revocation ordinance or resolution.

(3)(A) Any Indian tribe having jurisdiction over the Indian lands upon which a class III gaming activity is being conducted, or is to be conducted, shall request the state in which such lands are located to enter into negotiations for the purpose of entering into a Tribal-State compact governing the conduct of gaming activities. Upon receiving such a request, the State shall negotiate with the Indian tribe in good faith to enter into such a compact.

(B) Any State and any Indian tribe may enter into a Tribal-State compact governing gaming activities on the Indian lands of the Indian tribe, but such compact shall take effect only when notice of approval by the Secretary of such compact has been published by the Secretary in the Federal Register.

(C) Any Tribal-State compact negotiated under subparagraph (A) may include provisions relating to–

(i) the application of the criminal and civil laws and regulations of the Indian tribe or the State that are directly related to, and necessary for, the licensing and regulation of such activity;

(ii)   the allocation of criminal and civil jurisdiction between the State and the Indian tribe necessary for enforcement of such laws and regulations;

(iii)   the assessment by the State of such activities in such amounts as are necessary to defray the costs of regulating such activity;

(iv)   taxation by the Indian tribe of such activity in amounts comparable to amounts assessed by the State for comparable activities;

(v)   remedies for breach of contract;

(vi)   standards for the operation of such activity and maintenance of the gaming facility, including licensing; and

(vii)   any other subjects that are directly related to the operation of gaming activities.

(4)   Except for any assessments that may be agreed to under paragraph (3)(C)(iii) of this subsection, nothing in this section shall be interpreted as conferring upon a State or any of its political subdivisions authority to impose any tax, fee, charge, or other assessment upon an Indian tribe or upon any other person or entity authorized by an Indian tribe to engage in a class III activity. No State may refuse to enter into the negotiations described in paragraph (3)(A) based upon the lack of authority in such State or its political subdivision to impose such a tax, fee, charge, or other assessment.

(5)   Nothing in this subsection shall impair the right of an Indian tribe to regulate class III gaming on its Indian lands concurrently with the State, except to the extent that such regulation is inconsistent with, or less stringent than, the state laws and regulations made applicable by any Tribal-State compact entered into by the Indian tribe under paragraph (3) that is in effect.

(6)   The provisions of section 5 of the Act of January 2, 1951 (64 Stat.1135) shall not apply to any gaming conducted under a Tribal-State compact that–

(A) is entered into under paragraph (3) by a State in which gambling devices are legal, and

(B) is in effect.

(7)(A) The United States district courts shall have jurisdiction over–

(i) any cause of action initiated by an Indian tribe arising from the failure of a State to enter into negotiations with the Indian tribe for the purpose of entering into a Tribal-State compact under paragraph (3) or to conduct such negotiations in good faith,

(ii) any cause of action initiated by a State or Indian tribe to enjoin a class III gaming activity located on Indian lands and conducted in violation of any Tribal-State compact entered into under paragraph (3) that is in effect, and

(iii) any cause of action initiated by the Secretary to enforce the procedures prescribed under subparagraph (B)(vii).

(B)(i) An Indian tribe may initiate a cause of action describe in subparagraph (A)(i) only after the close of the 180-day period beginning on the date on which the Indian tribe requested the State to enter into negotiations under paragraph (3)(A).

(ii) In any action described in subparagraph (A)(i), upon the introduction of evidence by an Indian tribe that –

(I) a Tribal-State compact has not been entered into under paragraph (3), and

(II) the State did not respond to the request of the Indian tribe to negotiate such a compact or did not respond to such request in good faith, the burden of proof shall be upon the State to prove that the State has negotiated with the Indian tribe in good faith to conclude a Tribal-State compact governing the conduct of gaming activities.

(iii) If, in any action described in subparagraph (A)(i), the court finds that the State has failed to negotiate in good faith with the Indian tribe to conclude a Tribal-State compact governing the conduct of gaming activities, the court shall order the State and the

Indian Tribe to conclude such a compact within a 60-day period. In determining in such an action whether a State has negotiated in good faith, the court–

    (I)   may take into account the public interest, public safety, criminality, financial integrity, and adverse economic impacts on existing gaming activities, and

    (II)   shall consider any demand by the State for direct taxation of the Indian tribe or of any Indian lands as evidence that the State has not negotiated in good faith.

(iv) If a State and an Indian tribe fail to conclude a Tribal-State compact governing the conduct of gaming activities on the Indian lands subject to the jurisdiction of such Indian tribe within the 60-day period provided in the order of a court issued under clause (iii), the Indian tribe and the State shall each submit to a mediator appointed by the court a proposed compact that represents their last best offer for a compact. The mediator shall select from the two proposed compacts the one which best comports with the terms of this Act, and any other applicable Federal law and with the findings and order of the court.

(v) The mediator appointed by the court under clause (iv) shall submit to the State and the Indian tribe the compact selected by the mediator under clause (iv).

(vi) If a State consents to a proposed compact during the 60-day period beginning on the date on which the proposed compact is submitted by the mediator to the State under clause (v), the proposed compact shall be treated as a Tribal-State compact entered into under paragraph (3).

(vii) If the State does not consent during the 60-day period described in clause (vi) to a proposed compact submitted by a mediator under clause (v), the mediator shall notify the Secretary and the Secretary shall prescribe, in consultation with the Indian tribe procedures–

    (I)   which are consistent with the proposed compact selected by the mediator under clause (iv), the provisions of this Act, and the relevant provisions of the laws of the State, and

(II)   under which class III gaming may be conducted on Indian lands over which the Indian tribe has jurisdiction.

(8)(A)   The Secretary is authorized to approve any Tribal-State compact entered into between an Indian tribe and a State governing gaming on Indian lands of such Indian tribe.

(B) The Secretary may disapprove a compact described in subparagraph (A) only if such compact violates–

(i)   any provision of this Act,

(ii)   any other provision of Federal law that does not relate to jurisdiction over gaming on Indian lands, or

(ii)   the trust obligations of the United States to Indians.

(C) If the Secretary does not approve or disapprove a compact described in subparagraph (A) before the date that is 45 days after the date on which the compact is submitted to the Secretary for approval, the compact shall be considered to have been approved by the Secretary, but only to the extent the compact is consistent with the provisions of this Act.

(D) The Secretary shall publish in the Federal Register notice of any Tribal-State compact that is approved, or considered to have been approved, under this paragraph.

(9)   An Indian tribe may enter into a management contract for the operation of a class III gaming activity if such contract has been submitted to, and approved by, the Chairman.   The Chairman's review and approval of such contract shall be governed by the provisions of subsections (b), (c), (d), (f), (g), and (h) of section 12.

(e)   For purposes of this section, by not later than the date that is 90 days after the date on which any tribal gaming ordinance or resolution is submitted to the Chairman, the Chairman shall approve such ordinance or resolution if it meets the requirements of this section.   Any such ordinance or resolution not acted upon at the end of that 90-day period shall be considered to have been approved by the Chairman, but only to the extent such ordinance or resolution is consistent with the provisions of this Act.

MANAGEMENT CONTRACTS

Sec. 12. (A)(1)   Subject to the approval of the Chairman, an Indian tribe may enter into a management contract for the operation and management of a class II gaming activity that the Indian tribe may engage in under section 11(b)(1), but, before approving such contract, the Chairman shall require and obtain the following information;

(A) the name, address, and other additional pertinent background information on each person or entity (including individuals comprising such entity) having a direct financial interest in, or management responsibility for, such contract, and, in the case of a corporation, those individuals who serve on the board of directors of such corporation and each of its stockholders who hold (directly or indirectly) 10 percent or more of its issued and outstanding stock;

(B) a description of any previous experience that each person listed pursuant to subparagraph (A) has had with other gaming contracts with Indian tribes or with the gaming industry generally, including specifically the name and address of any licensing or regulatory agency with which such person has had a contract relating to gaming; and

(C) a complete financial statement of each person listed pursuant to subparagraph (A).

(2) Any person listed pursuant to paragraph (1)(A) shall be required to respond to such written or oral questions that the Chairman may propound in accordance with his responsibilities under this section.

(3) For purposes of this Act, any reference to the management contract described in paragraph (1) shall be considered to include all collateral agreements to such contract that relate to the gaming activity.

(b) The Chairman may approve any management contract entered into pursuant to this section only if he determines that it provides at least–

(1) for adequate accounting procedures that are maintained, and for verifiable financial reports that are prepared, by or for the tribal governing body on a monthly basis;

(2) for access to the daily operations of the gaming to appropriate tribal officials who shall also have a right to verify the daily gross revenues and income made from any such tribal gaming activity;

(3) for a minimum guaranteed payment to the Indian tribe that has preference over the retirement of development and construction costs;

(4) for an agreed ceiling for the repayment of development and construction costs;

(5) for a contract term not to exceed five years, except that, upon the request of an Indian tribe, the Chairman may authorize a contract term that exceeds five years but does not exceed seven years if the Chairman is satisfied that the capital investment required, and the income projections, for the particular gaming activity require the additional time; and

(6) for grounds and mechanisms for terminating such contract, but actual contract termination shall not require the approval of the Commission.

(c)(1) The Chairman may approve a management contract providing for a fee based upon a percentage of the net revenues of a tribal gaming activity if the Chairman determines that such percentage fee is reasonable in light of surrounding circumstances, Except as otherwise provided in this subsection, such fee shall not exceed 30 percent of the net revenues.

(2) Upon the request of an Indian tribe, the Chairman may approve a management contract providing for a fee based upon a percentage of the net revenues of a tribal gaming activity that exceeds 30 percent but not 40 percent of the net revenues if the Chairman is satisfied that the capital investment required, and

income projections, for such tribal gaming activity require the additional fee requested by the Indian tribe.

(d) By no later than the date that is 180 days after the date on which a management contract is submitted to the Chairman for approval, the Chairman shall approve or disapprove such contract on its merits. The Chairman may extend the 180-day period by not more than 90 days if the Chairman notifies the Indian tribe in writing of the reason for the extension. The Indian tribe may bring an action in a United States district court to compel action by the Chairman if a contract has not been approved or disapproved within the period required by this subsection.

(e) The Chairman shall not approve any contract if the Chairman determines that–

(1) any person listed pursuant to subsection (a)(1)(A) of this section–

(A) is an elected member of the governing body of the Indian tribe which is the party to the management contract;

(B) has been or subsequently is convicted of any felony or gaming offense;

(C) has knowingly and willfully provided materially important false statements or information to the Commission or the Indian tribe pursuant to this Act or has refused to respond to questions propounded pursuant to subsection (a)(2); or

(D) has been determined to be a person whose prior activities, criminal record if any, or reputation, habits, and associations pose a threat to the public interest or to the effective regulation and control of gaming, or create or enhance the dangers of unsuitable, unfair, or illegal practices, methods, and activities in the conduct of gaming or the carrying on of the business and financial arrangements incidental thereto;

(2) the management contractor has, or has attempted to, unduly interfere or influence for its gain or advantage any decision or process of tribal government relating to the gaming activity;

(3) the management contractor has deliberately or substantially failed to comply with the terms of the management contract or the tribal gaming ordinance or resolution adopted and approved pursuant to the Act; or

(4) a trustee, exercising the skill and diligence that a trustee is commonly held to, would not approve the contract.

(f) The Chairman, after notice and hearing, shall have the authority to require appropriate contract modifications or may void any contract if he subsequently determines that any of the provisions of this section have been violated.

(g) No management contract for the operation and management of a gaming activity regulated by this Act shall transfer or, in any other manner, convey any interest in land or other real property, unless specific statutory authority exists and unless clearly specified in writing in said contract.

(h) The authority of the Secretary under section 22103 of the Revised Statutes (25 U.S.C. 81), relating to management contracts regulated pursuant to this Act, is hereby transferred to the Commission.

(i) The Commission shall require a potential contractor to pay a fee to cover the cost of the investigation necessary to reach a determination required in subsection (e) of this section.

REVIEW OF EXISTING ORDINANCES AND CONTRACTS

Sec. 13. (a) As soon as practicable after the organization of the Commission, the Chairman shall notify each Indian tribe or management contractor who, prior to the enactment of this Act, adopted an ordinance or resolution authorizing class II gaming or class III gaming or entered into a management contract, that such ordinance, resolution, or contract, including all collateral agreements relating to the gaming activity, must be submitted for his review within 60 days of such notification. Any activity conducted under such ordinance, resolution, contract, or agreement shall be valid under this Act, or any amendment made by this Act, unless disapproved under this section.

(b)(1) By no later than the date that is 90 days after the date on which an ordinance or resolution authorizing class II gaming or class III gaming is submitted to the Chairman pursuant to subsection (a), the Chairman shall review such ordinance or resolution to determine if it conforms to the requirements of section 11(b) of this Act.

(2) If the Chairman determines that an ordinance or resolution submitted under subsection (a) conforms to the requirements of section 11(b), the Chairman shall approve it.

(3) If the Chairman determines that an ordinance or resolution submitted under subsection (a) does not conform to the requirements of section 11(b), the Chairman shall provide written notification of necessary modifications to the Indian tribe which shall have not more than 120 days to bring such ordinance or resolution into compliance.

(c)(1) Within 180 days after the submission of a management contract, including all collateral agreements, pursuant to subsection (a), the Chairman shall subject such contract to the requirements and process of section 12.

(2) If the Chairman determines that a management contract submitted under subsection (a), and the management contractor under such contract, meet the requirements of section 12, the Chairman shall approve the management contract.

(3) If the Chairman determines that a contract submitted under subsection (a), or the management contractor under a contract submitted under subsection (a), does not meet the requirements of section 12, the Chairman shall provide written notification to the parties to such contract of necessary modifications and the parties shall have not more than 120 days to come into compliance . If a management contract has been approved by the Secretary prior to the date of enactment of this Act, the parties shall have not more than 180 days after notification of necessary modifications to come into compliance.

CIVIL PENALTIES

Sec. 14. (a)(1) Subject to such regulations as may be prescribed by the Commission, the Chairman shall have authority to levy and collect appropriate civil fines, not to exceed $25,000 per violation, against the tribal operator of an Indian game or a management contractor engaged in gaming for any violation of any provision of this Act, any regulation prescribed by the Commission pursuant to this Act, or tribal regulations, ordinances, or resolutions approved under section 11 or 13.

(2) The Commission shall, by regulation, provide an opportunity for an appeal and hearing before the Commission on fines levied and collected by the Chairman.

(3) Whenever the Commission has reason to believe that the tribal operator of an Indian game or a management contractor is engaged in activities regulated by this Act, by regulations prescribed under this Act, or by tribal regulations, ordinances, or resolutions, approved under section 11 or 13, that may result in the imposition of a fine under subsection (a)(1), the permanent closure of such game, or the modification or termination of any management contract, the Commission shall provide such tribal operator or management contractor with a written complaint stating the acts or omissions which form the basis for such belief and the action or choice of action being considered by the Commission. The allegation shall be set forth in common and concise language and must specify the statutory or regulatory provisions alleged to have been violated, but may not consist merely of allegations stated in statutory or regulatory language.

(b)(1) The Chairman shall have power to order temporary closure of an Indian game for substantial violation of the provisions of this Act, of regulations prescribed by the Commission pursuant to this Act, or of tribal regulations, ordinances, or resolutions approved under section 11 or 13 of this Act.

(2) Not later than thirty days after the issuance by the Chairman of an order of temporary closure, the Indian tribe or management

contractor involved shall have a right to a hearing before the Commission to determine whether such order should be made permanent or dissolved. Not later than sixty days following such hearing, the Commission shall, by a vote of not less than two of its members, decide whether to order a permanent closure of the gaming operation.

(c) A decision of the Commission to give final approval of a fine levied by the Chairman or to order a permanent closure pursuant to this section shall be appealable to the appropriate Federal district court pursuant to chapter 7 of title 5, United State Code.

(d) Nothing in this Act precludes an Indian tribe from exercising regulatory authority provided under tribal law over a gaming establishment within the Indian tribe's jurisdiction if such regulation is not inconsistent with this Act or with any rules or regulations adopted by the Commission.

JUDICIAL REVIEW

Sec. 15. Decisions made by the Commission pursuant to sections 11, 12, 13, and 14 shall be final agency decisions for purposes of appeal to the appropriate Federal district court pursuant to chapter 7 of title 5, United States Code.

SUBPOENA AND DEPOSITION AUTHORITY

Sec. 16.(a) By a vote of not less than two members the Commission shall have the power to require by subpoena the attendance and testimony of witnesses and the production of all books, papers, and documents relating to any matter under consideration or investigation. Witnesses so summoned shall be paid the same fees and mileage that are paid witnesses in the courts of the United States.

(b) The attendance of witnesses and the production of books, papers, and documents, may be required from any place in the United States at any designated place of hearing. The Commission may request the Secretary to request the Attorney General to bring an action to enforce any subpoena under this section.

(c) Any court of the United States within the jurisdiction of which an inquiry is carried on may, in case of contumacy or refusal to obey a subpoena for any reason, issue an order requiring such person to appear before the Commission (and produce books, papers, or documents as so ordered) and give evidence concerning the matter in question and any failure to obey such order of the court may be punished by such court as a contempt thereof.

(d) A Commissioner may order testimony to be taken by deposition in any proceeding or investigation pending before the Commission at any stage of such proceeding or investigation. Such depositions may be taken before any person designated by the Commission and having power to administer oaths. Reasonable notice must first be given to the Commission in writing by the party or his attorney proposing to take such deposition, and, in cases in which a Commissioner proposes to take a deposition, reasonable notice must be given. The notice shall state the name of the witness and the time and place of the taking of his deposition. Any person may be compelled to appear and depose, and to produce books, papers, or documents, in the same manner as witnesses may be compelled to appear and testify and produce like documentary evidence before the Commission, as hereinbefore provided.

(e) Every person deposing as herein provided shall be cautioned and shall be required to swear (or affirm, if he so requests) to testify to the whole truth, and shall be carefully examined. His testimony shall be reduced to writing by the person taking the deposition, or under his direction, and shall, after it has been reduced to writing, be subscribed by the deponent. All depositions shall be promptly filed with the Commission.

(f) Witnesses whose depositions are taken as authorized in this section, and the persons taking the same, shall severally be entitled to the same fees as are paid for like services in the courts of the United States

INVESTIGATIVE POWERS

Sec. 17. (a) Except as provided in subsection (b), the Commission shall preserve any and all information received pursuant to this Act as confidential pursuant to the provisions of paragraphs (4) and (7) of section 552(b) of title 5, United States Code.

(b) The Commission shall, when such information indicates a violation of Federal, State, or tribal statues, ordinances, or resolutions, provide such information to the appropriate law enforcement officials.

(c) The Attorney General shall investigate activities associated with gaming authorized by this Act which may be a violation of Federal law.

COMMISSION FUNDING

Sec. 18. (a)(1) The Commission shall establish a schedule of fees to be paid to the Commission annually by each class II gaming activity that is regulated by this Act.

(2)(A) The rate of the fees imposed under the schedule established under paragraph (1) shall be–

(i) no less than 0.5 percent nor more than 2.5 percent of the first $1,500,000, and

(ii) no more than 5 percent of amounts in excess of the first $1,500,000,

of the gross revenues from each activity regulated by this Act.

(B) The total amount of all fees imposed during any fiscal year under the schedule established under paragraph (1) shall not exceed $1,500,000.

(3) The Commission, by a vote of not less than two of its members, shall annually adopt the rate of the fees authorized by this section which shall be payable to the Commission on a quarterly basis.

(4) Failure to pay the fees imposed under the schedule established under paragraph (1) shall, subject to the regulations of

the Commission, be grounds for revocation of the approval of the Chairman of any license, ordinance, or resolution required under this Act for the operation of gaming.

(5)   To the extent that revenue derived from fees imposed under the schedule established under paragraph (1) are not expended or committed at the close of any fiscal year, such surplus funds shall be credited to each gaming activity on a pro rata basis against such fees imposed for the succeeding year.

(6)   For purposes of this section, gross revenues shall constitute the annual total amount of money wagered, less any amounts paid out as prizes or paid for prizes awarded and less allowance for amortization of capital expenditures for structures.

(b)(1) The Commission, in coordination with the Secretary and in conjunction with the fiscal year of the United States, shall adopt an annual budget for the expenses and operation of the Commission,

(2)   The budget of the Commission may include a request for appropriations, as authorized by section 19, in an amount equal the amount of funds derived from assessments authorized by subsection (a) for the fiscal year preceding the fiscal year for which the appropriation request is made.

(3)   The request for appropriations pursuant to paragraph (2) shall be subject to the approval of the Secretary and shall be included as a part of the budget request of the Department of the Interior.

AUTHORIZATION OF APPROPRIATIONS

Sec. 19. (a) Subject to the provisions of section 18, there are hereby authorized to be appropriated such sums as may be necessary for the operation of the Commission.

(b)   Notwithstanding the provisions of section 18, there are hereby authorized to be appropriated not to exceed $2,000,000 to fund the operation of the Commission for each of the fiscal years beginning October 1, 1988, and October 1, 1989.

GAMING ON LANDS ACQUIRED AFTER
ENACTMENT OF THIS ACT

Sec. 20. (a)   Except as provided in subsection (b), gaming regulated by this Act shall not be conducted on lands acquired by the Secretary in trust for the benefit of an Indian tribe after the date of enactment of this Act unless–

(1)   such lands are located within or contiguous to the boundaries of the reservation of the Indian tribe on the date of enactment of this Act; or

(2)   the Indian tribe has no reservation on the date of enactment of this Act and–

(A)   such lands are located in Oklahoma and–

(i)   are within the boundaries of the Indian tribe's former reservation, as defined by the Secretary, or

(ii)   are contiguous to other land held in trust or restricted status by the United States for the Indian tribe in Oklahoma; or

(B)   such lands are located in a State other than Oklahoma and are within the Indian tribe's last recognized reservation within the State or States within which such Indian tribe is presently located.

(b)(1) Subsection (a) will not apply when–

(A)   the Secretary, after consultation with the Indian tribe and appropriate State and local officials, including officials of other nearby Indian tribes, determines that a gaming establishment on newly acquired lands would be in the best interest of the Indian tribe and its members, and would not be detrimental to the surrounding community, but only if the Governor of the State in which the gaming activity is to be conducted concurs in the Secretary's determination; or

(B)   lands are taken into trust as part of–

(i)   a settlement of a land claim,

(ii)   the initial reservation of an Indian tribe acknowledged by the Secretary under the Federal acknowledgment process, or

(iii)   the restoration of lands for an Indian tribe that is restored to Federal recognition.

(2)   Subsection (a) shall not apply to–

(A)   any lands involved in the trust petition of the St. Croix Chippewa Indians of Wisconsin that is the subject of the action filed in the United States District Court for the District of Columbia entitle St. Croix Chippewa Indians of Wisconsin v. United States, Civ. No. 86-2278, or

(B)   the interest of the Miccosukee Tribe of Indians of Florida in approximately 25 contiguous acres of land, more or less, in Dade County, Florida, located within one mile of the intersection of State Road Numbered 27 (also know as Krome Avenue) and the Tamiami Trail.

(3)   Upon request of the governing body of the Miccosukee Tribe of Indians of Florida, the Secretary shall, notwithstanding any other provision of law, accept the transfer by such Tribe to the Secretary of the interest of such tribe in the lands described in paragraph (2)(B) and the Secretary shall declare that such interests are held in trust by the Secretary for the benefit of such Tribe and that such interest are part of the reservation of such Tribe under sections 5 and 7 of the Act of June 18, 1934 (48 Stat. 985; 25 U.S.C. 465, 467), subject to any encumbrances and rights that are held at the time of such transfer by any person or entity other than such Tribe. The Secretary shall publish in the Federal Register the legal description of any lands that are declared held in trust by the Secretary under this paragraph.

(c) Nothing in this section shall affect or diminish the authority and responsibility of the Secretary to take land into trust.

(d)(1) The provisions of the Internal Revenue Code of 1986 (including sections 1441, 3402(q), 6041, and 6050I, and chapter 35 of such Code) concerning the reporting and withholding of taxes with respect to the winnings from gaming or wagering operations shall apply to Indian gaming operations conducted pursuant to this Act, or under a Tribal-State compact entered into under section 11(d)(3) that is in effect, in the same manner as such provisions apply to State gaming and wagering operations.

(2) The provisions of this subsection shall apply notwithstanding any other provision of law enacted before, on, or after the date of enactment of this Act unless such other provision of law specifically cites this subsection.

DISSEMINATION OF INFORMATION

Sec. 21. Consistent with the requirements of this Act, sections 1301, 1302 1303 and 1304 of title 18, United States Code, shall not apply to any gaming conducted by an Indian tribe pursuant to this Act.

SEVERABILITY

Sec. 22. In the event that any section or provision of this Act, or amendment made by this Act, is held invalid, it is the intent of Congress that the remaining sections or provisions of this Act, and amendments made by this Act, shall continue in full force and effect.

CRIMINAL PENALTIES

Sec. 23. Chapter 53 of title 18, United States Code, is Amended by adding at the end thereof the following new sections:

"§ 1166. Gambling in Indian country

"(a) Subject to subsection (c), for purposes of Federal law, all State laws pertaining to the licensing, regulation, or prohibition of gambling, including but not limited to criminal sanctions applicable thereto, shall apply in Indian country in the same manner and to the same extent as such laws apply elsewhere in the State.

"(b) Whoever in Indian country is guilty of any act or omission involving gambling, whether or not conducted or sanctioned by an Indian tribe, which, although not made punishable by any enactment of Congress would be punishable if committed or omitted within the jurisdiction of the State in which the act or omission occurred, under the laws governing the licensing, regulation, or prohibition of gambling in force at the time of such act or omission, shall be guilty of a like offense and subject to a like punishment.

"(c) For the purpose of this section, the term 'gambling' does not include–

"(1) class I gaming or class II gaming regulated by the Indian Gaming Regulatory Act, or

"(2) class III gaming conducted under a Tribal-State compact approved by the Secretary of the Interior under section 11(d)(8) of the Indian Gaming Regulatory Act that is in effect.

"(d) The United States shall have exclusive jurisdiction over criminal prosecutions of violations of State gambling laws that are made applicable under this section to Indian country, unless and Indian tribe pursuant to a Tribal-State compact approved by the Secretary of the Interior under section 11(d)(8) of the Indian Gaming Regulatory Act, or under any other provision of Federal law, has consented to the transfer to the State of criminal jurisdiction with respect to gambling on the lands of the Indian tribe.

"§ 1167. Theft from gaming establishments on Indian lands

"(a) Whoever abstracts, purloins, willfully misapplies, or takes and carries away with intent to steal, any money, funds, or other property of value of $1,000 or less belonging to an establishment operated by or for or licensed by an Indian tribe pursuant to an ordinance or resolution approved by the National Indian Gaming Commission shall be fined not more than $100,000 or be imprisoned for not more than one year, or both.

"(b) Whoever abstracts, purloins, willfully misapplies, or takes and caries away with intent to steal, any money, funds, or other property of a value in excess of $1,000 belonging to a gaming establishment operated by or for or licensed by an Indian tribe pursuant to an ordinance or resolution approved by the National Indian Gaming Commission shall be fined not more than $250,000, or imprisoned for not more than ten years, or both.

"§ 1168. Theft by officers or employees of gaming establishments on Indian lands

"(a) Whoever, being an officer, employee, or individual licensee of a gaming establishment operated by or for or licensed by an Indian tribe pursuant to an ordinance or resolution approved by the National Indian Gaming Commission, embezzles, abstracts, purloins, willfully misapplies, or takes and carries away with intent to steal, any moneys, funds, assets, or other property of such establishment of a value of $1,000 or less shall be fined not more than $250,000 and be imprisoned for not more than five years, or both;

"(b) Whoever, being an officer, employee, or individual licensee of a gaming establishment operated by or for or licensed by an Indian tribe pursuant to an ordinance or resolution approved by the National Indian Gaming Commission, embezzles, abstracts, purloins, willfully misapplies, or takes and carries away with intent to steal, any moneys, funds, assets, or other property of such establishment of a value in excess of $1,000 shall be fined not more than $1,000,000 or imprisoned for not more than twenty years, or both.".

CONFORMING AMENDMENT

Sec. 24. The table of contents for chapter 53 of title 18, United States Code, is amended by adding at the end thereof the following:

"1166.   Gambling in Indian country.
"1167.   Theft from gaming establishments on Indian lands.
"1168.   Theft by officers or employees of gaming establishments on Indian lands.".

Approved October 17, 1988.

C

CALIFORNIA TRIBAL COMPACT

Signed by Governor Gray Davis

September 10, 1999

TRIBAL-STATE GAMING COMPACT

Between the

XXXXXXX, a federally recognized Indian Tribe,

and the

STATE OF CALIFORNIA

This Tribal-State Gaming Compact is entered into on a government-to-government basis by and between the XXXXXXX, a federally-recognized sovereign Indian tribe (hereafter "Tribe"), and the State of California, a sovereign State of the United States (hereafter "State"), pursuant to the Indian Gaming Regulatory Act of 1988 (P. L. 100-497, codified at 18 U.S.C. Sec. 1166 et seq. and 25 U.S.C. Sec. 2701 et seq.) (hereafter "IGRA"), and any successor statute or amendments.

PREAMBLE

A. In 1988, Congress enacted IGRA as the federal statute governing Indian gaming in the United States. The purposes of IGRA are to provide a statutory basis for the operation of gaming by Indian tribes as a means of promoting tribal economic development, self-sufficiency, and strong tribal governments; to provide a statutory basis for regulation of Indian gaming adequate to shield it from organized crime and other corrupting influences; to ensure that the Indian tribe is the primary beneficiary of the gaming operation; to ensure that gaming is conducted fairly and honestly by both the operator and players; and to declare that the establishment of an independent federal regulatory authority for gaming on Indian lands, federal standards for gaming on Indian lands, and a National Indian Gaming Commission are necessary to meet congressional concerns.

B. The system of regulation of Indian gaming fashioned by Congress in IGRA rests on an allocation of regulatory jurisdiction among the three sovereigns involved: the federal government, the state in which a tribe has land, and the tribe itself. IGRA makes Class III gaming activities lawful on the lands of federally-recognized Indian tribes only if such activities are: (1) authorized by a tribal ordinance, (2) located in a state that permits such gaming for any purpose by any person, organization or entity, and (3) conducted in conformity with a gaming compact entered into between the Indian tribe and the state and approved by the Secretary of the Interior.

C. The Tribe is currently operating a tribal gaming casino offering Class III gaming activities on its land. On September 1, 1999, the largest number of Gaming Devices operated by the Tribe was 2,000.

D. The State enters into this Compact out of respect for the sovereignty of the Tribe; in recognition of the historical fact that Indian gaming has become the single largest revenue-producing activity for Indian tribes in the United States; out of a desire to terminate pending "bad faith" litigation between the Tribe and the State; to initiate a new era of tribal-state cooperation in areas of mutual concern; out of a respect for the sentiment of the voters of California who, in approving Proposition 5, expressed their belief that the forms of gaming authorized herein should be allowed; and in anticipation of voter approval of SCA 11 as passed by the California legislature.

E. The exclusive rights that Indian tribes in California, including the Tribe, will enjoy under this Compact create a unique opportunity for the Tribe to operate its Gaming Facility in an economic environment free of competition from the Class III gaming referred to in Section 4.0 of this Compact on non-Indian lands in California. The parties are mindful that this unique environment is of great economic value to the Tribe and the fact that income from Gaming Devices represents a substantial portion of the tribes' gaming revenues. In consideration for the exclusive rights enjoyed by the tribes, and in further consideration for the State's willingness to enter into this Compact, the tribes have agreed to provide to the State, on a sovereign-to-sovereign basis, a portion of its revenue from Gaming Devices.

F. The State has a legitimate interest in promoting the purposes of IGRA for all federally-recognized Indian tribes in California, whether gaming or non-gaming. The State contends that it has an equally legitimate sovereign interest in regulating the growth of Class III gaming activities in California. The Tribe and the State share a joint sovereign interest in ensuring that tribal gaming activities are free from criminal and other undesirable elements.

Section 1.0. PURPOSES AND OBJECTIVES.

The terms of this Gaming Compact are designed and intended to:

(a) Evidence the goodwill and cooperation of the Tribe and State in fostering a mutually respectful government-to-government relationship that will serve the mutual interests of the parties.

(b) Develop and implement a means of regulating Class III gaming, and only Class III gaming, on the Tribe's Indian lands to ensure its fair and honest operation in accordance with IGRA, and through that regulated Class III gaming, enable the Tribe to develop self-sufficiency, promote tribal economic development, and generate jobs and revenues to support the Tribe's government and governmental services and programs.

(c) Promote ethical practices in conjunction with that gaming, through the licensing and control of persons and entities employed in, or providing goods and services to, the Tribe's Gaming Operation and protecting against the presence or participation of persons whose criminal backgrounds, reputations, character, or associations make them unsuitable for participation in gaming, thereby maintaining a high level of integrity in tribal government gaming.

Sec. 2.0. DEFINITIONS.

Sec. 2.1. "Applicant" means an individual or entity that applies for a Tribal license or State certification.

Sec. 2.2. "Association" means an association of California tribal and state gaming regulators, the membership of which comprises up to two representatives from each tribal gaming agency of those tribes with whom the State has a gaming compact under IGRA, and up to two delegates each from the state Division of Gambling Control and the state Gambling Control Commission.

Sec. 2.3. "Class III gaming" means the forms of Class III gaming defined as such in 25 U.S.C. Sec. 2703(8) and by regulations of the National Indian Gaming Commission.

Sec. 2.4. "Gaming Activities" means the Class III gaming activities authorized under this Gaming Compact.

Sec. 2.5. "Gaming Compact" or "Compact" means this compact.

Sec. 2.6. "Gaming Device" means a slot machine, including an electronic, electromechanical, electrical, or video device that, for consideration, permits:

individual play with or against that device or the participation in any electronic, electromechanical, electrical, or video system to which that device

is connected; the playing of games thereon or therewith, including, but not limited to, the playing of facsimiles of games of chance or skill; the possible delivery of, or entitlement by the player to, a prize or something of value as a result of the application of an element of chance; and a method for viewing the outcome, prize won, and other information regarding the playing of games thereon or therewith.

Sec. 2.7. "Gaming Employee" means any person who (a) operates, maintains, repairs, assists in any Class III gaming activity, or is in any way responsible for supervising such gaming activities or persons who conduct, operate, account for, or supervise any such gaming activity, (b) is in a category under federal or tribal gaming law requiring licensing, (c) is an employee of the Tribal Gaming Agency with access to confidential information, or (d) is a person whose employment duties require or authorize access to areas of the Gaming Facility that are not open to the public.

Sec. 2.8. "Gaming Facility" or "Facility" means any building in which Class III gaming activities or gaming operations occur, or in which the business records, receipts, or other funds of the gaming operation are maintained (but excluding offsite facilities primarily dedicated to storage of those records, and financial institutions), and all rooms, buildings, and areas, including parking lots and walkways, a principal purpose of which is to serve the activities of the Gaming Operation, provided that nothing herein prevents the conduct of Class II gaming (as defined under IGRA) therein.

Sec. 2.9. "Gaming Operation" means the business enterprise that offers and operates Class III Gaming Activities, whether exclusively or otherwise.

Sec. 2.10. "Gaming Ordinance" means a tribal ordinance or resolution duly authorizing the conduct of Class III Gaming Activities on the Tribe's Indian lands and approved under IGRA.

Sec. 2.11. "Gaming Resources" means any goods or services provided or used in connection with Class III Gaming Activities, whether exclusively or otherwise, including, but not limited to, equipment, furniture, gambling devices and ancillary equipment, implements of gaming activities such as playing cards and dice, furniture designed primarily for Class III gaming activities, maintenance or security equipment and services, and Class III gaming consulting services. "Gaming Resources" does not include professional accounting and legal services.

Sec. 2.12. "Gaming Resource Supplier" means any person or entity who, directly or indirectly, manufactures, distributes, supplies, vends, leases, or otherwise purveys Gaming Resources to the Gaming Operation or Gaming Facility, provided that the Tribal Gaming Agency may exclude a purveyor of equipment or furniture that is not specifically designed for, and is distributed generally for use other than in connection with, Gaming Activities, if the purveyor is not otherwise a Gaming Resource Supplier as described by of Section 6.4.5, the compensation received by the purveyor is not grossly disproportionate to the value of the goods or services provided, and the purveyor is not otherwise a person who exercises a significant influence over the Gambling Operation.

Sec. 2.13. "IGRA" means the Indian Gaming Regulatory Act of 1988 (P. L. 100-497, 18 U.S.C. Sec. 1166 et seq. and 25 U.S.C. Sec. 2701 et seq.) any amendments thereto, and all regulations promulgated thereunder. Sec. 2.14. "Management Contractor" means any Gaming Resource Supplier with whom the Tribe has contracted for the management of any Gaming Activity or Gaming Facility, including, but not limited to, any person who would be regarded as a management contractor under IGRA.

Sec. 2.15. "Net Win" means "net win" as defined by American Institute of Certified Public Accountants.

Sec. 2.16. "NIGC" means the National Indian Gaming Commission.

Sec. 2.17. "State" means the State of California or an authorized official or agency thereof.

Sec. 2.18. "State Gaming Agency" means the entities authorized to investigate, approve, and regulate gaming licenses pursuant to the Gambling Control Act (Chapter 5 (commencing with Section 19800) of Division 8 of the Business and Professions Code).

Sec. 2.19. "Tribal Chairperson" means the person duly elected or selected under the Tribe's organic documents, customs, or traditions to serve as the primary spokesperson for the Tribe.

Sec. 2.20. "Tribal Gaming Agency" means the person, agency, board, committee, commission, or council designated under tribal law, including, but not limited to, an intertribal gaming regulatory agency approved to fulfill those functions by the National Indian Gaming Commission, as primarily responsible for carrying out the Tribe's regulatory responsibilities under IGRA and the Tribal Gaming Ordinance. No person employed in, or in connection with, the management, supervision, or conduct of any gaming activity may be a member or employee of the Tribal Gaming Agency.

Sec. 2.21. "Tribe" means the Dry Creek Rancheria, a federally-recognized Indian tribe, or an authorized official or agency thereof.

Sec. 3.0 CLASS III GAMING AUTHORIZED AND PERMITTED.

The Tribe is hereby authorized and permitted to engage in only the Class III Gaming Activities expressly referred to in Section 4.0 and shall not engage in Class III gaming that is not expressly authorized in that Section.

Sec. 4.0. SCOPE OF CLASS III GAMING.

Sec. 4.1. Authorized and Permitted Class III gaming.

The Tribe is hereby authorized and permitted to operate the following Gaming Activities under the terms and conditions set forth in this Gaming Compact.

(a) The operation of Gaming Devices.

(b) Any banking or percentage card game.

(c) The operation of any devices or games that are authorized under state law to the California State Lottery, provided that the Tribe will not offer such games through use of the Internet unless others in the state are permitted to do so under state and federal law.

(e) Nothing herein shall be construed to preclude negotiation of a separate compact governing the conduct of off-track wagering at the Tribe's Gaming Facility.

Sec. 4.2. Authorized Gaming Facilities.

The Tribe may establish and operate not more than two Gaming Facilities, and only on those Indian lands on which gaming may lawfully be conducted under the Indian Gaming Regulatory Act. The Tribe may combine and operate in each Gaming Facility any forms and kinds of gaming permitted under law, except to the extent limited under IGRA, this Compact, or the Tribe's Gaming Ordinance.

Sec. 4.3. Authorized number of Gaming Devices

Sec. 4.3.1 The Tribe may operate no more Gaming Devices than the larger of the following:

(a) A number of terminals equal to the number of Gaming Devices operated by the Tribe on September 1, 1999; or (b) Three hundred fifty (350) Gaming Devices.

Sec. 4.3.2. Revenue Sharing with Non-Gaming Tribes.

(a) For the purposes of this Section 4.3.2 and Section 5.0, the following definitions apply:

(i) A "Compact Tribe" is a tribe having a compact with the State that authorizes the Gaming Activities authorized by this Compact. Federally-recognized tribes that are operating fewer than 350 Gaming Devices are "Non-Compact Tribes." Non-Compact Tribes shall be deemed third party beneficiaries of this and other compacts identical in all material respects. A Compact Tribe that becomes a Non-Compact Tribe may not thereafter return to the status of a Compact Tribe for a period of two years becoming a Non-Compact Tribe.

(ii) The Revenue Sharing Trust Fund is a fund created by the Legislature and administered by the California Gambling Control Commission, as Trustee, for the receipt, deposit, and distribution of monies paid pursuant to this Section 4.3.2.

(iii) The Special Distribution Fund is a fund created by the Legislature for the receipt, deposit, and distribution of monies paid pursuant to Section 5.0.

Sec. 4.3.2.1. Revenue Sharing Trust Fund.

(a) The Tribe agrees with all other Compact Tribes that are parties to compacts having this Section 4.3.2, that each Non-Compact Tribe in the State shall receive the sum of $1.1 million per year. In the event there are insufficient monies in the Revenue Sharing Trust Fund to pay $1.1 million per year to each Non-Compact Tribe, any available monies in that

Fund shall be distributed to Non-Compact Tribes in equal shares. Monies in excess of the amount necessary to $1.1 million to each Non-Compact Tribe shall remain in the Revenue Sharing Trust Fund available for disbursement in future years.

(b) Payments made to Non-Compact Tribes shall be made quarterly and in equal shares out of the Revenue Sharing Trust Fund. The Commission shall serve as the trustee of the fund. The Commission shall have no discretion with respect to the use or disbursement of the trust funds. Its sole authority shall be to serve as a depository of the trust funds and to disburse them on a quarterly basis to Non-Compact Tribes. In no event shall the State's General Fund be obligated to make up any shortfall or pay any unpaid claims.

Sec. 4.3.2.2. Allocation of Licenses.

(a) The Tribe, along with all other Compact Tribes, may acquire licenses to use Gaming Devices in excess of the number they are authorized to use under Sec. 4.3.1, but in no event may the Tribe operate more than 2,000 Gaming Devices, on the following terms, conditions, and priorities:

(1). The maximum number of machines that all Compact Tribes in the aggregate may license pursuant to this Section shall be a sum equal to 350 multiplied by the number of Non-Compact tribes as of September 1, 1999, plus the difference between 350 and the lesser number authorized under Section 4.3.1.

(2) The Tribe may acquire and maintain a license to operate a Gaming Device by paying into the Revenue Sharing Trust Fund, on a quarterly basis, in the following amounts:

Number of Licensed Devices	Fee Per Device Per Annum
1–350	$0
351–750	$900
751–1250	$1950
1251–2000	$4350

(3) Licenses to use Gaming Devices shall be awarded as follows:

(i)   First, Compact Tribes with no Existing Devices (i.e., the number of Gaming Devices operated by a Compact Tribe as of September 1, 1999) may draw up to 150 licenses for a total of 500 Gaming Devices;

(ii)   Next, Compact Tribes authorized under Section 4.3.1 to operate up to and including 500 Gaming Devices as of September 1, 1999 (including tribes, if any, that have acquired licenses through subparagraph (i)), may draw up to an additional 500 licenses, to a total of 1000 Gaming Devices;

(iii)   Next, Compact Tribes operating between 501 and 1000 Gaming Devices as of September 1, 1999 (including tribes, if any, that have acquired licenses through subparagraph (ii)), shall be entitled to draw up to an additional 750 Gaming Devices;

(iv)   Next, Compact Tribes authorized to operate up to and including 1500 gaming devices (including tribes, if any, that have acquired licenses through subparagraph (iii)), shall be entitled to draw up to an additional 500 licenses, for a total authorization to operate up to

2000 gaming devices.

(v) Next, Compact Tribes authorized to operate more than 1500 gaming devices (including tribes, if any, that have acquired licenses through subparagraph (iv))., shall be entitled to draw additional licenses up to a total authorization to operate up to 2000 gaming devices.

(vi) After the first round of draws, a second and subsequent round(s) shall be conducted utilizing the same order of priority as set forth above. Rounds shall continue until tribes cease making draws, at which time draws will be discontinued for one month or until the Trustee is notified that a tribe desires to acquire a license, whichever last occurs.

(b) As a condition of acquiring licenses to operate Gaming Devices, a non-refundable one-time pre-payment fee shall be required in the amount of $1,250 per Gaming Device being licensed, which fees shall be deposited in the Revenue Sharing Trust Fund. The license for any Gaming Device shall be canceled if the Gaming Device authorized by the license is not in commercial operation within twelve months of issuance of the license.

Sec. 4.3.2.3. The Tribe shall not conduct any Gaming Activity authorized by this Compact if the Tribe is more than two quarterly contributions in arrears in its license fee payments to the Revenue Sharing Trust Fund.

Sec. 4.3.3. If requested to do so by either party after March 7, 2003, but not later than March 31, 2003, the parties will promptly commence negotiations in good faith with the Tribe concerning any matters encompassed by Sections 4.3.1 and Section 4.3.2, and their subsections.

SEC. 5.0 REVENUE DISTRIBUTION

Sec. 5.1.

(a) The Tribe shall make contributions to the Special Distribution Fund created by the Legislature, in accordance with the following schedule, but only with respect to the number of Gaming Devices operated by the Tribe on September 1, 1999:

Number of Terminals in Quarterly Device Base Percent of Average Gaming Device Net Win

1 - 200	0%
201 – 500	7%
501 – 1000	7% applied to the excess over 200 terminals, up to 500 terminals, plus 10% applied to terminals over 500 terminals, up to 1000 terminals.
1000+	7% applied to excess over 200, up to 500 terminals, plus 10% applied to terminals over 500, up to 1000 terminals, plus 13% applied to the excess above 1000 terminals.

(b) The first transfer to the Special Distribution Fund of its share of the gaming revenue shall made at the conclusion of the first calendar quarter
following the second anniversary date of the effective date of this Compact.

Sec. 5.2. Use of funds. The State's share of the Gaming Device revenue shall be placed in the Special Distribution Fund, available for appropriation by the Legislature for the following purposes: (a) grants, including any administrative costs, for programs designed to address gambling addiction; (b) grants, including any administrative costs, for the support of state and local government agencies impacted by tribal government gaming; (c) compensation for regulatory costs incurred by the State Gaming Agency and the state Department of Justice in connection with the implementation and administration of the Compact; (d) payment of shortfalls that may occur in the Revenue Sharing Trust Fund; and (e) any other purposes specified by the Legislature. It is the intent of the parties that Compact Tribes will be consulted in the process of identifying purposes for grants made to local governments.

Sec. 5.3.

(a) The quarterly contributions due under Section 5.1 shall be determined and made not later than the thirtieth (30th) day following the end of each calendar quarter by first determining the total number of all Gaming Devices operated by a Tribe during a given quarter ("Quarterly Device Base"). The "Average Device Net Win" is calculated by dividing the total Net Win from all terminals during the quarter by the Quarterly Terminal Base.

(b) Any quarterly contribution not paid on or before the date on which such amount is due shall be deemed overdue. If any quarterly contribution under Section 5.1 is overdue to the Special Distribution Fund, the Tribe shall pay to the Special Distribution Fund, in addition to the overdue quarterly contribution, interest on such amount from the date the quarterly contribution was due until the date such quarterly contribution (together with interest thereon) was actually paid at the rate of 1.0% per month or the maximum rate permitted by state law, whichever is less. Entitlement to such interest shall be in addition to any other remedies the State may have.

(c) At the time each quarterly contribution is made, the Tribe shall submit to the State a report (the "Quarterly Contribution Report") certified by an authorized representative of the Tribe reflecting the Quarterly Device Base, the Net Win from all terminals in the Quarterly Device Base (broken down by Gaming Device), and the Average Device Net Win.

(d) If the State causes an audit to be made pursuant to subdivision (c), and the Average Device Net Win for any quarter as reflected on such quarter's Quarterly Contribution Reports is found to be understated, the State will promptly notify the Tribe, and the Tribe will either accept the difference or provide a reconciliation satisfactory to the State. If the Tribe accepts the difference or does not provide a reconciliation satisfactory to the State, the Tribe must immediately pay the amount of the resulting deficiencies in the quarterly contribution plus interest on such amounts from the date they were due at the rate of 1.0% per month or the maximum rate permitted by applicable law, whichever is less.

(e) The Tribe shall not conduct Class III gaming if more than two quarterly contributions to the Special Distribution Fund are overdue.

Sec. 6.0. LICENSING.

Sec. 6.1. Gaming Ordinance and Regulations.

All Gaming Activities conducted under this Gaming Compact shall, at a minimum, comply with a Gaming Ordinance duly adopted by the Tribe and approved in accordance with IGRA, and with all rules, regulations, procedures, specifications, and standards duly adopted by the Tribal Gaming Agency.

Sec. 6.2. Tribal Ownership, Management, and Control of Gaming Operation.

The Gaming Operations authorized under this Gaming Compact shall be owned solely by the Tribe.

Sec. 6.3. Prohibition Regarding Minors

(a) Except as provided in subdivision (b), the Tribe shall not permit persons under the age of 18 years to be present in any room in which Class III Gaming Activities are being conducted unless the person is en-route to a non-gaming area of the Gaming Facility.

(b) If the Tribe permits the consumption of alcoholic beverages in the Gaming Facility, the Tribe shall prohibit persons under the age of 21 years from being present in any area in which Class III gaming activities are being conducted and in which alcoholic beverages may be consumed, to the extent required by the state Department of Alcoholic Beverage Control.

Sec. 6.4. Licensing Requirements and Procedures.

      Sec. 6.4.1. Summary of Licensing Principles.

All persons in any way connected with the Gaming Operation or Facility who are required to be licensed or to submit to a background investigation under IGRA, and any others required to be licensed under this Gaming Compact, including, but not limited to, all Gaming Employees and Gaming Resource Suppliers, and any other person having a significant influence over the Gaming Operation must be licensed by the Tribal Gaming Agency. The parties intend that the licensing process provided for in this Gaming Compact shall involve joint cooperation between the Tribal Gaming Agency and the State Gaming Agency, as more particularly described herein.

Sec. 6.4.2. Gaming Facility. (a) The Gaming Facility authorized by this Gaming Compact shall be licensed by the Tribal Gaming Agency in conformity with the requirements of this Gaming Compact, the Tribal Gaming Ordinance, and IGRA. The license shall be reviewed and renewed, if appropriate, every two years thereafter. Verification that this requirement has been met shall be provided by the Tribe to the State Gaming Agency every two years. The Tribal Gaming Agency's certification to that effect shall be posted in a conspicuous and public place in the Gaming Facility at all times.

(b) In order to protect the health and safety of all Gaming Facility patrons, guests, and employees, all Gaming Facilities of the Tribe constructed after the effective date of this Gaming Compact, and all expansions or modifications to a Gaming Facility in operation as of the effective date of this compact, shall meet the building and safety codes of the Tribe, which, as a condition for engaging in that construction, expansion, modification, or renovation, shall amend its existing building and safety codes if necessary, or enact such codes if there are none, so that they meet the standards of either the building and safety codes of any county within the boundaries of which the site of the Facility is located, or the Uniform Building Codes, including all uniform fire, plumbing, electrical, mechanical, and related codes then in effect provided that nothing herein shall be deemed to confer jurisdiction upon any county or the State with respect to any reference to such building and safety codes. Any such construction, expansion or modification will also comply with the federal Americans with Disabilities Act, P. L. 101-336, as amended, 42 U.S.C. § 12101 et seq.

(c) Any Gaming Facility in which gaming authorized by this Gaming Compact is conducted shall be issued a certificate of occupancy by the Tribal Gaming Agency prior to occupancy if it was not used for any Gaming Activities under IGRA prior to the effective date of this Gaming Compact, or, if it was so used, within one year thereafter. The issuance of this certificate shall be reviewed for continuing compliance every two years thereafter. Inspections by qualified building and safety experts shall be conducted under the direction of the Tribal Gaming Agency as the basis for issuing any certificate hereunder. The Tribal Gaming Agency shall determine and certify that, as to new construction or new use for gaming, the Facility meets the Tribe's building and safety code, or, as to facilities or portions of facilities that were used for the Tribe's Gaming Activities prior to this Gaming Compact, that the facility or portions thereof do not endanger the health or safety of occupants or the integrity of the Gaming Operation. The Tribe will not offer Class III gaming in a Facility that is constructed or maintained in a manner that endangers the health or safety of occupants or the integrity of the gaming operation.

(d) The State shall designate an agent or agents to be given reasonable notice of each inspection by the Tribal Gaming Agency's experts, which state agents may accompany any such inspection. The Tribe agrees to correct any Gaming Facility condition noted in an inspection that does not meet the standards set forth in subdivisions (b) and (c). The Tribal Gaming Agency and the State's designated agent or agents shall exchange any reports of an inspection within 10 days after completion of the report, which reports shall also be separately and simultaneously forwarded by both agencies to the Tribal Chairperson. Upon certification by the Tribal Gaming Agency's experts that a Gaming Facility meets applicable standards, the Tribal Gaming Agency shall forward the experts' certification to the State within 10 days of issuance. If the State's agent objects to that certification, the Tribe shall make a good faith effort to address the State's concerns, but if the State does not withdraw its objection, the matter will be resolved in accordance with the dispute resolution provisions of Section 9.0.

Sec. 6.4.3. Suitability Standard Regarding Gaming Licenses. (a) In reviewing an application for a gaming license, and in addition to any standards set forth in the Tribal Gaming Ordinance, the Tribal Gaming Agency shall consider whether issuance of the license is inimical to public health, safety, or welfare, and whether issuance of the license will undermine public trust that the Tribe's Gaming Operations, or tribal government gaming generally, are free from criminal and dishonest elements and would be conducted honestly. A license may not be issued unless, based on all information and documents submitted, the Tribal Gaming Agency is satisfied that the applicant is all of the following, in addition to any other criteria in IGRA or the Tribal Gaming Ordinance:

(a) A person of good character, honesty, and integrity.

(b) A person whose prior activities, criminal record (if any), reputation, habits, and associations do not pose a threat to the public interest or to the effective regulation and control of gambling, or create or enhance the dangers of unsuitable, unfair, or illegal practices, methods, or activities in the conduct of gambling, or in the carrying on of the business and financial arrangements incidental thereto.

(c) A person who is in all other respects qualified to be licensed as provided in this Gaming Compact, IGRA, the Tribal Gaming Ordinance, and any other criteria adopted by the Tribal Gaming Agency or the Tribe. An applicant shall not be found to be unsuitable solely on the ground that the applicant was an employee of a tribal gaming operation in California that was conducted prior to the effective date of this Compact.

Sec. 6.4.4. Gaming Employees.

(a) Every Gaming Employee shall obtain, and thereafter maintain current, a valid tribal gaming license, which shall be subject to biennial renewal; provided that in accordance with Section 6.4.9, those persons may be employed on a temporary or conditional basis pending completion of the licensing process.

(b) Except as provided in subdivisions (c) and (d), the Tribe will not employ or continue to employ, any person whose application to the State Gaming Agency for a determination of suitability, or for a renewal of such a determination, has been denied or has expired without renewal.

(c) Notwithstanding subdivision (a), the Tribe may retain in its employ a person whose application for a determination of suitability, or for a renewal of such a determination, has been denied by the State Gaming Agency, if: (i) the person holds a valid and current license issued by the Tribal Gaming Agency that must be renewed at least biennially; (ii) the denial of the application by the State Gaming Agency is based solely on activities, conduct, or associations that antedate the filing of the person's initial application to the State Gaming Agency for a determination of suitability; (iii) the person is not an employee or agent of any other gaming operation; and (iv) the person has been in the continuous employ of the Tribe for at least three years prior to the effective date of this Compact.

(d) Notwithstanding subdivision (a), the Tribe may employ or retain in its employ a person whose application for a determination of suitability, or for a renewal of such a determination, has been denied by the State Gaming Agency, if the person is an enrolled member of the Tribe, as defined in this subdivision, and if (i) the person holds a valid and current license issued by the Tribal Gaming Agency that must be renewed at least biennially; (ii) the denial of the application by the State Gaming Agency is based solely on activities, conduct, or associations that antedate the filing of the person's initial application to the State Gaming Agency for a determination of suitability; and (iii) the person is not an employee or agent of any other gaming operation. For purposes of this subdivision, "enrolled member" means a person who is either (a) certified by the Tribe as having been a member of the Tribe for at least five (5) years, or (b) a holder of confirmation of membership issued by the Bureau of Indian Affairs.

(e) Nothing herein shall be construed to relieve any person of the obligation to apply for a renewal of a determination of suitability as required by Section 6.5.6.

Sec. 6.4.5. Gaming Resource Supplier. Any Gaming Resource Supplier who, directly or indirectly, provides, has provided, or is deemed likely to provide at least twenty-five thousand dollars ($25,000) in Gaming Resources in any 12-month period, or who has received at least twenty-five thousand dollars ($25,000) in any consecutive 12-month period within the 24-month period immediately preceding application, shall be licensed by the Tribal Gaming Agency prior to the sale, lease, or distribution, or further sale, lease, or distribution, of any such Gaming Resources to or in connection with the Tribe's Operation or Facility. These licenses shall be reviewed at least every two years for continuing compliance. In connection with such a review, the Tribal Gaming Agency shall require the Supplier to update all information provided in the previous application. For purposes of Section 6.5.2, such a review shall be deemed to constitute an application for renewal. The Tribe shall not enter into, or continue to make payments pursuant to, any contract or agreement for the provision of Gaming Resources with any person whose application to the State Gaming Agency for a determination of suitability has been denied or has expired without renewal. Any agreement between the Tribe and a Gaming Resource Supplier shall be deemed to include a provision for its termination without further liability on the part of the Tribe, except for the bona fide repayment of all outstanding sums (exclusive of interest) owed as of, or payment for services or materials received up to, the date of termination, upon revocation or non-renewal of the Supplier's license by the Tribal Gaming Agency based on a determination of unsuitability by the State Gaming Agency.

Sec. 6.4.6. Financial Sources. Any person extending financing, directly or indirectly, to the Tribe's Gaming Facility or Gaming Operation shall be licensed by the Tribal Gaming Agency prior to extending that financing, provided that any person who is extending financing at the time of the execution of this Compact shall be licensed by the Tribal Gaming Agency within ninety (90) days of such execution. These licenses shall be reviewed at least every two years for continuing compliance. In connection with such a review, the Tribal Gaming Agency shall require the Financial Source to update all information provided in the previous application. For purposes of Section 6.5.2, such a review shall be deemed to constitute an application for renewal. Any agreement between the Tribe and a Financial Source shall be deemed to include a provision for its termination without further liability on the part of the Tribe, except for the bona fide repayment of all outstanding sums (exclusive of interest) owed as of the date of termination, upon revocation or non-renewal of the Financial Source's license by the Tribal Gaming Agency based on a determination of unsuitability by the State Gaming Agency. The Tribe shall not enter into, or continue to make payments pursuant to, any contract or agreement for the provision of financing with any person whose application to the State Gaming Agency for a determination of suitability has been denied or has expired without renewal. A Gaming Resource Supplier who provides financing exclusively in connection with the sale or lease of Gaming Resources obtained from that Supplier may be licensed solely in accordance with licensing procedures applicable, if at all, to Gaming Resource Suppliers. The Tribal Gaming Agency may, at its discretion, exclude from the licensing requirements of this section, financing provided by a federally regulated or state-regulated bank, savings and loan, or other federally- or state-regulated lending institution; or any agency of the federal, state, or local government; or any investor who, alone or in conjunction with others, holds less than 10% of any outstanding indebtedness evidenced by bonds issued by the Tribe.

Sec. 6.4.7. Processing Tribal Gaming License Applications. Each applicant for a tribal gaming license shall submit the completed application along with the required information and an application fee, if required, to the Tribal Gaming Agency in accordance with the rules and regulations of that agency. At a minimum, the Tribal Gaming Agency shall require submission and consideration of all information required under IGRA, including Section 556.4 of Title 25 of the Code of Federal Regulations, for licensing primary management officials and key employees. For applicants who are business entities, these licensing provisions shall apply to the entity as well as: (i) each of its officers and directors; (ii) each of its principal management employees, including any chief executive officer, chief financial officer, chief operating officer, and general manager; (iii) each of its owners or partners, if an unincorporated business; (iv) each of its shareholders who owns more than 10 percent of the shares of the corporation, if a corporation; and (v) each person or entity (other than a financial institution that the Tribal Gaming Agency has determined does not require a license under the preceding section) that, alone or in combination with others, has provided financing in connection with any gaming authorized under this Gaming Compact, if that person or entity provided more than 10 percent of (a) the start-up capital, (b) the operating capital over a 12-month period, or (c) a combination thereof. For purposes of this Section, where there is any commonality of the characteristics identified in clauses (i) to (v), inclusive, between any two or more entities, those entities may be deemed to be a single entity. Nothing herein precludes the Tribe or Tribal Gaming Agency from requiring more stringent licensing requirements.

Sec. 6.4.8. Background Investigations of Applicants.

The Tribal Gaming Agency shall conduct or cause to be conducted all necessary background investigations reasonably required to determine that the applicant is qualified for a gaming license under the standards set forth in Section 6.4.3, and to fulfill all requirements for licensing under IGRA, the Tribal Gaming Ordinance, and this Gaming Compact. The Tribal Gaming Agency shall not issue other than a temporary license until a determination is made that those qualifications have been met. In lieu of completing its own background investigation, and to the extent that doing so does not conflict with or violate IGRA or the Tribal Gaming Ordinance, the Tribal Gaming Agency may contract with the State Gaming Agency for the

conduct of background investigations, may rely on a state certification of non-objection previously issued under a gaming compact involving another tribe, or may rely on a State gaming license previously issued to the applicant, to fulfill some or all of the Tribal Gaming Agency's background investigation obligation. An applicant for a tribal gaming license shall be required to provide releases to the State Gaming Agency to make available to the Tribal Gaming Agency background information regarding the applicant. The State Gaming Agency shall cooperate in furnishing to the Tribal Gaming Agency that information, unless doing so would violate any agreement the State Gaming Agency has with a source of the information other than the applicant, or would impair or impede a criminal investigation, or unless the Tribal Gaming Agency cannot provide sufficient safeguards to assure the State Gaming Agency that the information will remain confidential or that provision of the information would violate state or federal law. If the Tribe adopts an ordinance confirming that Article 6 (commencing with section 11140) of Chapter 1 of Title 1 of Part 4 of the California Penal Code is applicable to members, investigators, and staff of the Tribal Gaming Agency, and those members, investigators, and staff thereafter comply with that ordinance, then, for purposes of carrying out its obligations under this Section, the Tribal Gaming Agency shall be considered to be an entity entitled to receive state summary criminal history information within the meaning of subdivision (b)(12) of section 11105 of the California Penal Code. The California Department of Justice shall provide services to the Tribal Gaming Agency through the California Law Enforcement Telecommunications System (CLETS), subject to a determination by the CLETS advisory committee that the Tribal Gaming Agency is qualified for receipt of such services, and on such terms and conditions as are deemed reasonable by that advisory committee.

Sec. 6.4.9. Temporary Licensing of Gaming Employees.

Notwithstanding anything herein to the contrary, if the applicant has completed a license application in a manner satisfactory to the Tribal Gaming Agency, and that agency has conducted a preliminary background investigation, and the investigation or other information held by that agency does not indicate that the applicant has a criminal history or other information in his or her background that would either automatically disqualify the applicant from obtaining a license or cause a reasonable person to investigate further before issuing a license, or is otherwise unsuitable for licensing, the Tribal Gaming Agency may issue a temporary license and may impose such specific conditions thereon pending completion of the applicant's background investigation, as the Tribal Gaming Agency in its sole discretion shall determine. Special fees may be required by the Tribal Gaming Agency to issue or maintain a temporary license. A temporary license shall remain in effect until suspended or revoked, or a final determination is made on the application. At any time after issuance of a temporary license, the Tribal Gaming Agency may suspend or revoke it in accor dance with Sections 6.5.1 or 6.5.5, and the State Gaming Agency may request suspension or revocation in accordance with subdivision (d) of Section 6.5.6.

Nothing herein shall be construed to relieve the Tribe of any obligation under Part 558 of Title 25 of the Code of Federal Regulations.

Sec. 6.5. Gaming License Issuance.

Upon completion of the necessary background investigation, the Tribal Gaming Agency may issue a license on a conditional or unconditional basis. Nothing herein shall create a property or other right of an applicant in an opportunity to be licensed, or in a license itself, both of which shall be considered to be privileges granted to the applicant in the sole discretion of the Tribal Gaming Agency. Sec. 6.5.1. Denial, Suspension, or Revocation of Licenses. (a) Any application for a gaming license may be denied, and any license issued may be revoked, if the Tribal Gaming Agency determines that the application is incomplete or deficient, or if the applicant is determined to be unsuitable or otherwise unqualified for a gaming license. Pending consideration of revocation, the Tribal Gaming Agency may suspend a license in accordance with Section 6.5.5. All rights to notice and hearing shall be governed by tribal law, as to which the applicant will be notified in writing along with notice of an intent to suspend or revoke the license.

(b) (i) Except as provided in paragraph (ii) below, upon receipt of notice that the State Gaming Agency has determined that a person would be unsuitable for licensure in a gambling establishment subject to the jurisdiction of the State Gaming Agency, the Tribal Gaming Agency shall promptly revoke any license that has theretofore been issued to the person; provided that the Tribal Gaming Agency may, in its discretion, re-issue a license to the person following entry of a final judgment reversing the determination of the State Gaming Agency in a proceeding in state court conducted pursuant to section 1085 of the California Civil Code. (ii) Notwithstanding a determination of unsuitability by the State Gaming Agency, the Tribal Gaming Agency may, in its discretion, decline to revoke a tribal license issued to a person employed by the Tribe pursuant to Section 6.4.4(c) or Section 6.4.4(d).

Sec. 6.5.2. Renewal of Licenses; Extensions; Further Investigation.

The term of a tribal gaming license shall not exceed two years, and application for renewal of a license must be made prior to its expiration. Applicants for renewal of a license shall provide updated material as requested, on the appropriate renewal forms, but, at the discretion of the Tribal Gaming Agency, may not be required to resubmit historical data previously submitted or that is otherwise available to the Tribal Gaming Agency. At the discretion of the Tribal Gaming Agency, an additional background investigation may be required at any time if the Tribal Gaming Agency determines the need for further information concerning the applicant's continuing suitability or eligibility for a license. Prior to renewing a license, the Tribal Gaming Agency shall deliver to the State Gaming Agency copies of all information and documents received in connection with the application for renewal.

Sec. 6.5.3. Identification Cards. The Tribal Gaming Agency shall require that all persons who are required to be licensed wear, in plain view at all times while in the Gaming Facility, identification badges issued by the Tribal Gaming Agency. Identification badges must display information including, but not limited to, a photograph and an identification number that is adequate to enable agents of the Tribal Gaming Agency to readily identify the person and determine the validity and date of expiration of his or her license.

Sec. 6.5.4. Fees for Tribal License.

The fees for all tribal licenses shall be set by the Tribal Gaming Agency.

Sec. 6.5.5. Suspension of Tribal License. The Tribal Gaming Agency may summarily suspend the license of any employee if the Tribal Gaming Agency determines that the continued licensing of the person or entity could constitute a threat to the public health or safety or may violate the Tribal Gaming Agency's licensing or other standards. Any right to notice or hearing in regard thereto shall be governed by Tribal law.

Sec. 6.5.6. State Certification Process.

(a) Upon receipt of a completed license application and a determination by the Tribal Gaming Agency that it intends to issue the earlier of a temporary or permanent license, the Tribal Gaming Agency shall transmit to the State Gaming Agency a notice of intent to license the applicant, together with all of the following: (i) a copy of all tribal license application materials and information received by the Tribal Gaming Agency from the applicant; (ii) an original set of fingerprint cards; (iii) a current photograph; and (iv) except to the extent waived by the State Gaming Agency, such releases of information, waivers, and other completed and executed forms as have been obtained by the Tribal Gaming Agency. Except for an applicant for licensing as a non-key Gaming Employee, as defined by agreement between the Tribal Gaming Agency and the State Gaming Agency, the Tribal Gaming Agency shall require the applicant also to file an application with the State Gaming Agency, prior to issuance of a temporary or permanent tribal gaming license, for a determination of suitability for licensure under the California Gambling Control Act. Investigation and disposition of that application shall be governed entirely by state law, and the State Gaming Agency shall determine whether the applicant would be found suitable for licensure in a gambling establishment subject to that Agency's jurisdiction. Additional information may be required by the State Gaming Agency to assist it in its background investigation, provided that such State Gaming Agency requirement shall be no greater than that which may be required of applicants for a State gaming license in connection with nontribal gaming activities and at a similar level of participation or employment. A determination of suitability is valid for the term of the tribal license held by the applicant, and the Tribal Gaming Agency shall require a licensee to apply for renewal of a determination of suitability at such time as the licensee applies for renewal of a tribal gaming license. The State Gaming Agency and the Tribal Gaming Agency (together with tribal gaming agencies under other gaming compacts) shall cooperate in developing standard licensing forms for tribal gaming license applicants, on a statewide basis, that reduce or eliminate duplicative or excessive paperwork, which forms and procedures shall take into account the Tribe's requirements under IGRA and the expense thereof.

(b) Background Investigations of Applicants. Upon receipt of completed license application information from the Tribal Gaming Agency, the State Gaming Agency may conduct a background investigation pursuant to state law to determine whether the applicant would be suitable to be licensed for association with a gambling establishment subject to the jurisdiction of the State Gaming Agency. If further investigation is required to supplement the investigation conducted by the Tribal Gaming Agency, the applicant will be required to pay the statutory application fee charged by the State Gaming Agency pursuant to California Business and Professions Code section 19941(a), but any deposit requested by the State Gaming Agency pursuant to section 19855 of that Code shall take into account reports of the background investigation already conducted by the Tribal Gaming Agency and the NIGC, if any. Failure to pay the application fee or deposit may be grounds for denial of the application by the State Gaming Agency. The State Gaming Agency and Tribal Gaming Agency shall cooperate in sharing as much background information as possible, both to maximize investigative efficiency and thoroughness, and to minimize investigative costs. Upon completion of the necessary background investigation or other verification of suitability, the State Gaming Agency shall issue a notice to the Tribal Gaming Agency certifying that the State has determined that the applicant would be suitable, or that the applicant would be unsuitable, for licensure in a gambling establishment subject to the jurisdiction of the State Gaming Agency and, if unsuitable, stating the reasons therefor.

(c) The Tribe shall monthly provide the State Gaming Agency with the name, badge identification number, and job descriptions of all non-key Gaming Employees.

(d) Prior to denying an application for a determination of suitability, the State Gaming Agency shall notify the Tribal Gaming Agency and afford the Tribe an opportunity to be heard. If the State Gaming Agency denies an application for a determination of suitability, that Agency shall provide the applicant with written notice of all appeal rights available under state law.

Sec. 7.0. COMPLIANCE ENFORCEMENT.

Sec. 7.1. On-Site Regulation.
It is the responsibility of the Tribal Gaming Agency to conduct on-site gaming regulation and control in order to enforce the terms of this Gaming Compact, IGRA, and the Tribal Gaming Ordinance with respect to Gaming Operation and Facility compliance, and to protect the integrity of the Gaming Activities, the reputation of the Tribe and the Gaming Operation for honesty and fairness, and the confidence of patrons that tribal government gaming in California meets the highest standards of regulation and internal controls. To meet those responsibilities, the Tribal Gaming Agency shall adopt and enforce regulations, procedures, and practices as set forth herein.

Sec. 7.2. Investigation and Sanctions.
The Tribal Gaming Agency shall investigate any reported violation of this Gaming Compact and shall require the Gaming Operation to correct the violation upon such terms and conditions as the Tribal Gaming Agency determines are necessary. The Tribal Gaming Agency shall be empowered by the Tribal Gaming Ordinance to impose fines or other sanctions within the jurisdiction of the Tribe against gaming licensees or other persons who interfere with or violate the Tribe's gaming regulatory requirements and obligations under IGRA, the Tribal Gaming Ordinance, or this Gaming Compact. The Tribal Gaming Agency shall report significant or continued violations of this Compact or failures to comply with its orders to the State Gaming Agency.

Sec. 7.3. Assistance by State Gaming Agency.
The Tribe may request the assistance of the State Gaming Agency whenever it reasonably appears that such assistance may be necessary to carry out the purposes described in Section 7.1, or otherwise to protect public health, safety, or welfare. If requested by the Tribe or Tribal Gaming Agency, the State Gaming Agency shall provide requested services to ensure proper compliance with this Gaming Compact. The State shall be reimbursed for its actual and reasonable costs of that assistance, if the assistance required expenditure of extraordinary costs.

Sec. 7.4. Access to Premises by State Gaming Agency; Notification; Inspections.
Notwithstanding that the Tribe has the primary responsibility to administer and enforce the regulatory requirements of this Compact, the State Gaming Agency shall have the right to inspect the Tribe's Gaming Facility with respect to Class III Gaming Activities only, and all Gaming Operation or Facility records relating thereto, subject to the following conditions:

Sec. 7.4.1. Inspection of public areas of a Gaming Facility may be made at any time without prior notice during normal Gaming Facility business hours.

Sec. 7.4.2. Inspection of areas of a Gaming Facility not normally accessible to the public may be made at any time during normal Gaming Facility business hours, immediately after the State Gaming Agency's authorized inspector notifies the Tribal Gaming Agency of his or her presence on the premises, presents proper identification, and requests access to the non-public areas of the Gaming Facility. The Tribal Gaming Agency, in its sole discretion, may require a member of the Tribal Gaming Agency to accompany the State Gaming Agency inspector at all times that the State Gaming Agency inspector is in a non-public area of the Gaming Facility. If the Tribal Gaming Agency imposes such a requirement, it shall require such member to be available at all times for those purposes and shall ensure that the member has the ability to gain immediate access to all non-public areas of the Gaming Facility. Nothing in this Compact shall be construed to limit the State Gaming Agency to one inspector during inspections.

Sec. 7.4.3. (a) Inspection and copying of Gaming Operation papers, books, and records may occur at any time, immediately after notice to the Tribal Gaming Agency, during the normal hours of the Gaming Facility's business office, provided that the inspection and copying of those papers, books or records shall not interfere with the normal functioning of the Gaming Operation or Facility. Notwithstanding any other provision of California law, all information and records that the State Gaming Agency obtains, inspects, or copies pursuant to this Gaming Compact shall be, and remain, the property solely of the Tribe; provided that such records and copies may be retained by the State Gaming Agency as reasonably necessary for completion of any investigation of the Tribe's compliance with this Compact.

(b)(i) The State Gaming Agency will exercise utmost care in the preservation of the confidentiality of any and all information and documents received from the Tribe, and will apply the highest standards of confidentiality expected under state law to preserve such information and documents from disclosure. The Tribe may avail itself of any and all remedies under state law for improper disclosure of information or documents. To the extent reasonably feasible, the State Gaming Agency will consult with representatives of the Tribe prior to disclosure of any documents received from the Tribe, or any documents compiled from such documents or from information received from the Tribe, including any disclosure compelled by judicial process, and, in the case of any disclosure compelled by judicial process, will endeavor to give the Tribe immediate notice of the order compelling disclosure and a reasonable opportunity to interpose an objection thereto with the court. (ii) The Tribal Gaming Agency and the State Gaming Agency shall confer and agree upon protocols for release to other law enforcement agencies of information obtained during the course of background investigations.

(c) Records received by the State Gaming Agency from the Tribe in compliance with this Compact, or information compiled by the State Gaming Agency from those records, shall be exempt from disclosure under the California Public Records Act.

Sec. 7.4.4. Notwithstanding any other provision of this Compact, the State Gaming Agency shall not be denied access to papers, books, records, equipment, or places where such access is reasonably necessary to ensure compliance with this Compact.

Sec. 7.4.5. (a) Subject to the provisions of subdivision (b), the Tribal Gaming Agency shall not permit any Gaming Device to be transported to or from the Tribe's land except in accordance with procedures established by agreement between the State Gaming Agency and the Tribal Gaming Agency and upon at least 10 days' notice to the Sheriff's Department for the county in which the land is located.

(b) Transportation of a Gaming Device from the Gaming Facility within California is permissible only if: (i) The final destination of the device is a gaming facility of any tribe in California that has a compact with the State; (ii) The final destination of the device is any other state in which possession of the device or devices is made lawful by state law or by tribal-state compact; (iii) The final destination of the device is another country, or any state or province of another country, wherein possession of the device is lawful; or (iv) The final destination is a location within California for testing, repair, maintenance, or storage by a person or entity that has been licensed by the Tribal Gaming Agency and has been found suitable for licensure by the State Gaming Agency.

(c) Gaming Devices transported off the Tribe's land in violation of this Section 7.4.5 or in violation of any permit issued pursuant thereto is subject to summary seizure by California peace officers.

Sec. 8.0. RULES AND REGULATIONS FOR THE OPERATION AND MANAGEMENT OF THE TRIBAL GAMING OPERATION.

Sec. 8.1. Adoption of Regulations for Operation and Management; Minimum Standards.
In order to meet the goals set forth in this Gaming Compact and required of the Tribe by law, the Tribal Gaming Agency shall be vested with the authority to promulgate, and shall promulgate, at a minimum, rules and regulations or specifications governing the following subjects, and to ensure their enforcement in an effective manner:

Sec. 8.1.1. The enforcement of all relevant laws and rules with respect to the Gaming Operation and Facility, and the power to conduct investigations and hearings with respect thereto, and to any other subject within its jurisdiction.

Sec. 8.1.2. Ensuring the physical safety of Gaming Operation patrons and employees, and any other person while in the Gaming Facility. Nothing herein shall be construed to make applicable to the Tribe any state laws, regulations, or standards governing the use of tobacco.

Sec. 8.1.3. The physical safeguarding of assets transported to, within, and from the Gaming Facility.

Sec. 8.1.4. The prevention of illegal activity from occurring within the Gaming Facility or with regard to the Gaming Operation, including, but not limited to, the maintenance of employee procedures and a surveillance system as provided below.

Sec. 8.1.5. The recording of any and all occurrences within the Gaming Facility that deviate from normal operating policies and procedures (hereafter "incidents"). The procedure for recording incidents shall: (1) specify that security personnel record all incidents, regardless of an employee's determination that the incident may be immaterial (all incidents shall be identified in writing); (2) require the assignment of a sequential number to each report; (3) provide for permanent reporting in indelible ink in a bound notebook from which pages cannot be removed and in which entries are made on each side of each page; and (4) require that each report include, at a minimum, all of the following:

 (a) The record number.
 (b) The date.
 (c) The time.
 (d) The location of the incident.
 (e) A detailed description of the incident.
 (f) The persons involved in the incident.
 (g) The security department employee assigned to the incident.

Sec. 8.1.6. The establishment of employee procedures designed to permit detection of any irregularities, theft, cheating, fraud, or the like, consistent with industry practice.

Sec. 8.1.7. Maintenance of a list of persons barred from the Gaming Facility who, because of their past behavior, criminal history, or association with persons or organizations, pose a threat to the integrity of the Gaming Activities of the Tribe or to the integrity of regulated gaming within the State.

Sec. 8.1.8. The conduct of an audit of the Gaming Operation, not less than annually, by an independent certified public accountant, in accordance with the auditing and accounting standards for audits of casinos of the American Institute of Certified Public Accountants.

Sec. 8.1.9. Submission to, and prior approval, from the Tribal Gaming Agency of the rules and regulations of each Class III game to be operated by the Tribe, and of any changes in those rules and regulations. No Class III game may be played that has not received Tribal Gaming Agency approval.

Sec. 8.1.10. Addressing all of the following:

 (a) Maintenance of a copy of the rules, regulations, and procedures for each game as played, including, but not limited to, the method of play and the odds and method of determining amounts paid to winners;

 (b) Specifications and standards to ensure that information regarding the method of play, odds, and payoff determinations shall be visibly displayed or available to patrons in written form in the Gaming Facility;

 (c) Specifications ensuring that betting limits applicable to any gaming station shall be displayed at that gaming station;

 (d) Procedures ensuring that in the event of a patron dispute over the application of any gaming rule or regulation, the matter shall be handled in accordance with, industry practice and principles of fairness, pursuant to the Tribal Gaming Ordinance and any rules and regulations promulgated by the Tribal Gaming Agency.

Sec. 8.1.11. Maintenance of a closed-circuit television surveillance system consistent with industry standards for gaming facilities of the type and scale operated by the Tribe, which system shall be approved by, and may not be modified without the approval of, the Tribal Gaming Agency. The Tribal

Gaming Agency shall have current copies of the Gaming Facility floor plan and closed-circuit television system at all times, and any modifications thereof first shall be approved by the Tribal Gaming Agency.

Sec. 8.1.12. Maintenance of a cashier's cage in accordance with industry standards for such facilities.

Sec. 8.1.13. Specification of minimum staff and supervisory requirements for each Gaming Activity to be conducted.

Sec. 8.1.14. Technical standards and specifications for the operation of Gaming Devices and other games authorized herein to be conducted by the Tribe, which technical specifications may be no less stringent than those approved by a recognized gaming testing laboratory in the gaming industry.

Sec. 8.2. State Civil and Criminal Jurisdiction. Nothing in this Gaming Compact affects the civil or criminal jurisdiction of the State under Public Law 280 (18 U.S.C. Sec. 1162; 28 U.S.C. Sec. 1360) or IGRA, to the extent applicable. In addition, criminal jurisdiction to enforce state gambling laws is transferred to the State pursuant to 18 U.S.C. § 1166(d), provided that no Gaming Activity conducted by the Tribe pursuant to this Gaming Compact may be deemed to be a civil or criminal violation of any law of the State.

Sec. 8.3. (a) The Tribe shall take all reasonable steps to ensure that members of the Tribal Gaming Agency are free from corruption, undue influence, compromise, and conflicting interests in the conduct of their duties under this Compact; shall adopt a conflict-of-interest code to that end; and shall ensure the prompt removal of any member of the Tribal Gaming Agency who is found to have acted in a corrupt or compromised manner.

(b) The Tribe shall conduct a background investigation on a prospective member of the Tribal Gaming Agency, who shall meet the background requirements of a management contractor under IGRA; provided that, if such official is elected through a tribal election process, that official may not participate in any Tribal Gaming Agency matters under this Compact unless a background investigation has been concluded and the official has been found to be suitable. If requested by the tribal government or the Tribal Gaming Agency, the State Gaming Agency may assist in the conduct of such a background investigation and may assist in the investigation of any possible corruption or compromise of a member of the agency.

Sec. 8.4. In order to foster statewide uniformity of regulation of Class III gaming operations throughout the state, rules, regulations, standards, specifications, and procedures of the Tribal Gaming Agency in respect to any matter encompassed by Sections 6.0, 7.0, or 8.0 shall be consistent with regulations adopted by the State Gaming Agency in accordance with Section 8.4.1. Chapter 3.5 (commencing with section 11340) of Part 1 of Division 3 of Title 2 of the California Government Code does not apply to regulations adopted by the State Gaming Agency in respect to tribal gaming operations under this Section.

Sec. 8.4.1. (a) Except as provided in subdivision (d), no State Gaming Agency regulation shall be effective with respect to the Tribe's Gaming Operation unless it has first been approved by the Association and the Tribe has had an opportunity to review and comment on the proposed regulation. (b) Every State Gaming Agency regulation that is intended to apply to the Tribe (other than a regulation proposed or previously approved by the Association) shall be submitted to the Association for consideration prior to submission of the regulation to the Tribe for comment as provided in subdivision (c). A regulation that is disapproved by the Association shall not be submitted to the Tribe for comment unless it is re-adopted by the State Gaming Agency as a proposed regulation, in its original or amended form, with a detailed, written response to the Association's objections. (c) Except as provided in subdivision (d), no regulation of the State Gaming Agency shall be adopted as a final regulation in respect to the Tribe's Gaming Operation before the expiration of 30 days after submission of the proposed regulation to the Tribe for comment as a proposed regulation, and after consideration of the Tribe's comments, if any. (d) In exigent circumstances (e.g., imminent threat to public health and safety), the State Gaming Agency may adopt a regulation that becomes effective immediately. Any such regulation shall be accompanied by a detailed, written description of the exigent circumstances, and shall be submitted immediately to the Association for consideration. If the regulation is disapproved by the Association, it shall cease to be effective, but may be re-adopted by the State Gaming Agency as a proposed regulation, in its original or amended form, with a detailed, written response to the Association's objections, and thereafter submitted to the Tribe for comment as provided in subdivision (c). (e) The Tribe may object to a State Gaming Agency regulation on the ground that it is unnecessary, unduly burdensome, or unfairly discriminatory, and may seek repeal or amendment of the regulation through the dispute resolution process of Section 9.0.

Sec. 9.0. DISPUTE RESOLUTION PROVISIONS.

Sec. 9.1. Voluntary Resolution; Reference to Other Means of Resolution.
In recognition of the government-to-government relationship of the Tribe and the State, the parties shall make their best efforts to resolve disputes that occur under this Gaming Compact by good faith negotiations whenever possible. Therefore, without prejudice to the right of either party to seek injunctive relief against the other when circumstances are deemed to require immediate relief, the parties hereby establish a threshold requirement that disputes between the Tribe and the State first be subjected to a process of meeting and conferring in good faith in order to foster a spirit of cooperation and efficiency in the administration and monitoring of performance and compliance by each other with the terms, provisions, and conditions of this Gaming Compact, as follows:

(a) Either party shall give the other, as soon as possible after the event giving rise to the concern, a written notice setting forth, with specificity, the issues to be resolved.

(b) The parties shall meet and confer in a good faith attempt to resolve the dispute through negotiation not later than 10 days after receipt of the notice, unless both parties agree in writing to an extension of time.

(c) If the dispute is not resolved to the satisfaction of the parties within 30 calendar days after the first meeting, then either party may seek to have the dispute resolved by an arbitrator in accordance with this section, but neither party shall be required to agree to submit to arbitration.

(d) Disagreements that are not otherwise resolved by arbitration or other mutually acceptable means as provided in Section 9.3 may be resolved in the United States District Court where the Tribe's Gaming Facility is located, or is to be located, and the Ninth Circuit Court of Appeals (or, if those federal courts lack jurisdiction, in any state court of competent jurisdiction and its related courts of appeal). The disputes to be submitted to court action include, but are not limited to, claims of breach or violation of this Compact, or failure to negotiate in good faith as required by the terms of this Compact. In no event may the Tribe be precluded from pursuing any arbitration or judicial remedy against the State on the grounds that the Tribe has failed to exhaust its state administrative remedies. The parties agree that, except in the case of imminent threat to the public health or safety, reasonable efforts will be made to explore alternative dispute resolution avenues prior to resort to judicial process.

Sec. 9.2. Arbitration Rules.
Arbitration shall be conducted in accordance with the policies and procedures of the Commercial Arbitration Rules of the American Arbitration Association, and shall be held on the Tribe's land or, if unreasonably inconvenient under the circumstances, at such other location as the parties may agree. Each side shall bear its own costs, attorneys' fees, and one-half the costs and expenses of the American Arbitration Association and the arbitrator, unless the arbitrator rules otherwise. Only one neutral arbitrator may be named, unless the Tribe or the State objects, in which case a panel of three arbitrators (one of whom is selected by each party) will be named. The provisions of Section 1283.05 of the California Code of Civil Procedure shall apply; provided that no discovery authorized by that section may be conducted without leave of the arbitrator. The decision of the arbitrator shall be in writing, give reasons for the decision, and shall be binding. Judgment on the award may be entered in any federal or state court having jurisdiction thereof.

Sec. 9.3. No Waiver or Preclusion of Other Means of Dispute Resolution.

This Section 9.0 may not be construed to waive, limit, or restrict any remedy that is otherwise available to either party, nor may this Section be construed to preclude, limit, or restrict the ability of the parties to pursue, by mutual agreement, any other method of dispute resolution, including, but not limited to, mediation or utilization of a technical advisor to the Tribal and State Gaming Agencies; provided that neither party is under any obligation to agree to such alternative method of dispute resolution.

Sec. 9.4. Limited Waiver of Sovereign Immunity.

(a) In the event that a dispute is to be resolved in federal court or a state court of competent jurisdiction as provided in this Section 9.0, the State and the Tribe expressly consent to be sued therein and waive any immunity therefrom that they may have provided that:

(1) The dispute is limited solely to issues arising under this Gaming Compact;

(2) Neither side makes any claim for monetary damages (that is, only injunctive, specific performance, including enforcement of a provision of this Compact requiring payment of money to one or another of the parties, or declaratory relief is sought); and

(3) No person or entity other than the Tribe and the State is party to the action, unless failure to join a third party would deprive the court of jurisdiction; provided that nothing herein shall be construed to constitute a waiver of the sovereign immunity of either the Tribe or the State in respect to any such third party.

(b) In the event of intervention by any additional party into any such action without the consent of the Tribe and the State, the waivers of either the Tribe or the State provided for herein may be revoked, unless joinder is required to preserve the court's jurisdiction; provided that nothing herein shall be construed to constitute a waiver of the sovereign immunity of either the Tribe or the State in respect to any such third party.

(c) The waivers and consents provided for under this Section 9.0 shall extend to civil actions authorized by this Compact, including, but not limited to, actions to compel arbitration, any arbitration proceeding herein, any action to confirm or enforce any judgment or arbitration award as provided herein, and any appellate proceedings emanating from a matter in which an immunity waiver has been granted. Except as stated herein or elsewhere in this Compact, no other waivers or consents to be sued, either express or implied, are granted by either party.

Sec. 10.0. PUBLIC AND WORKPLACE HEALTH, SAFETY, AND LIABILITY.

Sec. 10.1.

The Tribe will not conduct Class III gaming in a manner that endangers the public health, safety, or welfare; provided that nothing herein shall be construed to make applicable to the Tribe any state laws or regulations governing the use of tobacco.

Sec. 10.2. Compliance.

For the purposes of this Gaming Compact, the Tribal Gaming Operation shall:

(a) Adopt and comply with standards no less stringent than state public health standards for food and beverage handling. The Gaming Operation will allow inspection of food and beverage services by state or county health inspectors, during normal hours of operation, to assess compliance with these standards, unless inspections are routinely made by an agency of the United States government to ensure compliance with equivalent standards of the United States Public Health Service. Nothing herein shall be construed as submission of the Tribe to the jurisdiction of those state or county health inspectors, but any alleged violations of the standards shall be treated as alleged violations of this Compact.

(b) Adopt and comply with standards no less stringent than federal water quality and safe drinking water standards applicable in California; the Gaming Operation will allow for inspection and testing of water quality by state or county health inspectors, as applicable, during normal hours of operation, to assess compliance with these standards, unless inspections and testing are made by an agency of the United States pursuant to, or by the Tribe under express authorization of, federal law, to ensure compliance with federal water quality and safe drinking water standards. Nothing herein shall be construed as submission of the Tribe to the jurisdiction of those state or county health inspectors, but any alleged violations of the standards shall be treated as alleged violations of this Compact.

(c) Comply with the building and safety standards set forth in Section 6.4.

(d) Carry no less than five million dollars ($5,000,000) in public liability insurance for patron claims, and that the Tribe provide reasonable assurance that those claims will be promptly and fairly adjudicated, and that legitimate claims will be paid; provided that nothing herein requires the Tribe to agree to liability for punitive damages or attorneys' fees. On or before the effective date of this Compact or not less than 30 days prior to the commencement of Gaming Activities under this Compact, whichever is later, the Tribe shall adopt and make available to patrons a tort liability ordinance setting forth the terms and conditions, if any, under which the Tribe waives immunity to suit for money damages resulting from intentional or negligent injuries to person or property at the Gaming Facility or in connection with the Tribe's Gaming Operation, including procedures for processing any claims for such money damages; provided that nothing in this Section shall require the Tribe to waive its immunity to suit except to the extent of the policy limits set out above.

(e) Adopt and comply with standards no less stringent than federal workplace and occupational health and safety standards; the Gaming Operation will allow for inspection of Gaming Facility workplaces by state inspectors, during normal hours of operation, to assess compliance with these standards, unless inspections are regularly made by an agency of the United States government to ensure compliance with federal workplace and occupational health and safety standards. Nothing herein shall be construed as submission of the Tribe to the jurisdiction of those state inspectors, but any alleged violations of the standards shall be treated as alleged violations of this Compact.

(f) Comply with tribal codes and other applicable federal law regarding public health and safety.

(g) Adopt and comply with standards no less stringent than federal laws and state laws forbidding employers generally from discriminating in the employment of persons to work for the Gaming Operation or in the Gaming Facility on the

basis of race, color, religion, national origin, gender, sexual orientation, age, or disability; provided that nothing herein shall preclude the tribe from giving a preference in employment to Indians, pursuant to a duly adopted tribal ordinance.

(h) Adopt and comply with standards that are no less stringent than state laws prohibiting a gaming enterprise from cashing any check drawn against a federal, state, county, or city fund, including but not limited to, Social Security, unemployment insurance, disability payments, or public assistance payments.

(i) Adopt and comply with standards that are no less stringent than state laws, if any, prohibiting a gaming enterprise from providing, allowing, contracting to provide, or arranging to provide alcoholic beverages, or food or lodging for no charge or at reduced prices at a gambling establishment or lodging facility as an incentive or enticement.

(j) Adopt and comply with standards that are no less stringent than state laws, if any, prohibiting extensions of credit.

(k) Provisions of the Bank Secrecy Act, P. L. 91-508, October 26, 1970, 31 U.S.C. Sec. 5311–5314, as amended, and all reporting requirements of the Internal Revenue Service, insofar as such provisions and reporting requirements are applicable to casinos.

Sec. 10.2.1. The Tribe shall adopt and, not later than 30 days after the effective date of this Compact, shall make available on request the standards described in subdivisions (a)–(c) and (e)–(k) of Section

10.2 to which the Gaming Operation is held. In the absence of a promulgated tribal standard in respect to a matter identified in those subdivisions, or the express adoption of an applicable federal statute or regulation in lieu of a tribal standard in respect to any such matter, the applicable state statute or regulation shall be deemed to have been adopted by the Tribe as the applicable standard.

Sec. 10.3 Participation in state statutory programs related to employment.

(a) In lieu of permitting the Gaming Operation to participate in the state statutory workers' compensation system, the Tribe may create and maintain a system that provides redress for employee work-related injuries through requiring insurance or self-insurance, which system must include a scope of coverage, availability of an independent medical examination, right to notice, hearings before an independent tribunal, a means of enforcement against the employer, and benefits comparable to those mandated for comparable employees under state law. Not later than the effective date of this Compact, or 60 days prior to the commencement of Gaming Activities under this Compact, the Tribe will advise the State of its election to participate in the statutory workers' compensation system or, alternatively, will forward to the State all relevant ordinances that have been adopted and all other documents establishing the system and demonstrating that the system is fully operational and compliant with the comparability standard set forth above. The parties agree that independent contractors doing business with the Tribe must comply with all state workers' compensation laws and obligations.

(b) The Tribe agrees that its Gaming Operation will participate in the State's program for providing unemployment compensation benefits and unemployment compensation disability benefits with respect to employees employed at the Gaming Facility, including compliance with the provisions of the California Unemployment Insurance Code, and the Tribe consents to the jurisdiction of the state agencies charged with the enforcement of that Code and of the courts of the State of California for purposes of enforcement.

(c) As a matter of comity, with respect to persons employed at the Gaming Facility, other than members of the Tribe, the Tribal Gaming Operation shall withhold all taxes due to the State as provided in the California Unemployment Insurance Code and the Revenue and Taxation Code, and shall forward such amounts as provided in said Codes to the State.

Sec. 10.4. Emergency Service Accessibility. The Tribe shall make reasonable provisions for adequate emergency fire, medical, and related relief and disaster services for patrons and employees of the Gaming Facility.

Sec. 10.5. Alcoholic Beverage Service. Standards for alcohol service shall be subject to applicable law.

Sec. 10.6. Possession of firearms shall be prohibited at all times in the Gaming Facility except for state, local, or tribal security or law enforcement personnel authorized by tribal law and by federal or state law to possess fire arms at the Facility.

Sec. 10.7. Labor Relations.

Notwithstanding any other provision of this Compact, this Compact shall be null and void if, on or before October 13, 1999, the Tribe has not provided an agreement or other procedure acceptable to the State for addressing organizational and representational rights of Class III Gaming Employees and other employees associated with the Tribe's Class III gaming enterprise, such as food and beverage, housekeeping, cleaning, bell and door services, and laundry employees at the Gaming Facility or any related facility, the only significant purpose of which is to facilitate patronage at the Gaming Facility.

Sec. 10.8. Off-Reservation Environmental Impacts.

Sec. 10.8.1. On or before the effective date of this Compact, or not less than 90 days prior to the commencement of a Project, as defined herein, the Tribe shall adopt an ordinance providing for the preparation, circulation, and consideration by the Tribe of environmental impact reports concerning potential off-Reservation environmental impacts of any and all Projects to be commenced on or after the effective date of this Compact. In fashioning the environmental protection ordinance, the Tribe will make a good faith effort to incorporate the policies and purposes of the National Environmental Policy Act and the California Environmental Quality Act consistent with the Tribe's governmental interests.

Sec. 10.8.2.

(a) Prior to commencement of a Project, the Tribe will:

    (1) Inform the public of the planned Project;

    (2) Take appropriate actions to determine whether the project will have any significant adverse impacts on the off-Reservation environment;

    (3) For the purpose of receiving and responding to comments, submit all environmental impact reports concerning the proposed Project to the State Clearinghouse in the Office of Planning and Research and the county board of supervisors, for distribution to the public.

    (4) Consult with the board of supervisors of the county or counties within which the Tribe's Gaming Facility is located, or is to be located, and, if the Gaming Facility is within a city, with the city council, and if requested by the board or council, as the case may be, meet with them to discuss mitigation of significant adverse off-Reservation environmental impacts;

    (5) Meet with and provide an opportunity for comment by those members of the public residing off-Reservation within the vicinity of the Gaming Facility such as might be adversely affected by proposed Project.

(b) During the conduct of a Project, the Tribe shall:

    (1) Keep the board or council, as the case may be, and potentially affected members of the public apprized of the project's progress; and

    (2) Make good faith efforts to mitigate any and all such significant adverse off-Reservation environmental impacts.

(c) As used in Section 10.8.1 and this Section 10.8.2, the term "Project" means any expansion or any significant renovation or modification of an existing Gaming Facility, or any significant excavation, construction, or development associated with the Tribe's Gaming Facility or proposed Gaming Facility and the term "environmental impact reports" means any environmental assessment, environmental impact report, or environmental impact statement, as the case may be.

Sec. 10.8.3. (a) The Tribe and the State shall, from time to time, meet to review the adequacy of this Section 10.8, the Tribe's ordinance adopted pursuant thereto, and the Tribe's compliance with its obligations under Section 10.8.2, to ensure that significant adverse impacts to the off-Reservation environment resulting from projects undertaken by the Tribe may be avoided or mitigated.

(b) At any time after January 1, 2003, but not later than March 1, 2003, the State may request negotiations for an amendment to this Section 10.8 on the ground that, as it presently reads, the Section has proven to be inadequate to protect the off-Reservation environment from significant adverse impacts resulting from Projects undertaken by the Tribe or to ensure adequate mitigation by the Tribe of significant adverse off-Reservation environmental impacts and, upon such a request, the Tribe will enter into such negotiations in good faith.

(c) On or after January 1, 2004, the Tribe may bring an action in federal court under 25 U.S.C. Sec. 2710(d)(7)(A)(i) on the ground that the State has failed to negotiate in good faith, provided that the Tribe's good faith in the negotiations shall also be in issue. In any such action, the court may consider whether the State's invocation of its rights under subdivision (b) of this Section 10.8.3 was in good faith. If the State has requested negotiations pursuant to subdivision (b) but, as of January 1, 2005, there is neither an agreement nor an order against the State under 25 U.S.C. Sec. 2710(d)(7)(B)(iii), then, on that date, the Tribe shall immediately cease construction and other activities on all projects then in progress that have the potential to cause adverse off-Reservation impacts, unless and until an agreement to amend this Section 10.8 has been concluded between the Tribe and the State.

Sec. 11.0. EFFECTIVE DATE AND TERM OF COMPACT.

Sec. 11.1. Effective Date.

This Gaming Compact shall not be effective unless and until all of the following have occurred:

(a) The Compact is ratified by statute in accordance with state law;

(b) Notice of approval or constructive approval is published in the Federal Register as provided in 25 U.S.C. 2710(d)(3)(B); and

(c) SCA 11 is approved by the California voters in the March 2000 general election.

Sec. 11.2. Term of Compact; Termination.

Sec. 11.2.1. Effective. (a) Once effective this Compact shall be in full force and effect for state law purposes until December 31, 2020.

(b) Once ratified, this Compact shall constitute a binding and determinative agreement between the Tribe and the State, without regard to voter approval of any constitutional amendment, other than SCA 11, that authorizes a gaming compact.

(c) Either party may bring an action in federal court, after providing a sixty (60) day written notice of an opportunity to cure any alleged breach of this Compact, for a declaration that the other party has materially breached this Compact. Upon issuance of such a declaration, the complaining party may unilaterally terminate this Compact upon service of written notice on the other party. In the event a federal court determines that it lacks jurisdiction over such an action, the action may be brought in the superior court for the county in which the Tribe's Gaming Facility is located. The parties expressly waive their immunity to suit for purposes of an action under this subdivision, subject to the qualifications stated in Section 9.4(a).

Sec. 12.0. AMENDMENTS; RENEGOTIATIONS.

Sec. 12.1. The terms and conditions of this Gaming Compact may be amended at any time by the mutual and written agreement of both parties.

Sec. 12.2. This Gaming Compact is subject to renegotiation in the event the Tribe wishes to engage in forms of Class III gaming other than those games authorized herein and requests renegotiation for that purpose, provided that no such renegotiation may be sought for 12 months following the effective date of this Gaming Compact.

Sec. 12.3. Process and Negotiation Standards. All requests to amend or renegotiate this Gaming Compact shall be in writing, addressed to the Tribal Chairperson or the Governor, as the case may be, and shall include the activities or circumstances to be negotiated, together with a statement of the basis supporting the request. If the request meets the requirements of this Section, the parties shall confer promptly and determine a schedule for commencing negotiations within 30 days of the request. Unless expressly provided otherwise herein, all matters involving negotiations or other amendatory processes under Section 4.3.3(b) and this Section 12.0 shall be governed, controlled, and conducted in conformity with the provisions and requirements of IGRA, including those provisions regarding the obligation of the State to negotiate in good faith and the enforcement of that obligation in federal court. The Chairperson of the Tribe and the Governor of the State are hereby authorized to designate the person or agency responsible for conducting the negotiations, and shall execute any documents necessary to do so.

Sec. 12.4. The Tribe shall have the right to terminate this Compact in the event the exclusive right of Indian tribes to operate Gaming Devices in California is abrogated by the enactment, amendment, or repeal of a state statute or constitutional provision, or the conclusive and dispositive judicial construction of a statute or the state Constitution by a California appellate court after the effective date of this Compact, that Gaming Devices may lawfully be operated by another person, organization, or entity (other than an Indian tribe pursuant to a compact) within California.

Sec. 13.0 NOTICES.

Unless otherwise indicated by this Gaming Compact, all notices required or authorized to be served shall be served by first-class mail at the following addresses:

Governor
State Capitol
Sacramento, California 95814

Tribal Chairperson
XXXXXXX
P. O. Box 4234
Palm Springs, CA 91509

Sec. 14.0. CHANGES IN IGRA.

This Gaming Compact is intended to meet the requirements of IGRA as it reads on the effective date of this Gaming Compact, and when reference is made to the Indian Gaming Regulatory Act or to an implementing regulation thereof, the referenced provision is deemed to have been incorporated into this Compact as if set out in full. Subsequent changes to IGRA that diminish the rights of the State or the Tribe may not be applied retroactively to alter the terms of this Gaming Compact, except to the extent that federal law validly mandates that retroactive application without the State's or the Tribe's respective consent

Sec. 15.0. MISCELLANEOUS.

Sec. 15.1. Third Party Beneficiaries.
Except to the extent expressly provided under this Gaming Compact, this Gaming Compact is not intended to, and shall not be construed to, create any right on the part of a third party to bring an action to enforce any of its terms.
Sec. 15.2. Complete agreement; revocation of prior requests to negotiate.
This Gaming Compact, together with all addenda and approved amendments, sets forth the full and complete agreement of the parties and supersedes any prior agreements or understandings with respect to the subject matter hereof.
Sec. 15.3. Construction. Neither the presence in another tribal-state compact of language that is not included in this Compact, nor the absence in this Compact of language that is present in another tribal-state compact shall be a factor in construing the terms of this Compact.
Sec. 15.4. Most Favored Tribe. If, after the effective date of this Compact, the State enters into a Compact with any other tribe that contains more favorable provisions with respect to any provisions of this Compact, the State shall, at the Tribe's request, enter into the preferred compact with the Tribe as a superseding substitute for this Compact; provided that the duration of the substitute compact shall not exceed the duration of this Compact.
Sec. 15.6. Representations. By entering into this Compact, the Tribe expressly represents that, as of the date of the Tribe's execution of this Compact: (a) the undersigned has the authority to execute this Compact on behalf of his or her tribe and will provide written proof of such authority and ratification of this Compact by the tribal governing body no later than October 9, 1999; (b) the Tribe is (i) recognized as eligible by the Secretary of the Interior for special programs and services provided by the United States to Indians because of their status as Indians, and (ii) recognized by the Secretary of the Interior as possessing powers of self-government. In entering into this Compact, the State expressly relies upon the foregoing representations by the Tribe, and the State's entry into the Compact is expressly made contingent upon the truth of those representations as of the date of the Tribe's execution of this Compact. Failure to provide written proof of authority to execute this Compact or failure to provide written proof of ratification by the Tribe's governing body will give the State the opportunity to declare this Compact null and void.

IN WITNESS WHEREOF, the undersigned sign this Compact on behalf of the **STATE OF CALI-FORNIA** and the **XXXXXXX**.

Done at Sacramento, California, this 10th day of September 1999.

STATE OF CALIFORNIA　　　　　**XXXXXXX**

By Gray Davis
Governor of the State of California

By Johnny Carswell
Chairperson of the Xxxxxxx

D

FEDERALLY RECOGNIZED GAMING TRIBES

Reprinted with permission of:

National Indian Gaming Commission
1441 L St. NW Suite 9100
Washington, DC 20005
PH: 202-632-7003
FAX: 202-632-7066
www.nigc.gov

ALASKA

Klawock Cooperative Association
Metlakatla Indian Community

ARIZONA

Ak Chin Indian Community
Cocopah Indian Tribe
Colorado River Indian Tribes
Fort McDowell Mohave-Apache Indian Community
Gila River Indian Community
Pascua Yaqui Tribe of Arizona
Quechan Indian Tribe
Salt River Pima-Maricopa Indian Community
San Carlos Apache Tribe
Tohono O'odham Nation
Tonto Apache Tribe
White Mountain Apache Tribe
Yavapai Apache Tribe
Yavapai-Prescott Indian Tribe

CALIFORNIA

Agua Caliente Band of Cahuilla Indians
Auberry Big Sandy Rancheria
Augustine Band of Mission Indians
Barona Band of Mission Indians
Big Valley Rancheria of Pomo Indians
Bishop Paiute Tribe
Cabazon Band of Mission Indians
Cahto Tribe of the Laytonville Rancheria
Cahuilla Band of Mission Indians
Chemehuevi Indian Tribe
Chicken Ranch Band of Me-Wuk Indians
Colusa Band of Wintun Indians
Coyote Valley Band of Pomo Indians
Dry Creek Rancheria Band of Pomo Indians
Elk Valley Rancheria

Fort Mojave Tribal Council
Hoopa Valley Tribe
Hopland Band of Pomo Indians
Jackson Rancheria Band of Miwuk Indians
Lake Miwok Indian Nation of the Middletown Rancheria
Mooretown Rancheria
Morongo Band of Mission Indians
Pala Band of Mission Indians
Pit River Tribe
Redding Rancheria
Rincon San Luiseno Band of Mission Indians
Robinson Rancheria of Pomo Indians
Rumsey Indian Rancheria
San Manuel Band of Mission Indians
Santa Rosa Band of Tachi Indians of the Santa Rosa Rancheria
Santa Ynez Band of Mission Indians
Sherwood Valley Rancheria
Smith River Rancheria
Soboba Band of Mission Indians
Susanville Indian Rancheria
Sycuan Band of Mission Indians
Table Mountain Rancheria
Temecula Band of Luiseno Mission Indians
Trinidad Rancheria
Tule River Tribe of the Tule River Indian Reservation
Twenty Nine Palms Band of Mission Indians
Tyme Maidu Tribe of the Berry Creek Rancheria
Viejas Band of Mission Indians

COLORADO

Southern Ute Indian Tribe
Ute Mountain Ute Tribe

CONNECTICUT

Mashantucket Pequot Tribal Nation
Mohegan Tribe of Indians of Connecticut

FLORIDA

    Miccosukee Business Committee
    Seminole Tribe

IDAHO

    Coeur d'Alene Tribe
    Kootenai Tribe of Idaho
    Nez Perce Tribe
    Shoshone-Bannock Tribes

IOWA

    Sac & Fox Tribe of Mississippi in Iowa

KANSAS

    Iowa Tribe of Kansas and Nebraska
    Kickapoo Nation in Kansas
    Prairie Band Potawatomi
    Sac and Fox Nation of Missouri

LOUISIANA

    Chitimacha Tribe of Louisiana
    Coushatta Tribe of Louisiana
    Tunica-Biloxi Tribe of Louisiana

MICHIGAN

    Bay Mills Indian Community
    Grand Traverse Band of Ottawa/Chippewa Indians
    Hannahville Indian Community
    Keweenaw Bay Indian Community
    Lac Vieux Desert Band of Lake Superior Chippewa Indians
    Little River Band of Ottawa Chippewa
    Little Traverse Bay Bands of Odawa Indians
    Saginaw Chippewa Indian Tribe
    Sault Ste. Marie Tribe of Chippewa Indians

MINNESOTA

Bois Forte Band of Chippewas
Fond du Lac Reservation Business Committee
Grand Portage Band of Chippewa Indians
Leech Lake Band of Chippewa Indians
Lower Sioux Indian Community
Mille Lacs Band of Chippewa Indians
Prairie Island Indian Community
Red Lake Band of Chippewa Indians
Shakopee Mdewakanton Sioux Community
Upper Sioux Community
White Earth Band of Chippewa Indians

MISSISSIPPI

Mississippi Band of Choctaw Indians

MISSOURI

Eastern Shawnee Tribe of Oklahoma

MONTANA

Assiniboine & Sioux Tribes of the Fort Peck Reservation
Blackfeet Tribe of Indians
Chippewa Cree Tribe of the Rocky Boy's Reservation
Confederated Salish and Kootenai Tribes of the Flathead Rese
Crow Indian Tribe
Fort Belknap Indian Community
Northern Cheyenne Tribe

NEBRASKA

Omaha Tribe of Nebraska
Santee Sioux Tribe of Nebraska
Winnebago Tribe of Nebraska

NEVADA

Las Vegas Paiute Tribe
Moapa Band of Paiutes

NEW MEXICO

Mescalero Apache Tribe
Pueblo of Acoma
Pueblo of Isleta
Pueblo of Laguna
Pueblo of Pojoaque
Pueblo of San Felipe
Pueblo of San Juan
Pueblo of Sandia
Pueblo of Santa Ana
Pueblo of Taos
Pueblo of Tesuque

NEW YORK

Oneida Nation of New York
Seneca Nation of Indians
St. Regis Mohawk Tribe

NORTH CAROLINA

Eastern Band of Cherokee Indians

NORTH DAKOTA

Spirit Lake Sioux Nation
Standing Rock Sioux Tribe
Three Affiliated Tribes of the Fort Berthold Reservation
Turtle Mountain Band of Chippewa Indians

OKLAHOMA

Absentee-Shawnee Tribe of Oklahoma
Cherokee Nation of Oklahoma
Cheyenne and Arapaho Tribes of Oklahoma
Chickasaw Nation of Oklahoma
Choctaw Nation of Oklahoma
Citizen Band Potawatomi Indians of Oklahoma
Comanche Indian Tribe
Delaware Tribe of Western Oklahoma
Ft. Sill Apache Tribe of Oklahoma

Iowa Tribe of Oklahoma
Kaw Nation of Oklahoma
Kickapoo Tribe of Oklahoma
Miami Tribe of Oklahoma
Modoc Tribe of Oklahoma
Muscogee (Creek) Nation
Osage Nation
Otoe-Missouria Tribe of Oklahoma
Ponca Tribe of Oklahoma
Quapaw Tribe of Oklahoma
Seminole Nation of Oklahoma
Seneca-Cayuga Tribe of Oklahoma
Thlopthlocco Tribal Town
Tonkawa Tribe of Oklahoma

OREGON

Burns Paiute Tribe
Confederated Tribes of the Grand Ronde Community
Confederated Tribes of the Siletz Indians of Oregon
Confederated Tribes of the Umatilla Indian Reservation
Confederated Tribes of the Warm Springs Reservation of Or
Coquille Indian Tribe
Cow Creek Band of Umpqua Indians
Klamath Tribes

SOUTH DAKOTA

Cheyenne River Sioux Tribe
Crow Creek Sioux Tribe
Flandreau Santee Sioux Tribe
Lower Brule Sioux Tribe
Oglala Sioux Tribe
Rosebud Sioux Tribe
Sisseton-Wahpeton Sioux Tribe
Yankton Sioux Tribe

TEXAS

Kickapoo Traditional Tribe of Texas

WASHINGTON

Confederated Tribes and Bands of the Yakama Indian Nation
Confederated Tribes of the Chehalis Reservation
Confederated Tribes of the Colville Reservation
Jamestown S'Klallam Tribe
Lummi Nation
Makah Indian Tribe of the Makah Indian Reservation
Muckleshoot Indian Tribe
Nisqually Indian Tribe
Nooksack Indian Tribe
Port Gamble S'Klallam Tribe
Puyallup Tribe of Indians
Shoalwater Bay Indian Tribe
Spokane Tribe of Indians
Squaxin Island Tribe
Suquamish Tribe
Swinomish Indian Tribal Community
Tulalip Tribes of Washington
Upper Skagit Indian Tribe

WISCONSIN

Bad River Band of Lake Superior Tribe of Chippewa Indians
Forest County Potawatomi Community
Ho-Chunk Nation
Lac Courte Oreilles Band of Lake Superior Chippewas
Lac du Flambeau Band of Lake Superior Chippewa Indians
Menominee Indian Tribe of Wisconsin
Oneida Tribe of Indians of Wisconsin
Red Cliff Band of Lake Superior Chippewas
Sokaogon Chippewa Community
St. Croix Chippewa Indians of Wisconsin
Stockbridge-Munsee Community

WYOMING

Northern Arapaho Tribe of the Wind River Indian Reservation

Contributors

Tim Carlson

Tim Carlson is presently one of three principals in the MoVada Group, serving as its C.E.O. The MoVada Group has recently completed an agreement with the Fort Mojave Tribe to lease 1,000 acres to be developed as a planned recreational community, with commercial and residential sites, recreational area and hotel sites in the State of Nevada. Mr. Carlson's background is in economic development.

Anthony Chamblin

Anthony Chamblin is Executive Vice President of the Association of Racing Commissioners International in Lexington, Kentucky. Mr. Chamblin is a published author and has represented various racing industry organizations before Congressional and State legislative panels.

William R. Eadington

William R. Eadington is a Professor of Economics at the University of Nevada, Reno, and the Director of the Institute for the Study of Gambling and Commercial Gaming. Professor Eadington has long been involved in research relating to legalization and regulation of commercial gaming throughout the world. He also served as the Conference Chairman for the North American Conference on the Status of Indian Gaming.

Nora Garcia

Nora Garcia has served as Chairperson for the Fort Mojave Indian Tribe since 1985 and has worked continuously for the Tribal Council since 1975 in various capacities. She also serves as First Vice-President to the Inter-Tribal Council of Arizona; First Vice-President to the Indian Development District of Arizona; Secretary for the Fort Mojave Development Board; and is a member of the Colorado River Task Force.

Wendell George

Wendell George is the Chairman of the Planning Committee for the Colville Business Council of the Colville Confederated Tribes of the State of Washington. The Planning Committee is responsible for the development of a Bingo project for the tribe which has operated for past three years and is now building a million dollar facility to expand the operation. They are now in the process of negotiating a compact with the State of Washington to define Class III gaming on the reservation. Under Mr. George's direction, the Planning

Committee is also involved in the development of Roosevelt Recreation Enterprise on Lake Roosevelt and has long been involved in comprehensive land use planning for the tribe.

John R. Mills

John Mills is an Associate Professor of Accounting at the College of Business Administration of the University of Nevada, Reno and is a Certified Public Accountant. Dr. Mills is the author of several articles and he is an active member of several committees and boards including the American Accounting Association, National Association of Accountants, and the Board of Trustees for the Nevada Certified Public Accountants Foundation for Education and Research.

Harold A. Monteau

Harold Monteau is currently the Tribal Attorney for the Chippewa-Cree Tribe of the Rocky Boy's Reservation, Box Elder, Montana. He previously served as the Tribal Attorney to the Confederated Salish and Kootenai Tribes of the Flathead Reservation, Pablo, Montana. He is a graduate of the University of New Mexico School of Law in Albuquerque, New Mexico.

Judith A. Osborne

Judith A. Osborne, a graduate of the Faculty of Law, University of Edinburgh and of the Centre for Criminology, University of Toronto, is an Associate Professor of Criminology at Simon Fraser University, British Columbia. A co-author of a study of the constitutional validity of

Canada's gambling laws, she is currently engaged in a larger study of gambling and the law in Canada.

Harry Reid

Senator Harry Reid has served in the U.S. Senate for the state of Nevada since 1986. He is a former lieutenant governor of Nevada, as well as having previously chaired the Nevada Gaming Commission. Before being elected to the U.S. Senate, Senator Reid served two terms in the House of Representatives representing the Southern District of Nevada.

James E. Ritchie

James E. Ritchie is engaged in the private practice of law in Washington, D.C., specializing in the area of statutory and regulatory control of legalized gaming throughout the world, and the impact of tax policy on gaming. He is the advisor to various legislative jurisdictions on policy issues raised by gaming measures. He previously served as Executive Director of the Presidential Commission on the Review of the National Policy Toward Gambling.

I. Nelson Rose

I. Nelson Rose is recognized as one of the nation's leading authorities on gambling law. He is the author of over fifty articles on the subject, as well as the landmark 1986 book, *Gambling and the Law*. He is currently a tenured Associate Professor of Law at Whittier College School of Law in Los Angeles, California.

Jerome H. Skolnick

Dr. Jerome Skolnick is a Professor of Law and Criminology at the University of California-Berkeley, and he serves as Chair for the Center for the Study of Law and Society. Dr. Skolnick has served on the faculties of Yale Law School, the University of Chicago and the University of California-San Diego. He is the author of *House of Cards: Legalization and Control of Casino Gambling* and *America's Problems: Social Issues and Public Policy*; and co-authored *Crisis in American Institutions* (6th edition). Dr. Skolnick received his Ph.D. in Sociology from Yale University.

Vina A. Starr

Vina A. Starr is a native Indian lawyer who specializes in the practice of Indian Self-Government law. She is a graduate of the University of British Columbia Law School and a member of the Faculty of Law at the University of British Columbia. Ms. Starr is presently in the private practice of law.

William N. Thompson

William N. Thompson is a Professor of Public Administration and Management at the College of Business and Economics at the University of Nevada, Las Vegas. He has served as a gaming consultant to the President's Commission on Organized Crime, the Tourism Company of Puerto Rico, as well as various other organizations. Professor Thompson is the author of numerous gaming related articles and is co-author of *The Last Resort - Campaigns for Casinos in the American States* (1989).

B.W. "Butch" Tongate

B.W. "Butch" Tongate serves as a legislative consultant to the law firm of O'Connor and Hannan in Washington, D.C. specializing in gaming initiatives and legislation. He formerly worked as a lobbyist in Washington, D.C. dealing directly with the Act to Regulate Gaming on Indian Lands.

Eddie L. Tullis

Eddie Tullis is the Chairman of the Poarch Band of Creek Indians in Atmore, Alabama, a position he has held since 1976. He also serves as the Chairman for the National Advisory Council on Indian Education (NACIE). Mr. Tullis serves on a number of councils and committees including the American Indian Employment and Training Coalition, Americans for Indian Opportunity, American Indian and Alaska Native Advisory Committee, United South and Eastern Tribes, and the National Congress of American Indians.

Stewart L. Udall

Stewart Udall is the former United States Secretary of the Interior serving for eight years during the administrations of Presidents John F. Kennedy and Lyndon B. Johnson. He is the author of *The Quiet Crisis*, *Agenda for Tomorrow*, and *The Inland Empire: Coronado and the Spanish Legacy*. Mr. Udall now lives in Santa Fe, New Mexico where he writes and practices law.